PABLO NERUDA
The Poetics of Prophecy

PABLO NERUDA

The Poetics of Prophecy

Enrico Mario Santí

Cornell University Press

Ithaca and London

This book has been published with the aid of a grant from the Hull Memorial Publication Fund of Cornell University.

Copyright © 1982 by Cornell University Press

All rights reserved. Except for brief quotations in a review, this book, or parts thereof, must not be reproduced in any form without permission in writing from the publisher. For information address Cornell University Press, 124 Roberts Place, Ithaca, New York 14850.

First published 1982 by Cornell University Press.
Published in the United Kingdom by Cornell University Press Ltd.,
Ely House, 37 Dover Street, London W1X 4HQ.

International Standard Book Number 0-8014-1472-5
Library of Congress Catalog Card Number 82-4878
Printed in the United States of America
Librarians: Library of Congress cataloging information appears on the last page of the book.

Permission to quote in translation from *Canto General, Odas Elementales, Estravagario, Plenos Poderes,* and *Confieso que he vivido: Memorias* granted by Farrar, Straus & Giroux, Inc., and Souvenir Press Ltd. This translation copyright © 1982 Farrar, Straus & Giroux, Inc.

Permission to quote in translation from *Estravagario* and *Alturas de Macchu Picchu* granted by Farrar, Straus & Giroux, Inc., Jonathan Cape, Ltd., and the Estate of Pablo Neruda. This translation copyright © 1982 Farrar, Straus & Giroux, Inc.

Permission to translate into English portions of *Residencia en la tierra,* © Pablo Neruda, has been granted by Carmen Balcells Agencia Literaria on behalf of Mrs. Matilde Neruda and by New Directions Publishing Corp., publisher of *Residence on Earth.* Translated by Enrico Mario Santí, copyright © 1982 by Cornell University Press.

The paper in this book is acid-free, and meets the guidelines for permanence and durability of the Committee on Production Guidelines for Book Longevity of the Council on Library Resources.

Para Pura

Contents

	Acknowledgments	9
	Introduction	13
1	Vision and Time	24
2	Vision and Conversion	66
3	Prophecy of Writing	104
4	Politics of the Book	176
5	Apocalypse	206
	Postscript	237
	Bibliography	243
	Index	253

Acknowledgments

This book is a reading of the work of a Latin American poet and of its dialogue with the Western literary tradition. The book's genesis was, fittingly enough, a series of intense conversations with Emir Rodríguez Monegal, my teacher and friend, in whose seminars on Latin American literature at Yale I discovered the value of open critical discussion. Although this book bears little resemblance to the Ph.D. dissertation I wrote some years ago, it retains Professor Monegal's belief that the meaning of Latin American literature lies in the form of its debate with the Western tradition, and that the critic's principal task is to study that form. What I have to say about the poetry of Pablo Neruda constitutes a testimony to that fundamental and now shared conviction. No less responsible for my intellectual formation at Yale was José Juan Arrom, in whose "Renaissance Workshops" I discovered the meaning of human community.

In the completion of this book I was aided by a study leave, during the spring semester of 1980, from Cornell University's College of Arts and Sciences. My thanks to Alain Seznec, Dean of the College, and to Philip Lewis, then chairman of my department, for helping me to secure that leave. Other colleagues at Cornell and elsewhere contributed with their support, ideas, and suggestions, among them Ciriaco Morón Arroyo, Roberto González Echevarría, David I. Grossvogel, John W. Kronik, Juan Loveluck, William Luis, Alfred A. MacAdam, Félix Martínez Bonati, Robert Pring-Mill, Enrique Pupo-Walker, Alastair Reid, and Eliana Suárez-Rivero. Some chapters were first delivered as lectures, in March 1980, before the Humanities Faculty of the

Acknowledgments

University of Puerto Rico, Río Piedras. My thanks to José Ramón de la Torre, Dean of the Faculty, and to Federico and Ramón Luis Acevedo, Eduardo Forastieri-Braschi, José Luis Vega, and especially my dear friends Arturo Echavarría-Ferrari and Luce López-Baralt for the many kindnesses extended to me during my visit and for their contributions to a discussion that made me rethink a number of issues. I owe many a special debt to my colleague and friend Giuseppe Mazzotta, whose knowledge of Dante and poetic traditions proved invaluable to the clarification of my views on Neruda, and to Sandor Goodhart, of the University of Michigan, who performed a true labor of love during the revision of the manuscript. During the last stages of my writing I was fortunate to have the practical and moral support of Carlos Cano, of the University of South Florida, and Andrés Ordoño, the University Librarian. To John Crispin and J. Richard Andrews, former teachers at Vanderbilt University, I owe my greatest debts. They introduced me to Hispanic literature and encouraged me to carry a sense of discovery to my graduate studies.

The dedication of this book to my wife, Olga, can only in part express the depth of my gratitude to her.

Earlier versions of Chapters 4 and 5 and of the Postscript appeared in the journals *Symposium, Hispanic Review,* and *Zona Franca,* respectively. My thanks go to the editors of those journals for allowing me to use these essays in revised form. Unless otherwise noted, all references to Neruda's works are based on the fourth Losada edition (1973) of his *Obras completas;* roman and arabic numbers in the text refer to volume and page numbers of that edition. All English translations of this and other foreign works are mine. For permission to quote in translation from Neruda's works I thank Farrar, Straus & Giroux, New Directions Publishing Corp., Souvenir Press Ltd., Jonathan Cape, Ltd., and Carmen Balcells Agencia Literaria, agent for the estate of Pablo Neruda. Quotations from the Bible are based on the King James and Casiodoro de Reina versions.

Enrico Mario Santí

Ithaca, New York

PABLO NERUDA
The Poetics of Prophecy

Introduction

> If you ask me what my poetry is, I must answer: I don't know.
> But if you ask my poetry it'll tell you who I am.
> —Pablo Neruda, 1943

There is no longer any need to introduce Pablo Neruda to the English-speaking world. Years before he received the Nobel Prize in 1971, translations of his major poetry had made his work familiar to readers in this country and abroad. With the exception of Jorge Luis Borges, who is often mentioned as Neruda's antithesis, no Latin American author is better known, and the importance of his poetry has been acknowledged even by those who disagree with his literature or his politics. A Communist for most of his life, Neruda remained in the limelight until 1973, when the coup that toppled the Marxist government of Chilean president Salvador Allende precipitated his death after a long illness. Since then, his fame has steadily grown. New translations and readers' guides, in English and Spanish, have continued to appear, making all further introductions redundant. I have written this book in the belief that a critical study is long overdue and with a view toward reading Neruda's poetry through some of the lessons taught by recent literary theory.

That a poetics of prophecy underlies Neruda's major poetry has been the unstated assumption of most criticism. Often compared to Walt Whitman, the "American Bard," Neruda is perhaps his most direct heir in Latin America. Not all of Neruda's many modes and styles fit this rubric, of course, but a prophetic voice is what defines the major Neruda, and it is this voice, I believe, that will win him a place in literary history. While for many people, prophecy is a term of empty praise when applied to Neruda, for some it remains a synonym for his poetry of social or political content. Still others shun the term altogether, fearing that its religious connotation clashes with his politics, without realizing that prophecy embodies a rhetoric in which religion and politics merge. In this book I make this often unstated assumption the focus of a sustained inquiry.[1] In close readings of a few key poems, from *Residencia en la tierra* (1931, 1935, 1947) to *La espada encendida* (1970), I attempt to trace the prophetic strain in Neruda's poetry and its gradual shift from visionary to political to apocalyptic mode. The general aim of this book is to probe Neruda's sense of prophecy as the significant metaphor for modern poetry, and to dwell on the formal versions of that sense. I am not exclusively concerned with a religious reading of the poetry, unless religion is understood at its widest and most unorthodox level. Nor is this a study of Neruda's treatment of social or political themes, although politics is one of its central concerns. The principal subject of this book, then, is neither religion nor politics but rhetoric. To speak of prophecy in the work of a modern poet requires us to investigate his place in the Romantic or modern tradition and to assess how that tradition informs the poetry's rhetorical fabric.

By a poetics of prophecy I broadly mean the poetry's management of this formal dialogue, the presence of "tradition" within the poet's "individual talent." By poetics in particular, I do not mean the sum of a poet's theories or the logical argument he may mount within a discursive canon—his formal prose essays or his informal remarks about his craft. Poetics describes the troubled presence of the poet's intention in poetic form—not the fulfillment of that intention but the space *in between* intention and fulfillment—the X ray, so to speak, of poetic desire. Similarly, by prophecy I do not mean its occasional connotation of augury or prediction but rather its more precise sense of knowledge by vision or revelation. Thus broadly understood, the term "prophecy" describes not simply the predictive posture that one normally associates with the figure of the biblical proph-

---

[1] Emir Rodríguez Monegal was the first to suggest this inquiry in his essay "El sistema del poeta," *Revista Iberoamericana*, 39 (1973), 41–72; now part of his *Neruda: El viajero inmóvil* (1966; 2d rev. ed. Caracas: Monte Avila, 1977), pp. 447–467. More recently, Gastón Soublette's monograph attempts a similar reading; see *Pablo Neruda: Profeta de América* (Santiago de Chile: Nueva Universidad, 1980).

Introduction

et, but the more general and less specialized figure of the poet in the act of articulating significant and sometimes absolute knowledge. Prophecy unveils not the future but the absolute, and so a poetics of prophecy describes the desire to present absolute knowledge in poetic form.

It should be clear at the outset that my focus of interest is the *representation* of that knowledge and not the poet's actual thought. There is no poetics apart from the poem—despite the objections of sedulous critics and a few minor poets. Each of the five chapters of this book may be read as an essay on Neruda's formal adoption of the prophetic mode as mediated by the Romantic tradition. It was the Romantics who, as M. H. Abrams puts it, "represented themselves in the traditional persona of the philosopher-seer or the poet-prophet," and who used this persona in order to dramatize the imminence of "a renovated earth."[2] Neruda's poetry reminds us constantly of a prophetic speaker because of its deliberate adoption of a prophetic mode. That is, the prophetic tradition, from its Greek and Hebrew antecedents to its modern counterparts, provides Neruda with a set of literary conventions, a mode of writing or *écriture*, within which he unfolds his own language as if attempting to join with the central current of Western poetry. Such deliberateness itself betrays the adoption of an alien code and defines a peculiar link to literary history. From the standpoint of Latin America's informed marginality, Neruda's texts assert a prophetic mode only to exaggerate its conventionality and thereby expose its rhetorical fabric: "The Nephew of the West" was Neruda's self-description in the preface to *Cantos Ceremoniales* (1962). Such a kinship, however, cannot be measured simply in terms of parody, in the sense of a mocking imitation. It constitutes, rather, the metaphor for all belated adoptions and specifically for the troubled use of a Western model by all Latin American authors. What is more, that historical kinship implies a telling gloss on prophecy itself.

At its etymological root, to prophesy means to speak on behalf of someone or something, be it an inspiring god, nation, or muse. The prophet is the one who speaks, yet his speech derives its authority not from an inner reservoir, but from an out-

[2]*Natural Supernaturalism: Tradition and Revolution in Romantic Literature* (New York: Norton, 1971), p. 12.

side and sometimes alien source. Our sense of drama tells us that the prophet must be a self-assured, inspired spokesman. And yet both of these key adjectives (self-assured, inspired) subvert from within the very stability that they seemingly promote. Prophecy dramatizes, above all, a lack in the intentional speaking subject who is reduced by an overpowering external discourse to a mere agent or instrument—Moses relying on Aaron's eloquence, the Pythia stuttering at the oracle, Shelley faltering before the West Wind. If at times the prophet *appears* to foretell the future, it is not because he simply "sees" forthcoming events but because the power of the language that infuses him, in the thrust to establish a dialogue with absolute values, disrupts his temporal structure as a perceiving and expressing subject and replaces it with a whole new series of temporal relations. "The prophetic word," writes Maurice Blanchot, "is primary, but is always preceded by another word to which it responds, repeating it, as if every word would begin by answering."[3]

Neruda's version of prophetic dialogue is his poetry's commerce with poetic tradition. Through it speaks not only the Spirit of the Age or the Genius of Place but the Spirit and Genius of the Library. Yet even in this his poems prove no different from all other prophetic texts, which rely on the past for their authority as much as or more than on an inspiring otherness. Borges remarked once, in reference to Nietzsche's Zarathustra, that the prophet could allow himself to use only the first-person pronoun. "Prophetic style disallows the use of quotation marks or erudite references to books and authors."[4] Borges' point was that Nietzsche had skillfully manipulated a prophetic voice so as to avoid having to acknowledge his precursors' "discovery" of the eternal return. Beyond the obvious temporal aporia, the implication was that the line between prophecy and heresy is not always so clear as one may think, since the prophet derives his seemingly singular authority from a network of earlier texts. The prophet speaks, that is, *as if* on his own self-assured behalf all the while he is echoing the phantoms of earlier "discoveries."

[3]*Le Livre à venir* (Paris: Gallimard, 1959), p. 103.
[4]*Historia de la eternidad* (1936; Buenos Aires: Emecé, 1953), p. 83.

Introduction

I may seem to be arguing for a Borgesian Neruda, so to speak, for a prophet lost in a labyrinth who remained blind to the "real" issues of human history. Yet one need not reduce prophecy to a grammatical mirage, as Borges mischievously attempts to do, to realize that a less mystified understanding of the concept brings out some of the central issues of modern poetry. For the dilemma of the modern poet, since Romanticism, is that he must work as a solitary individual, new to the world, recreating the world for himself and inventing a new language to express it in, when in fact the mode of writing he adopts includes his response to the tradition in which he is working. And for the modern Latin American poet, working within a marginal literature and therefore exposed to a greater spectrum of traditions, that response will be more overt, even as he points to his marginality as the one true guarantee of an authentic invention. Nor does a reading of Neruda's dialogue with poetic tradition imply a neglect of the issues of history, a charge that does not apply even to Borges' deceptively "escapist" texts. Such a dialogue brings out, on the contrary, the historicity of Neruda's major poetry, the ultimately political nature of his manipulations of literary history, and makes for a message far more compelling than the vapid critical platitudes that often take the place of that message. Prophecy embodies a language of authenticity not only in summoning men to abide by the principles of their faith, but in doing so with the weight of tradition and with a charged discourse that strips away the fictions of innovation.

Such a reading challenges, at the very least, the anti-intellectual image that Neruda himself fostered and that continues to prevail among many of his admirers, if not among many critics. As early as 1929 Neruda was opposing Borges' "worry over the problems of culture and society" to his own "contempt for culture" and his preference for "a knowledge without antecedents" and "a physical absorption of the world."[5] Five years later, Federico García Lorca, a poet who cultivated the same image, introduced Neruda to the Spanish public

---

[5]My translation from Pablo Neruda and Héctor Eandi, *Correspondencia durante "Residencia en la tierra,"* ed. Margarita Aguirre (Buenos Aires: Sudamericana, 1980), p. 46.

as "a poet closer to death than to philosophy." Neruda's subsequent politicization, his successive conversions to social, "Americanist," and socialist-realist poetic modes, and his later whimsical verse were all versions of the same image of the poet as magus of immediacy. The trouble with such a celebrity image is that while it satisfies the curiosity of a few journalists, it often blurs a knowledge of the very texts that ostensibly sustain it. The criticism of Neruda has often succumbed to the allure of this celebrity image and its premises have invariably been affected by it. Not that Neruda's anti-intellectualism should be simply ignored so that one may read his poetry in sterile isolation; it should be situated as part of a broader rhetorical strategy that defines his role within the framework of modernity. For Neruda's quest after a "physical absorption of the world" and his "conversion" to politics are themselves the signs of his modernity, the symptoms of what Paul de Man calls "a desire to wipe out whatever came earlier, in the hope of reaching at last a point that could be called a true present, a point of origin that marks a new departure."[6]

One of the aims of this book, then, is to restore a sense of distance to the criticism of Neruda. To this end I have focused on prophecy, the central metaphor for modern poetry, not only because it is crucial for an understanding of Neruda's major works, but because it strikes at the heart of what I believe to be the principal cause of critical mystification. An assessment of Neruda's modernity cannot be limited to his genial discoveries, as it were, cannot stop with a recognition of his invention; it must also trace the erratic response that modernity, no less than prophecy, imposes. For at the very moment when the modern poet rejects the past in favor of an immediate present, he is forced to acknowledge his anteriority, the phantoms of literary history, so as not to sever the temporal basis of his claim to an origin, the body of literary modernity. And so "the more radical the rejection of anything that came before, the greater the dependence on the past."[7]

Similarly, my concern with poetics as a critical category re-

---

[6]Paul de Man, *Blindness and Insight: Essays in the Rhetoric of Contemporary Criticism* (New York: Oxford University Press, 1971), p. 148.
[7]Ibid., p. 161.

Introduction

flects the pursuit of a more realistic evaluation. That a poetics grounds a poet's utterances and that it can be safely recovered by the skillful interpreter is the almost inescapable assumption of every reading of poetry. We read poems not just to understand a particular text but to retrieve the poet's thought, his "vision of the world," his "ideology." Yet the nature of a poetics, not unlike the nature of ideology itself, is that it remains always partially hidden to both poet and reader, much as the structure of a language remains unthought by its native speakers. Poetics, then, is not simply the answer to the question that the poem poses, but the space where the poet's desire plays itself out—the trace of an origin whose loss the poem dramatizes. Like the ever-elusive answer in the epigraph at the head of this Introduction, a poetics can be "known" only in the mode of error. In fact, to summon a poetics may amount to undertaking the same kind of discreet reading that prophecy prescribes. For to insist on a "poetics of prophecy," as this book does, is to risk redundancy. As prophecy describes a lack in the speaking subject by locating the origin of his message outside of him, so poetics assumes the kind of reading that exposes the discordance of intention and origin that underlies all poetic discourse. In actual practice, this concern with poetics takes the form of a dialectic interplay of text and context, or of poem and autobiographical pronouncement. The most systematic formulation of this interplay is undertaken in Chapter 3, the book's physical and conceptual center, which is devoted to a reading of *Alturas de Macchu Picchu* (1946).

The early three-volume cycle of *Residencia en la tierra* (*Residence on Earth*) set the pattern that has dominated the criticism of Neruda in later years. The exotic allure of Neruda's four-year sojourn in the Far East (during which most of the poems of the first book were written), along with the alleged influence of an incipient surrealism, which at the time was relatively strong in Chile, crystallized a rarefied image for the poet which went hand in hand with the elliptical density of his poetic style. Amado Alonso, the first of Neruda's major critics, saw this style as "a dark sense of life" ruled by "a visionary feeling" that exposed "the slow decomposition of all existence."[8] Alonso

---

[8] *Poesía y estilo de Pablo Neruda: Interpretación de una poesía hermética* (1940; Buenos Aires: Sudamericana, 1968), pp. 19, 32.

wrote these words in 1940, five years after Neruda had published the first two books and well after he had abjured the *Residencia* poems following his experience in the Spanish Civil War. A Spaniard, Alonso elaborated his study in close consultation with Neruda and while living in Argentina, where he published it. Alonso's crucial insight was to identify Neruda's early visionary strain, but the exclusively negative message he derived from these early poems reflected a superficial acquaintance with modern poetry as well as a docile adoption of Neruda's prejudices against his earlier work. The interest that *Residencia en la tierra* held for Alonso was primarily that of a case study in what he called "modern poetic obscurity," which, viewed in the context of Neruda's style, became the formal or external counterpart of an emotional or internal turbulence. Hence his subtitle, "An Interpretation of a Hermetic Poetry."

Whether in fact Alonso's pioneer reading amounted to an "interpretation," in the traditional sense of the reconstitution of an argument, seems more open to question. "Stylistics interests itself," Alonso wrote elsewhere, in "the aesthetico-poetic consequences of an author's vision of the world—not... its philosophico-rational aspects," and in the irreducibly literary dimension "seen most easily in the case of lyrical poems" that are ordered "according not to rational knowledge but to a personal vision of factual elements."[9] What Alonso achieved, then, was not strictly a reading but a cross-section survey of the peculiarities of Neruda's style, a style in which hermeticism becomes the formal counterpart of a negative thematics and both, in turn, become the "expression" of internal turbulence. The trouble with such an "interpretation," of course, is not that it is false, in the sense of being aberrant or far-fetched, but that it is incomplete, based as it is on a partial survey that concentrated on the poetry's linguistic devices to the exclusion of its argument. However obscure the poetry of *Residencia* may have been originally, Alonso's dispersive survey, as determined by his application of a stylistics methodology, rendered it more obscure still. It could be said that instead of "an interpretation of a hermetic

---

[9]"The Stylistic Interpretation of Literary Texts" (1942), in *Velocities of Change*, ed. Richard Macksey (Baltimore: Johns Hopkins University Press, 1974), pp. 61–62.

Introduction

poetry," Alonso more properly achieved "a hermetic interpretation of poetry." And if Alonso's partial views prevailed eventually, it was partly because his was the first sustained attempt at the practical criticism of a contemporary Hispanic poet, partly because at the time it seemed to be the only logical critical response to Neruda's political conversion.

My own reading of *Residencia en la tierra*, which comprises the first two chapters of this book, attempts to reconstitute the argument that Alonso's "interpretation" laid aside. More than a negative world view, what is at stake in this textual construct is the rescue from time of a visionary self by an idolatrous conception of writing. Thus the first two volumes tell the story of prophecy gone wrong, and the second volume, especially, shows the monstrosity that writing becomes when it is put at the service of a self-centered enterprise. In showing how this project determines a fundamental change in the speaker, I propose a reading of the well-known conversion poems in *Tercera residencia* that eschews the traditional recourse to a biographical explication.

That a subtle complicity between poet and critic has permeated readings of *Residencia en la tierra* is confirmed in part by the recurrence of such a biographical fallacy in most of the criticism devoted to Neruda since Alonso's time. Given the nature of conversion, this recourse to biography has been to some extent inevitable. When applied to *Tercera residencia*, however, such a solution has concealed the rhetorical failure of its conversion texts. And in the case of *Alturas de Macchu Picchu*, Neruda's definitive conversion text, the loss of critical distance has become the principal obstacle to the assessment of the poem's meditation on history. Partly as a result of the biographical reading that Neruda himself encouraged in his accounts of his visit to Machu Picchu in 1943, partly owing to the climate of cultural nationalism in which the poem was written, critical readings have erected a monument to its ostensible dramatization of the cause of Latin American identity without realizing that, as an allegory, it both embodies that cause and denounces its ideal presuppositions. By unfolding what I call a "prophecy of writing," in which the activities of reading and interpretation themselves become political metaphors, the poem at once gains access to a Western historical consciousness and calls into question the metaphysical assumptions that render that consciousness possible. The poem's rhetorical gesture is one of exile, not cultural identity, and it is exile that explains the role it plays within the sequence of *Canto General* (1950).

Neruda's discovery of allegory would lead him, three years later, to fashion in *Canto General* an analogy to sacred scripture similar to Whitman's *Leaves of Grass* or Hugo's *Légende des siècles*, a kind of Latin American bible that dramatizes the politics of the Book. What is fundamental about this Book, I propose in Chapter 4, is not its recording of Neruda's quarrel with Gabriel González Videla, the then-president of Chile under whose persecution Neruda finished writing his book, but its dramatic use of biblical rhetoric to rewrite Latin American history and thus heighten political urgency. And far from being at odds with Neruda's Marxist politics, the rhetoric of biblical prophecy confirms an affinity with Marxism, which is heir to the prophetic tradition.

I devote what may seem disproportionate attention to *Alturas de Macchu Picchu,* a single poem, in contrast with the relatively brief time I spend on *Canto General,* the book that contains it. Yet unless we dwell first on the rhetorical implications of *Alturas,* which becomes the source for much of Neruda's subsequent poetry, we shall fail to grasp the underlying argument of *Canto General*. As the poem dramatizes the transformation of an idolatrous, ironic writing that is identified with *Residencia en la tierra,* so it also embodies the beginnings of a historical recuperation whose comprehensive metaphor is the Book. And as the poem's allegory disavows in advance all comprehensive claims, so *Canto General* wields this metaphor only to recoil from it in the end in order to avoid representing an apocalypse by revolution. In a fifth and final chapter, devoted to Neruda's late apocalyptic mode, I explore the rhetorical implications of this avoidance and attempt to locate its delayed representation in *La espada encendida* (1970), Neruda's last prophetic book, which dramatizes an internalized apocalypse.

We may thus regard the course of Neruda's poetics of prophecy as one poet's reenactment of the Romantic imagination, according to the pattern suggested by Abrams, whereby "faith in an apocalypse by revelation [is] replaced by faith in an apocalypse by revolution, and this now [gives] way to faith in an

Introduction

apocalypse by imagination or cognition."[10] What such a pattern ignores, of course, is that these Romantic modes, at least where Neruda is concerned, turn out to be interdependent rather than simply sequential, and therefore that a "poetics" cannot account fully for the margin of visionary error to which all prophecy is subject. In a brief Postscript on Neruda's most powerful late poem I attempt to deal with this question as part of a fable of the modern author.

[10] *Natural Supernaturalism*, p. 334.

1

Vision and Time

> I awake; but between me and nature remains a veil, a subtle tissue: a mosquito net. Behind it, things have taken their place in the world: brides receive their flowers, debtors their bills. Where am I? [III, 627]

I

Thus begins "Diurno de Singapore," one of a dozen newspaper articles that Neruda sent back to Chile while en route to the Far East in 1927. Behind the "mosquito net," a veil separating poet and world, subject and object, all things assume their place and elude his grasp. The final question lends itself to two discrete interpretations. A literal reading, provided further in the same paragraph, simply locates the poet in space: "I'm in Singapore." But another, rhetorical option would instead leave the relation between subject and veil unclear. Where is he, in fact, in relation to that "subtle tissue"? What position can the poet assume, where can he stand, in a world whose order somehow excludes him?

The above passage and its attendant questions may serve as a springboard for our discussion of *Residencia en la tierra*, the three-book cycle on which Neruda's reputation as a visionary poet rests. It is in these books that we can identify what I here call the visionary mode, the interplay of subject and object as the basis of poetic perception. All prophetic poetry, I have argued, is visionary in the sense of an imaginative statement predicated on the mimesis of revelation. But to speak of a visionary mode in particular implies recognition of a privileged perception in the speaker and its role in the poem's rhetorical structure. In visionary poetry the revelation of an object's truth stems from the perception of an alienated subject. In the above passage, for example, the speaker's visual range, isolated by the mosquito net, allows him to perceive two significant scenes that are related by the punctuation as sequential events. The sudden invasion of daylight accounts for the specifically visual experience, while the veil is but the symbol of the visionary process: the re*vel*ation or un*veil*ing of the object through the *re*veiling of language.

The term "visionary mode" is at once a restrictive and a comprehensive name for modernist poetics, a conception of the poet as an alienated subject who conveys images claimed to be truthful and significant. Such artistic truth, as Frank Kermode notes, "is unrelated to, and more exalted than, that of positivist science or any observation depending upon the discursive reason."[1] The representation of this truth determines, in turn, a distinct rhetorical effect insofar as the mode depends on the dramatic presence of a passive prophetic speaker or persona. This passive speaker, more an agent than an instrument, is concerned with insightful perception and with knowledge that transforms obscure feelings into clear ideas. Thus the visionary mode identifies what throughout literary history has been variously described as "spots of time" (Wordsworth), "moments privilégiés" (Proust), "epiphanies" (Joyce), or even the Russian formalists' notion of art as defamiliarization—in short, the modernist concept of art as the fresh rearrangement of reality.[2] Each of these formulas has a distinct structure of its own, of course, and my intention in lumping them together is to emphasize their common tenet: that visionary truth is inextricably linked to the artist's estrangement. That meaning was perhaps summarized best by Rimbaud, who in a memorable phrase claimed he was a seer because he was an *other*. "Car *je* est un autre" (For *I* is an other), he wrote to Paul Demeny in a phrase whose

---

[1] *Romantic Image* (New York: Vintage, 1964), p. 45. On the aesthetics of nondiscursivity, see A. G. Lehmann, *The Symbolist Aesthetic in France, 1885–1895*, 2d ed. (Oxford: Basil Blackwell, 1968), esp. pp. 74–80.

[2] For an account of these visionary "moments," see M. H. Abrams, *Natural Supernaturalism: Tradition and Revolution in Romantic Literature* (New York: Norton, 1971), pp. 409–62. Fredric Jameson argues for the inclusion of the Russian formalists' notion of estrangement, *ostranenie*, among these modernist moments in *The Prison-House of Language* (Princeton: Princeton University Press, 1972), pp. 54–57.

grammatical violence concealed a whole theory of poetic vision.[3] The subject's self-distancing—that is, his own internal discontinuity or *dédoublement*—alienates the object in such a way that it prompts its rearrangement in inordinate, perhaps superior, ways unseen by normal eyes.

The assumption that *Residencia en la tierra* is ultimately guided by a visionary poetics has with varying degrees of explicitness governed critical readings since Amado Alonso's groundbreaking study.[4] A visionary syntax or poetic logic can in fact be isolated in the three-book cycle. Each of these books can be read as a stage in the poet's reasoned probe into the subject-object dichotomy that underlies the visionary experience. Time, both as existential concern and aesthetic principle, plays a crucial role in this experience as it urges the self's preservation within an aesthetic project. That is, writing provides a haven for the poetic self against the passage of time, but as it does so it turns that self into a lifeless idol. The three books of *Residencia en la tierra* show the dramatic evolution of a prophetic speaker; by focusing on this dramatic change, we can outline the logic of conversion with which the *Residencia* cycle is brought to a close.

II

A "residence on earth" can be that only for someone not of this earth, someone who is alien or at least alienated. The poet is a guest, a newly arrived visitor, and his "residence" becomes the occasion for either fresh discovery or reacquaintance. From the very title, then, the book insists on the subject's distance from the object and the object's reconstitution in a new light.

Although the earliest poems of *Residencia* date from as far back as 1925, when Neruda was still living in Chile, it was not until he took up residence in Burma, two years later, that he began to

[3] Arthur Rimbaud, *Complete Works: Selected Letters*, ed. and trans. Wallace Fowlie (Chicago: University of Chicago Press, 1966), p. 304. On Rimbaud and the visionary tradition, see Gwendolyn Bays, *The Orphic Vision: Seer Poets from Novalis to Rimbaud* (Lincoln: University of Nebraska Press, 1964).

[4] *Poesía y estilo de Pablo Neruda* (1940; Buenos Aires: Sudamericana, 1968). Beyond Alonso, the two studies that have gone furthest in establishing this visionary filiation are Alfredo Lozada, *El monismo agónico de Pablo Neruda* (Mexico City: B. Costa Amic, 1971), and Emir Rodríguez Monegal, *Neruda: El viajero inmóvil* (1966; 2d rev. ed., Caracas: Monte Avila, 1977), esp. pp. 254-82.

give shape to the first book, which covers the years up to 1931.⁵ Neruda's alienation can be explained by the bleak circumstances in which he found himself at the time. His meager salary as honorary consul in Rangoon was hardly enough to survive on, and his physical isolation, removed as he was from a familiar geography and climate, was only made worse by his linguistic estrangement. English was the lingua franca of diplomacy in the Far East then (as it still is today) and he was living among people who never had heard Spanish, let alone spoke or understood it. There is even a pathetic letter from this period in which Neruda begged the Spanish poet Rafael Alberti to rush him a dictionary because he feared he was forgetting his native tongue. Indeed, one can hardly slight the linguistic import of Neruda's alienation, since in many ways *Residencia en la tierra* is just that—an estranged poet's refuge within the resources of his own language, a kind of poetic "last stand" within the one residence he knew best.⁶

Yet for all the importance of the language barrier, we must not overlook the broader alienating context of Neruda's personal clash with the East. It is a commonplace that Neruda, unlike other writers who have lived for a time in Asia and adapted to it with much more ease (such as Octavio Paz), was never willing or able to understand Eastern modes of life and thought. "Distance and a deep silence," he wrote years later, "separated me from the world, and I could not bring myself to enter wholeheartedly the alien world around me."⁷ Often, however, this acknowledgment is accompanied by a view of the poetry as the result of an intellectual impermeability, as irrational exercises,

---

⁵On Neruda's circumstances during these early years, see his *Memoirs*, trans. Hardie St. Martin (New York: Farrar, Straus & Giroux, 1976), pp. 71-110; Rodríguez Monegal, *Neruda*, pp. 67-93; and René de Costa, *The Poetry of Pablo Neruda* (Cambridge: Harvard University Press, 1979), pp. 58-104.

⁶An echo of this linguistic alienation appears in *La Barcarola* (1967): "Asia negra, tiniebla del bosque / . . . / De pronto se inmovilizaron las ruedas, bajaron los desconocidos / y allí me quedé, occidental, en la soledad de la selva: / allí sin salir de aquel carro perdido en la noche, con veinte años de edad / esperando la muerte, refugiado en mi idioma" (Black Asia, the forest's shadow / . . . / Suddenly, the wheels stopped, the strangers stepped down / and there I stayed, a Western man, in the jungle's solitude: / refusing to come out of that coach, lost in the night, twenty years old, / waiting for death, taking refuge in my language) (III, 180).

⁷*Memoirs*, p. 97.

that is, whose ostensible hermeticism excludes the possibility of representation. To support this view critics invoke the influence of an incipient surrealism, which was fairly strong in Chile at the time that Neruda wrote the first poems, and Neruda's own rejection of *Residencia en la tierra* after his involvement in the Spanish Civil War and his political conversion. Of the two, Neruda's rejection has provided much critical mileage. For in denouncing poetic abstruseness as a symptom of social inauthenticity, Neruda seemed to underscore the moral underside of hermeticism, in addition to explaining, if only from the vantage point of a personal crisis, the reasons for his conversion.[8] To my knowledge, the influence that Neruda's self-disparagement may have had on the criticism of *Residencia en la tierra* has never been broached. Nor for that matter has it ever been questioned that an inability to adopt an Eastern mode of thought necessarily determines an irrational style. It could be shown, I think, that there has existed a subtle but pervasive complicity between Neruda's political prejudices and the arguments often used to approach this early poetry. The issue is not, obviously, that Neruda's opinions should be discarded, but that they should be judged as defensive gestures that form part of a broader rhetorical strategy.

These distinctions need to be made clear, and the issue of alienation itself viewed dialectically, if we are to avoid making unwarranted assumptions. For neither a careful reading of the poems nor the extant documents of this period support the argument for irrationality that has gone unchallenged for so long. On the contrary, both poems and documents point up a nondiscursive though orderly probe of the poet's alienation and the knowledge it affords. It is the knowledge that Neruda displays, for example, in another of his articles in *La Nación*, in which he

---

[8]Neruda's renunciation of *Residencia* began almost immediately after his involvement in the Spanish Civil War, as attested by the poems of conversion of *España en el corazón* (1938). Among the many prose texts in which he declared his rejection, perhaps the best known is Alfredo Cardona Peña, "Pablo Neruda: Breve historia de sus libros," *Cuadernos Americanos*, 54 (1950), 257–89, reprinted, in slightly revised form, in *Pablo Neruda y otros ensayos* (Mexico City: De Andrea, 1955), pp. 7–84. The assumption of a coincidence between linguistic hermeticism and moral irresponsibility permeates Alonso's influential *Poesía y estilo de Pablo Neruda*.

remarks that "these places only require constant knowledge and attention" and that "in India human beings form no part of the landscape and there is no discontinuity between oneself and Nature as in the Contemporary West." Neruda concludes by noting that "everything here seems to be in ruins and tearing itself apart, but in truth strong elemental and living links join these appearances with almost secret and almost undying connections."[9] We may therefore view Neruda's goal in these poems as an attempt to understand those "secret and undying connections" not despite but because of his view that they constitute a dilemma for the Western observer who has internalized an epistemology based on irony and distance. It should be clear that by irony I mean not only the linguistic tension stemming from a disparity between intention and expression. I mean, principally, the phenomenology of Romantic irony, which prescribes the estrangement of the self and the consciousness of an absolute subjectivity as the means to knowledge. It is that knowledge, in fact, that appears at every turn in Neruda's correspondence with Héctor Eandi and José Santos González Vera, writer friends who at the time lived in Buenos Aires and Santiago de Chile: "I believe myself incapable of any communication"; "I've surrounded myself with a certain secret atmossphere." The most pathetic of such remarks appears in a letter he wrote to Eandi in 1930: "At the time I can feel nothing I can perceive, everything seems not empty of meaning but abounding in it. I do feel that all things have already found meaning by themselves, that I form no part of them and that I have nothing to penetrate them with."[10]

The title *Residencia en la tierra* thus provides a governing metaphor for an ironic distance between subject and object which, beginning with "Galope muerto," its first poem, elaborates what I should like to call a "scene of writing"—a textual

---

[9] My translation from "Oriente y Oriente," *La Nación* (Santiago de Chile), February 7, 1929, as reprinted in Juan Loveluck, "Tributo y despedida, Pablo Neruda (1904–1973): 'Más notas sobre Neruda en Oriente,'" *Hispania*, 57 (1974), 977.

[10] Unless otherwise noted, I quote and translate from Pablo Neruda–Héctor Eandi, *Correspondencia durante "Residencia en la tierra,"* ed. Margarita Aguirre (Buenos Aires: Sudamericana, 1980), pp. 78–79.

theater where the self dramatizes its relationship with the writing process.[11] The title of this first poem provides an important link to the book's title, as if the redundancy of the phrase "residencia en la tierra" contained an ironic paradox from which "Galope muerto," the following title phrase, stems. Implicit in the latter, which constitutes an oxymoron or antithetical metaphor, is a translation of the English "dead gallop," a horse's wild run. The Spanish "galope muerto," however, does not convey this figurative meaning; it signifies the antithetical sense of a dead or silent sound. The starting point of the poem, and therefore of the book, is this paradoxical, impossible experience, which originates in the irony of the two titles. Thus juxtaposed, they yield a contextual argument: (1) the subject's ironic distance causes (2) the paradox of a silent sound. This paradox is a vision.

I of course extend the definition of vision to encompass an aural mode. Privileged perception includes sound as well as sight, clairaudience as well as clairvoyance. This first poem can, in fact, be read as the narration of the passage from clairaudience to clairvoyance, hearing to sight, or "audition" to vision, as it recasts the experience of unheard sound, as it were, into intelligible imagery. What seems crucial, in any case, is that this particular communication depends on the title's double rhetorical deviation as both oxymoron and translation, a deviation that signals a retreat from referential meaning and a plunge into a purely linguistic realm. The title pointedly tells us, in other words, that the experience about to be told will prepare the ground for a visionary space that is made up solely of language—the only space in which visions can properly occur.

My explication of the first two titles may seem unduly labored but it is designed to convey that what in the past has been taken

---

[11] I borrow the term "scene of writing" from Jacques Derrida's essay "Freud and the Scene of Writing," in *Writing and Difference*, trans. Alan Bass (1967; Chicago: University of Chicago Press, 1978), pp. 196-231, where it is used to describe some of Freud's meditations on the unconscious. My own use differs from Derrida's in its emphasis of the dramatic component of the forces of writing. For readings of "Galope muerto" see Amado Alonso, *Poesía y estilo*, pp. 192-200; Lozada, *El monismo agónico*, pp. 215-21; and John Felstiner, "Translating Pablo Neruda's "Galope muerto,'" *PMLA*, 93 (1978), 185-98, now part of his *Translating Neruda: The Way to Macchu Picchu* (Stanford, Calif.: Stanford University Press, 1980), pp. 60-83.

Vision and Time

to be a baffling "hermeticism" is nothing more than a rich linguistic density that becomes clear if words are simply read in context. "Galope muerto" refers to nothing more than what is says: a dead, impossible sound. It is an aural rather than a visual revelation, the first of a series of poems in *Residencia* on the theme of the poet's gifted sense of hearing. Thus in the passage from the title to the first line the reader must supply the copula that the experience assumes: "Galope muerto *es*"

> Como cenizas, como mares poblándose,
> en la sumergida lentitud, en lo informe,
> o como se oyen desde lo alto de los caminos
> cruzar las campanadas en cruz,
> teniendo ese sonido ya aparte del metal,
> confuso, pesando, haciéndose polvo
> en el mismo molino de las formas demasiado lejos,
> o recordadas o no vistas,
> y el perfume de las ciruelas que rodando a tierra
> se pudren en el tiempo, infinitamente verdes. [I, 169]

> Like ashes, like seas populating / in the submerged slowness, in the unformed, / or as one hears from high atop the roads / the church bells crossing, / having that sound already apart from the metal, / confused, weighty, turning into dust / in the same windmill of forms too far away / or remembered or not seen, / and the perfume of plums, which, rolling down to earth, / rot in time, infinitely green.

Both the anxious tone and the obsessive simile clauses dramatize a desire to transpose indefinite sound into visual terms. Yet the choppy quality of these similes implies as well the sound's resistance to discursive form. Other sounds—the echo of ringing bells, for example—appear as possible substitutes, along with the images of faintly remembered or unseen shapes. The series culminates in the image of rotting green plums, which, like the title image, constitutes an oxymoron. The first stanza, then, arranges a sequence of image options in an order of viability that culminates, fittingly, in a visual version of the aural paradox described in the title.

After this initial success, the aural experience continues, and so does the poem. Far from being an isolated event, the muted sound appears everywhere, surrounding the speaker as in a state of siege:

> Aquello todo tan rápido, tan viviente,
> inmóvil sin embargo, como la polea loca en sí misma,
> esas ruedas de los motores, en fin.
> Existiendo como las puntadas secas en las costuras del árbol,
> callado, por alrededor, de tal modo,
> mezclando todos los limbos sus colas.
> Es que de dónde, por dónde, en qué orilla?
> El rodeo constante, incierto, tan mudo,
> como las lilas alrededor del convento
> o la llegada de la muerte a la lengua del buey
> que cae a tumbos, guardabajo, y cuyos cuernos quieren
>   sonar. [I, 169]

> All that so fast, so living, / immobile, however, like the pulley crazily turning on itself, / those engine wheels, that is. / Existing like the dried stitches in the seams of the tree, / silent, around, just so, / all the limbs mixing their tails. / It's just from where to where, on what shore? / The constant round, uncertain, so mute, / like the lilacs surrounding the convent / or the arrival of death at the tongue of the ox, / who drops his guard, and whose horns want to sound.

The surrounding objects, described with similar oxymorons (they are both "rápido" and "inmóvil"), appear spread out in a circular pattern. The first stanza suggests a circle in the image of "molino de las formas," which makes no sense until we encounter other circular images: "polea," "rodeo constante," "lilas alrededor del convento." These are images of circular or cyclical activity, an endless life-death process to which the speaker, who assumes a central position, bears witness.[12] Along with a common circular pattern these objects share a strange silence, an uncanny stillness that is enough to arrest the speaker's momentum and persuade him to pose the experience in far more cautious terms. The encompassing indefinite pronouns, for example, turn out to be "callado," the siege of reality becomes "tan mudo," and as death overcomes the tongue of the

---

[12] Lozada, *El monismo agónico*, pp. 218–20.

Vision and Time

falling ox its horns become a pair of muffled trumpets. The speaker discovers, that is, a voice buried under surrounding matter. His mission now, as in the first stanza, is to translate that "dead gallop" into yet another intelligible description, which the three questions pinpointing the origin of the experience are designed to prepare.

> Por eso, en lo inmóvil, deteniéndose, percibir,
> entonces, como aleteo inmenso, encima,
> como abejas muertas o números,
> ay, lo que mi corazón pálido no puede abarcar,
> en multitudes, en lágrimas saliendo apenas
> y esfuerzos humanos, tormentas,
> acciones negras descubiertas de repente
> como hielos, desorden vasto,
> oceánico, para mí que entro cantando,
> como con una espada entre indefensos. [I, 169-70]

> For this reason, in the stillness, stopping, to perceive, / then, like wing beats immense, above, / like dead bees or numbers, / oh, what my pale heart cannot bear, / in multitudes, in tears hardly flowing / and human efforts, storms, black actions suddenly discovered / like ice, vast disorder, / oceanic, for me who enter singing, / as with a sword among the defenseless.

Despite his anxiety—reflected by this point in a virtually telegraphic syntax that confutes grammatical coherence—the speaker resolves to confront the disordered human frailty that he alone perceives in sudden pangs of vision. Like the one-eyed king in the country of the blind, he is a singer amid mute objects, a competent translator of their silence, and consequently an armed prophet whose voice is a sword. But these credentials by themselves cannot account for the nature of the original sound, whose origin he seeks now in explicit terms:

> Ahora bien, de qué está hecho ese surgir de palomas
> que hay entre la noche y el tiempo, como una barranca
>   húmeda?
> Ese sonido ya tan largo
> que cae listando de piedras los caminos,
> más bien, cuando sólo una hora
> crece de improviso, extendiéndose sin tregua. [I, 170]

Pablo Neruda: The Poetics of Prophecy

> Well now, of what is that upsurge of pigeons made, / existing between night and time like a damp ravine? / That sound already so long / that it stripes the roads with stones as it falls, / rather, when only one hour / grows suddenly, extending without end.

The question—which, as John Felstiner notes, is one of only two complete sentences in the poem—restates the mystery.[13] Both "ese surgir de palomas" and "ese sonido ya tan largo," equated as they are by the same demonstrative pronoun, refer to the "dead gallop" whose effect on the speaker is a feeling of boundless temporality. The last stanza, finally, hints at the answer:

> Adentro del anillo del verano
> una vez los grandes zapallos escuchan,
> estirando sus plantas conmovedoras,
> de eso, de lo que solicitándose mucho,
> de lo lleno, oscuros de pesadas gotas.   [I, 170]
>
> Inside the ring of summer / once the great calabash trees listen / stretching their moving plants, / of that, of what asking much, / of the full, obscure with heavy drops.

The origin remains inside the "anillo del verano," a comprehensive circle that encloses all the circular objects in a single structure. Within it, "los grandes zapallos" listen to one another as if engaged in a cosmic conversation whose subject is perhaps the very answer to the riddle that prompts the poem. The latter image, typical of the early Neruda, echoes the passage in Baudelaire's "Correspondances" in which the "forest of symbols" casts an amused glance at the unsuspecting speaker. The final genitive clauses attempt to answer the question that was posed in the previous stanza. And yet, suspended until now, that answer is no clearer than the question itself. In the end, that is, we have learned no more than we knew at the beginning, with the possible exception, perhaps, that we know that the mysterious sound has accosted the speaker to the point of impeding his articulation of the quest. The origin of the haunting

---

[13]Felstiner, "Translating Pablo Neruda's 'Galope muerto,'" p. 91.

Vision and Time

experience, and thus the reason for the poem, remain beyond the speaker's reach, behind reality's encircling veil.

"Galope muerto" is the most apposite introduction to the visionary poetics of *Residencia en la tierra*, a fact that perhaps explains its leading position in the book. The poem deals with the discovery of the visionary vocation, and its echo of Baudelaire's famous text is appropriate, as Neruda seems to be responding with a postsymbolist poetics of his own. The two poems share a view of the poet as a reader or decoder of signs, but they propose radically different readings. For Baudelaire, reality enjoys a religious stability afforded by Nature's "temple," an aesthetic monad or ultimate symbol in which the poet places his faith as the means to ensure the accuracy of his reading of the world's "gloomy and deep unity." In Neruda's postmodern text, on the other hand, reality is no less gloomy or deep, but it hardly affords the unity or stability that Baudelaire enjoys: the "temple" has turned into "ashes." Baudelaire trusts that his poem will fuse word and thing by means of the proper symbol—a confidence whose formal correlative is the traditional sonnet of his argument. Neruda dramatizes a radical linguistic distrust by showing the gap that exists between word and thing—there being no longer an aesthetic unity that can support this language—and by making the search for a visual analogy the very subject of his poem. The poem's truncated, disjointed structure is the formal counterpart of the failure of that search. "Galope muerto" may, in fact, be the extreme version of the theme that Michel Foucault identifies at the root of classical representation—the anguish of the poet who "beneath the language of signs and beneath the interplay of their precisely delineated distinctions... strains his ears to catch that 'other language,' the language without words or discourse, of resemblance." The modern poet thus fulfills what Foucault calls an "allegorical role" in attempting to read that "other language," "another deeper discourse, which recalls the time when words glittered in the universal resemblance of things."[14]

That "Galope muerto" achieves its effect by dramatizing the visionary's anxiety is evident enough. But it would be wrong, I

---

[14]Michel Foucault, *The Order of Things* (New York: Random House, 1973), p. 49-50.

think, further to attribute the poem's disjointed form, as Alfredo Lozada suggests, to an intuitive source.[15] Rather than attempt to describe the empirical conditions of the writing subject, it seems safer to notice that the lack of a culminating vision signals a self-reflection that calls attention to the visionary process itself. Because of its disjointed form, as if it were the nervous stenography of a visionary session, the poem can yield only a trace of the manner in which it came about. The subject sees, in this sense, not only the object but also himself in the act of seeing and recording. He is a witness to his own witnessing, as it were, and the poem becomes a visionary cinema in which he plays the dual role of spectator and actor, audience and protagonist.

Self-reflection is what Amado Alonso called "auto-exégesis," self-exegesis or commentary, to explain those frequent moments in *Residencia en la Tierra* when the poetry turns to explaining itself.[16] As a critical tool the term is too limiting, as we shall see, but for the moment it serves to remind us that in *Residencia en la tierra* self-commentary varies in degree from poem to poem. In "Galope muerto," for example, the self-reflexive gesture is never dramatized overtly but remains implicit in the poem's disjointedness. This use of self-reflexive form dates back to *Tentativa del hombre infinito* (1925), Neruda's first long poem, in which the visionary speaker at times intrudes into the narrative to describe himself as a seer and to tell of his efforts to produce the text. As we read the poem we are left with the impression of automatic writing flowing directly from the unconscious without any guidance from the creative faculties. And yet its argument, as Jaime Alazraki and others have shown, is hardly capricious insofar as it structures a "visionary voyage," Neruda's contribution to a well-known poetic tradition.[17] "Galope muerto," then,

---

[15]Lozada, *Monismo agónico*, p. 222 and passim. Félix Martínez Bonati has shown how Alonso's confusion of the real and the textual authors is in part responsible for creating the image of Neruda as an "eruptive" poet. See his *La estructura de la obra literaria* (1961; Barcelona: Seix Barral, 1972), pp. 158–63.

[16]See Alonso, *Poesia y estilo*, pp. 30–31.

[17]Jaime Alazraki, "El surrealismo de *Tentativa del hombre infinito*," *Hispanic Review*, 40 (1972), 31–39; Luis F. González Cruz, "El viaje trascendente de Pablo Neruda: Una lectura de *Tentativa del hombre infinito*," *Symposium*, 32 (1978), 197–207, and de Costa, *Poetry of Pablo Neruda*, pp. 41–57. Alain Sicard has read the poem as an exercise in self-reflexive form: "La eternidad en el instante: Un análisis de *Tentativa del hombre infinito*," *Anales de la Universidad de Chile*, 129 (1971), 107–16, now part of his *El pensamiento poético de Pablo Neruda*, trans. Pilar Ruiz Va (1977; Madrid: Gredos, 1981), pp. 63–98.

Vision and Time

belongs to this earlier experimental stage, in which self-exegesis is a by-product of formal disjointedness.

"Arte poética" is perhaps the best illustration of this self-reflexive poetics, as its title suggests. And the further fact that it occupies a central position within the first book, the seventeenth of thirty-three poems, should convince us of its importance. For these reasons it seems best to discuss it now, profit from its centrality, and backtrack later. It begins by locating the speaker in an imaginary space:

> Entre sombra y espacio, entre guarniciones y doncellas,
> dotado de corazón singular y sueños funestos
> precipitadamente pálido, marchito en la frente
> y con luto de viudo furioso por cada día de vida   [I, 184]

> Between shadow and space, between garrisons and damsels, / gifted with a singular heart and dismal dreams / precipitously pallid, with withered forehead / and with a furious widower's mourning each day of life

While the first set of images denotes opposite states of perception—"sombra y espacio," confusion and clarity—the second set assigns the speaker the role of a hero breaking down garrisons to rescue damsels in distress. This self-adulation is complemented by the claim to "gifts," the traits of the Romantic artist and particularly those of the *poète maudit*—a unique heart, a peculiar paleness, and a daily death-in-life. The portrait is stock Romantic, to be sure, and it recalls one text in particular, Gérard de Nerval's "El desdichado" ("le ténébreux, le veuf, l'inconsolé" [the gloomy, the widower, the disconsolate]), to which the fourth line seems to allude. Nor should the irony of the self-portrait escape us. It reworks conventional Romantic traits in order to heighten the speaker's diffidence yet preserve tonal coherence. The alliteration in "*p*reci*p*itadamente *p*álido," for example, exaggerates the speaker's paleness enough to turn the portrait into a caricature. Following these lines are two instances of seeing and hearing which, together with the ensuing simile clauses, recall the desperate series in "Galope muerto." This time, however, the additional number heightens the desperate tone as the speaker gropes for the correct analogy. The last of them reveals

Pablo Neruda: The Poetics of Prophecy

> ... un olor de casa sola
> en la que los huéspedes entran de noche perdidamente ebrios,
> y hay un olor de ropa tirada al suelo, y
> una ausencia de flores,
> —posiblemente de otro modo aún menos melancólico—[I, 185]

> a smell of solitary house / which guests enter at night hopelessly drunk, / and there's a smell of clothes thrown on the floor, and / an absence of flowers, / —perhaps in another still less melancholy way—

The "solitary house" is but the "residence on earth" appearing here in spatial splendor, though it seems to be no more than an anonymous guesthouse that lodges the speaker's drunken friends, or perhaps the wraiths of vision. Its grotesque symbol is a bundle of dirty clothes, whose odor has displaced that of the Mallarméan bouquet, which, fittingly, is absent from the scene. By thus spatializing the subject's alienation, the last simile marks a climactic juncture that is quickly filled by a self-reflexive statement. In this statement, a dramatic aside, the speaker views the preceding anguish in ironic retrospect and lumps the first half of the poem into a single unit, a kind of free-verse sonnet (fourteen lines), as if reflecting upon it in an aftermath of vision. In addition to the fact that it appears at a crucial juncture, the importance of this ironic statement lies in its use of such a charged adjective as "melancólico," about which I shall say more later. For the moment we should note that it carries most of the weight of the irony and that it refers less to the speaker's weakness than to his perception of the formal inadequacy of his writing. The poem so far is too sad, he seems to say, too literary, perhaps, to capture my meaning. It is this ironic statement that underscores and thus uncovers all of the preceding Romantic themes. And in characterizing the poem as "melancólico," it denounces the literary conventionality of the description, which thus blocks the speaker's desire for authenticity, and pleads for a more immediate rendering of the same experience.

But to attempt a different and less desperate beginning leads ultimately to the same state of things. While the fifteenth line discredits melancholy expression, the ensuing argument returns to it:

Vision and Time

> pero, la verdad, de pronto, el viento que azota mi pecho,
> las noches de sustancia infinita caídas en mi dormitorio,
> el ruido de un día que arde con sacrificio
> me piden lo profético que hay en mí, con melancolía,
> y un golpe de objetos que llaman sin ser respondidos
> hay, y un movimiento sin tregua, y un nombre confuso. [I, 185]

> but, the truth, suddenly, the wind that beats upon my breast, / the nights of infinite substance fallen in my bedroom, / the noise of a day that burns with sacrifice / ask me, with melancholy, for all the prophecy there is in me, / and there's a thump of objects that call without answer, / and a ceaseless movement, and a confused name.

The "truth" that now takes hold is the prophetic power of the same Romantic language denounced earlier. It reappears along with an entirely different imagery: an inspiring wind, nights of revelation, voices promising days of self-sacrifice. The new imagery counters the previous somber sequence, so that both series represent the opposite cognitive poles ("sombra y espacio") to which the first line had alluded. It would appear, then, that such a shift has made the speaker advance from melancholy sickness to prophetic health. And yet the speaker still insists on linking "truth" with melancholy. The abiding question of these lines has thus been the apparent contradiction that confutes the preceding ironic reversal and the attendant shift of images. Emir Rodríguez Monegal's reading, for example, refuted Alonso's earlier interpretation, which had offered the view that melancholy permeates the entire poem, including the end. Monegal countered that both the image shift and the explicit claim to prophecy preclude a melancholy ending.[18] But even a sensitive debate such as this leaves unexplained the seemingly contradictory association of melancholy and prophecy.

To understand the precise sense of this association we need to shift our attention to the long history of melancholy as a literary concept. Melancholy was "black bile," one of the four humors that regulated the body's emotional system, according to ancient

---

[18]See Rodríguez Monegal, *Neruda,* pp. 449–55. Alonso's reading appears in *Poesía y estilo,* pp. 37–39 and 63–69.

medicine. The melancholic personality belonged to the sad and contemplative person whose excess of black bile was thought to induce fits of depression and, in extreme cases, madness. Once melancholy was identified as the source of emotional disturbances, it became part of the mythology of poetic inspiration. Natural philosophers, among them Aristotle, explained poetic frenzy as a melancholic seizure and thus made melancholy known as the painful reward that poet-prophets heroically endured. What in "Arte poética" seems to be a contradiction, then, can be easily explained as a function of this intellectual convention. In fact, once understood in its philological density, the reference to melancholy explains not only the recurring interplay of dark and light imagery throughout Neruda's poetry, but the mythology that underlies the entire visionary mode, its conventions and its structure of vision as estrangement.[19]

Instead of discrediting the role of melancholy, the shift of images affirms it by attributing it to a prophetic function. The last two lines revert to the initial sequence of unheeded objects, secret movements, and confused language. The pun in which the verb "hay" coincides with the interjection "ay!" prepares us for the less obvious one at the end, in which "un *nombre* confuso" (a confused name) sounds the same as "un *hombre* confuso" (a confused man). Whereas the first pun echoes the earlier one in the fifth line, where the interjection plays against the verb, the second pun points out, as did the rhetorical divergences of "Galope muerto," that both the subject and his literary product are purely linguistic entities. And the appearance of both puns in the last line further implies that the reversal to the initial somber state depends on this purely linguistic

---

[19]For exhaustive studies of melancholy in Western thought see Fritz Saxl, Erwin Panofsky, and Raymond Klibansky, *Saturn and Melancholy* (London: Thomas Nelson, 1964), and Giorgio Agamben, *Stanze, la parola e il fantasma nella cultura occidentale* (Turin: Einaudi, 1977). The extent of the paradox inherent in the theme can be gathered from a couple of examples from literary history. Milton's *Il Penseroso*, perhaps the *locus classicus* of the tradition, ends by noting: "Till old experience do attain / To something like Prophetic strain / These pleasures Melancholy give / and I with thee will choose to live." Nerval's "El desdichado," which is echoed in "Arte poética," invokes a fitting image in its last lines: "Ma seule étoile est morte, et mon luthe constellé / porte le Soleil noir de la Melancholie" (My only star is dead, and my starred lute / bears the black Sun of Melancholy). For an interesting reading of the tradition, see Bridget Gellert Lyons, *Voices of Melancholy* (New York: Norton, 1971).

Vision and Time

realm in which man and word, verb and interjection, are kept separate and distinct. The cyclical movement makes the poem end where it began, thus indicating that the previous image shift had been a temporary though still necessary stage of illumination within a consistently somber and confused cycle.

"Arte poética" clarifies the uses of irony and prophecy. Irony and reflexiveness, accordingly, become one and the same. The strategic location of the single most ironic line in the poem suggests that prophetic truth or poetic knowledge stems from a previous self-consciousness, which has arisen from the ruins of visionary exhaustion. As such, irony would seem to be a kind of "pause that refreshes," a fictional mediation whereby the alienated speaker holds in check the power of negativity and is thus able to posit a future reconciliation of spirit and world. Yet far from signaling a reparation, the ironic moment marks a temporal disjunction that exposes the speaker's facticity. That is, the speaker recognizes his inauthenticity; but just as two wrongs can never make a right, knowledge of one's inauthenticity cannot neutralize bad faith. Irony, like allegory, enacts what Paul de Man has called a "rhetoric of temporality," an authentic experience of time "which seen from the point of view of the self engaged in the world, is a negative one."[20] Caught between a consciousness of infinity and temporal facticity, the visionary poet recognizes his own limits and allows that knowledge to subvert the empirical claims of prophecy—that "truth" which

---

[20]Paul de Man, "The Rhetoric of Temporality," in *Interpretation: Theory and Practice*, ed. Charles S. Singleton (Baltimore: Johns Hopkins University Press, 1969), p. 207. For an opposite, dialectical view of irony and melancholy, see Jean Starobinski, "Ironie et mélancholie (I): Le Théatre de Carlo Gozzi" and "Ironie et mélancholie (II): *La Princesse de Brambilla* de E. T. A. Hoffmann," *Critique*, 227 and 228 (1966), 291-308 and 438-57. Whether we follow de Man or Starobinski, the speaker's temporal predicament remains part of the melancholy rhetoric, so to speak, which leads directly into irony. Thus melancholy, irony, and time seem to be the three vertices of a conceptual triangle in visionary poetry. "The melancholic primarily suffers from the contradiction between time and infinity, while at the same time giving a positive value to his own sorrow *sub specie aeternitatis*, since he feels that through his very melancholy he has a share in eternity.... Thus it can be understood how in modern man 'Humour,' in the sense of a limitation of the Self, developed alongside that of Melancholy which had become a feeling of an enhanced self;... one could be humorous about Melancholy itself, and by so doing bring out the tragic elements yet more strongly" (Saxl et al., *Saturn and Melancholy*, p. 235). For similar comments see Lyons, *Voices of Melancholy*, p. 150.

suddenly takes hold after the ironic break. Such a subversion of prophetic "truth" allows the speaker to invoke a self-conscious fictionality as the grounds for vision. This explains both the poem's circular structure, which dramatizes an endless process leading to no synthesis, and the speaker's identification, here as well as in "Galope muerto," with the written text, an identification that exposes the poem's fictionality and suspends a union between self and world.

Even the keenest commentators on *Residencia en la tierra* have been reluctant to recognize its ironic content, as if pointing to it would somehow denigrate Neruda's achievement. In his remarks about "self-exegesis," for example, Amado Alonso was sensitive enough to notice this ironic strain, but he invariably explained it away, using Crocean categories, as an anomaly owing to a disjunction of intuition and feeling. A rhetorical model not only seems to go further in explicating these moments, but it helps to identify Neruda's affinity with such Romantic ironists as Baudelaire, Novalis, and Heine. For what Romantic irony identifies is precisely that dissonant gesture evident in the authorial disruptions of whatever realistic illusions the text may create.

The other issue that "Arte poética" clarifies is prophecy. The poem shows the coincidence of a Romantic imagery with the speaker's claim to prophetic identity. Thus by providing a secular, or at least nonbiblical, context, it views prophecy as vision: not a speaking *before* or prediction, but a speaking *forth* or revelation, a mission with more of a rhetorical than an exclusively religious sense. This crucial insight coincides with a strategy of characterization that exploits the dramatic potential of such a title. That is, the speaker's identification of himself as a prophet renders his dramatic presence more immediate than the plainer label "mystic" or "visionary" could do. Such a deliberately dramatic gesture cannot help seeming forced, an authorial disruption groping for a suitable label. For prophecy is, finally, the fiction that identifies the visionary act. Once the visionary subject acknowledges his own facticity and discloses the degree to which his status depends on fiction, all visions are exposed as similar constructs that depend on a system of literary conventions.

Vision and Time

II

"The poet should not just do exercises," Neruda wrote to Héctor Eandi in November 1929. "There's a mandate for him—to penetrate life and make it prophetic. The poet ought to be a superstition, a mythic being."[21] The statement recalls the arguments of both "Galope muerto" and "Arte poética," although, as we have seen, the poems themselves go beyond Neruda's plea for the creation of impressive visionary speakers. Nor was Neruda's rejection of poetry as "exercise" as total or as innocent as it may seem. One could perhaps infer from the date of the letter that his injunction was a veiled reference to the Spanish poets of the Generation of 1927—García Lorca, Jorge Guillén, and Rafael Alberti, among others—who adhered vaguely to a notion of art as sport, or perhaps to Ortega y Gasset's description of the avant-garde poet, in *The Dehumanization of Art* (1925), as an intellectual athlete. One might venture further that Neruda's adverse reaction stemmed from his brief stopover in Madrid in 1927, while en route to the Far East, when he was probably slighted by the ruling poetic intelligentsia. And yet Neruda's contact with these poets was not so extensive during this first visit to Spain, nor were these men so devoted to the abstract imagism that Neruda was then rejecting, as to bear out the argument. Neruda devotes a mere three lines of his memoirs to his four-day visit to the Spanish capital, hardly an indication that he attached great importance to that first trip.[22] Furthermore, and contrary to popular distortions of literary history, Ortega and such poets as García Lorca and Guillén were committed instead to a *re*humanization of art which would profit from the innovations of the European avant-garde without losing sight of human values and expression. Their affinity to Neruda would be attested to years later when Ortega published three poems from *Residencia en la tierra* in *Revista de Occidente* and the Spanish poet defended Neruda against the charges of plagiarism that were raised in 1934 by his fellow Chilean Vicente Huidobro.[23]

[21]Neruda-Eandi, *Correspondencia*, p. 60.
[22]See *Memoirs*, p. 67.
[23]For the details of this quarrel, see Rodríguez Monegal, *Neruda*, pp. 106-7.

Pablo Neruda: The Poetics of Prophecy

It was in fact to Huidobro, along with the earlier ultraist movement, and not to his more immediate Spanish counterparts, that Neruda seems to have referred in his warning to Eandi. Ultraism had been the Hispanic equivalent and synthesis of the various imagist schools that had sprung up all over Europe in the century's first two decades. Typical of the avant-garde, it conceived of the artist as an intellectual athlete and of poetry especially as the most cerebral of games. Huidobro, a Chilean poet who in pre–World War I Paris had contributed to Pierre Reverdy's *Nord-Sud* review, soon became the "ambassador" of the French avant-garde in Hispanic circles, and it was largely through his agency, as well as through his claim to having fathered a new poetic school that he called Creationism, that ultraism acquired its fame and resonance. "Any serious artistic school," Huidobro had written in 1925, "must begin with a period of search in which intelligence directs the artist's efforts."[24] Analysis, logical structure, and lucid thought patterns were Huidobro's ingredients for the modern poem. His poetry, like that of the ultraists, readily mixed them to create surprising visual effects through metaphor—what the English at the time called Imagism. Later in the same letter to Eandi, Neruda pointedly alludes to Huidobro by complaining that "people have lost all temperament and devote themselves to intellectual exercise, with pleasure, as if it were a sport," adding further that "even so, all of them seem rather mediocre players." And the allusion seems more pointed still when he charges that "for some time poets' intelligence has cut all human links to what they say; cordiality and friendship toward the poetic message have fled the world."

In referring to poetic "exercise," then, Neruda rejects one cerebral poetry, associated with Huidobro, for another, which he calls prophetic and whose function is "to penetrate life." This is the poetry he claims to have written in *Residencia en la tierra*. What seems suspect about such a dichotomy, however, is its deliberate ease—Neruda's claim that his own poetry penetrates life and his implication that Huidobro's slights it. For Neruda's poetry was less immediate than his letter to Eandi implies, and Huidobro's was less cold and calculating than Huidobro himself

---

[24]Vicente Huidobro, *Manifestes* (Paris: Revue Mondiale, 1925), p. 46.

Vision and Time

claimed. Both, in fact, are versions of the same modernist poetics. Like Neruda, Huidobro sought to write a poetry that captured the unusual traits of objects and thereby altered and refreshed the reader's perception. Like Huidobro, Neruda wrote (at least in *Residencia en la tierra*) a difficult, often baffling poetry, which attests to his skill as a craftsman. Their opposition stems not from conflicting purposes, as Neruda seems to have believed, but from divergent simulations of the poetic experience. While Huidobro's revelations proceed swiftly, in almost mathematical fashion, seeming to result from an intense but orderly cerebral juggling, Neruda's prophetic utterances simulate all the anguish associated with the visionary experience. Neruda's neo-Romanticism, it seems, attempts to correct Huidobro's militant avant-gardism, but his own corrective gesture cannot help leading to a misreading of his precursor, as if mirroring the distortions to which the avant-garde itself subjected Romantic art. For contrary to the claims often made by modernist writers, "the cult of novelty and even of the strange," as Renato Poggioli notes, "was an exquisitely romantic phenomenon even before it became typically avant garde." "Instead of being reciprocal opposites," Romanticism and the avant-garde "came to appear as relatives, reacting to the humanistic and classical opposition in similar ways."[25] And so the poet may not have to do exercises, as Neruda claims, but the reader of *Residencia en la tierra* does, as much as or more in fact than when reading Huidobro's cerebral lyrics. In their textual strategies, at least, Neruda and Huidobro appear to be relatives, though they would have been the first to deny any kinship.

Neruda's antagonism toward Huidobro lasted throughout his life and at times even reached the violence of a true "anxiety of influence" (to use Harold Bloom's term), as when he obliquely disparaged Huidobro's well-known dictum that "the poet is a little god" in his Nobel Prize speech.[26] My concern with Neruda's statements in his correspondence, however, is aimed less at documenting this adverse relationship, interesting as it is, than

---

[25] *The Theory of the Avant Garde* (1962; New York: Harper & Row, 1971), pp. 50–51.
[26] See *Toward the Splendid City*, Nobel Lecture (New York: Farrar, Straus & Giroux, 1972), pp. 22–23. Neruda betrays the same anxiety in his seldom-quoted lecture, "Algunas reflexiones improvisadas sobre mis trabajos" (I, 712).

at pointing up the differential role that prophecy assumed at the time he wrote the poems of *Residencia en la tierra*. Invoking prophecy seems to have helped him to clear a creative space of his own and to distinguish his poetics from an ostensibly frivolous one, such as he judged Huidobro's to be. It is this differential role, I think, that explains the explicit references to prophecy in at least two other poems of *Residencia*. One of them, "Colección nocturna," dramatizes the appearance of prophecy in the form of an angel spreading an ominous "alimento profético" (prophetic nourishment) (I, 178). The reference occurs in the prelude to a dream vision that describes a catalogue of incongrous images in a familiar tone. Following a parade of motley figures and objects (the "colección nocturna" or night collection), the speaker announces the coming of day and admits that the entire vision has been a waking dream that creates the illusion of a bridge between subject and object: "un poco de cada oficio, un resto humillado trabaja su parte en nuestro interior" (a little of each job, a humiliated leftover does its work inside of us) (I, 179). "Communicaciones desmentidas," the second of five prose poems included in the first book, also invokes prophecy in its opening line: "Aquellos días extraviaron mi sentido profético" (Those days misled my prophetic sense) (I, 189). This time, however, the reference forms part of the speaker's struggle to preserve an identity that is dramatized, as in "Arte poética," as a Romantic self-caricature. The poet's faculties are once again stamped upon by melancholy, besieged by circular objects that render him an armed prophet: "aguardo el tiempo militarmente, y con el florete de la aventura manchado de sangre olvidada" (I await time in a military style, and with the adventure's foil stained with forgotten blood) (I, 190). Both of these poems advance prophecy as the principle underlining the visionary mode. Yet neither one approaches the power of such poems as "Galope muerto" and "Arte poética," both of which exploit a deft characterization and the unfolding of a visionary epistemology. In the case of "Arte poética," this epistemology proposes an analogy between the object's cyclical patterns and the structure of visionary discourse. As an order-preserving structure, the cycle constitutes the pattern inherent both in the object and in perception, in reality and in the discourse that identifies it.

It is this sense of vision as an activity that preserves order against temporal dispersion that Neruda repeatedly underscores in his letters to Eandi and José Santos González Vera. Despite the unreliable vagueness of this correspondence, which at times betrays the self-deprecation of a fledgling poet, there are moments of genuine insight in these letters, as when Neruda describes the poems as having "the same movement, the same pressure... developed in the same region of my head, like the same type of insistent waves." Scarcely a month had elapsed when the same description, cast in a similar redundant style, reappears: "I've completed almost an entire book of poems: *Residencia en la tierra*, and you will see how I'm able to isolate my expression, making it waver constantly among dangers, and what solid uniform substance I use to make the same force appear insistently." And the same terms appear again a year later, in yet another letter to Eandi, which calls the book "a heap of very monotonous verse" and "something very uniform, one single thing begun over and over, as if eternally and unsuccessfully rehearsed." What strikes one immediately about these statements it the recurrence of such key adjectives as "same," "uniform," "single," and "insistent," all of which convey the idea of singular unity or substance. They are all meant, obviously, as descriptions of the tonal uniformity that links the various parts of the book and provides it with an overall coherence. They describe, that is, an external integrative principle, a cycle, which functions at the broadest level of the book as a unit. Yet the same terms imply as well an internal cyclic principle that concerns the representation, within individual poems, of objective circular structures. Both external and internal cyclic principles coexist in these statements and both could be said to structure the form of *Residencia en la tierra*.[27]

What concerns me now is the way these two cyclic principles

[27]See Rodríguez Monegal, *Neruda*, p. 78, and Neruda–Eandi, *Correspondencia*, pp. 34, 38. In a 1964 lecture, thirty years after writing this letter, Neruda described his poetic career as a quest after "a cyclic poem" and told of wishing to write poetry "that would go beyond a single moment toward broader units" (III, 714). Even if by then Neruda's idea of cyclical structure had become a metaphor for an encyclopedic form that is more closely approached by such a book as *Canto General* (1950) than by the brief lyrics of *Residencia*, the statements in his earlier correspondence still ring too loudly to be ignored. In retrospect they appear to be the origin of the "cyclic ambition" that was barely adumbrated during this time. For the rhetorical implications of Neruda's encyclopedic project, see Chapter 4, below.

actually work to form what I earlier called the book's poetic logic or visionary syntax. I shall begin this inquiry with a reading of "Unidad" (Unity), the fifth poem in the book. The presence of an external cyclic sense depends, as we shall see, on the arrangement of the poems, but in the case of "Unidad" it plays a crucial role because of the poem's own internal cyclic sense. The title itself alludes to the achievement of ultimate cyclicality:

> Hay algo denso, unido, sentado en el fondo,
> repitiendo su número, su señal idéntica.
> Cómo se nota que las piedras han tocado el tiempo,
> en su fina materia hay olor a edad,
> y el agua que trae el mar, de sal y sueño.   [I, 173]

> There is something dense, united, seated in the back / repeating its number, its identical sign. / How one notices that the stones have touched time, / in its delicate matter there's a smell of age, / and the water that the sea brings, of salt and dream.

The first two lines, we should note, echo Neruda's statements in his letters. Repetition and sameness become the signs of a cyclical presence that the next three lines translate as an unrelenting temporal process. Noticing this sign—what the poem puts metaphorically as "olor a edad"—becomes the poet's duty, as it is to register the surrounding circular pattern:

> Me rodea una misma cosa, un solo movimiento:
> el peso del mineral, la luz de la piel,
> se pegan al sonido de la palabra noche:
> la tinta del trigo, del marfil, del llanto,
> las cosas de cuero, de madera, de lana,
> envejecidas, desteñidas, uniformes,
> se unen en torno a mí como paredes.   [I, 173]

> One same thing surrounds me, a single movement: / the weight of the mineral, the light of skin, / adhere to the sound of the word night; / the ink of wheat, of ivory, of weeping, / the things made of leather, of wood, of wool, / grown old, faded, uniform, / gather around me like walls.

The tone is decidedly less desperate and the catalogue itself less deranged than in "Galope muerto." The stanza aligns

Vision and Time

symmetrical triads of genitive clauses and adjectives, and it is this order that the last line identifies as an immuring fortress. Finally, the third and last stanza summarizes the form of the object as well as the subject's position in relation to it:

> Trabajo sordamente, girando sobre mí mismo,
> como el cuervo sobre la muerte, el cuervo de luto.
> Pienso, aislado en lo extremo de las estaciones,
> central, rodeado de geografía silenciosa:
> una temperatura parcial cae del cielo,
> un extremo imperio de confusas unidades
> se reúne rodeándome.   [I, 173]

> I work deafly [engrossed], gyrating upon myself, / like the crow over death, the mourning crow. / I think, isolated in the extreme of seasons, / central, surrounded by silent geography: / a partial temperature falls from the sky, / an extreme empire of confused items / reunites surrounding me.

The punning adverb of visionary work ("sordamente") implies both stealth and silence, which join to qualify the subject's own wheellike structure as homologous to the object's. This new description echoes the turning pulley of "Galope muerto," but its pointed difference signals the speaker's self-assertion as a result of his growing linguistic self-consciousness. Despite its bewilderment, the siege affords a clarity of vision whose climax the colon at the end of the fourth line discreetly anticipates. It is nothing less than a descent from heaven, though who or what descends we are not told. The compendious image of "confusas unidades" itself approaches the status of an oxymoron and conveys the cognitive tension we have encountered before. The image principally dramatizes the speaker's ability to discern a pattern where there appears to be none and to extract meaning from a set of otherwise unrelated objects. The last line all but reasserts, with a fitting measure of redundance, a circular order that consists of siege and repetition and that recalls the "anillo del verano" (ring of summer) of "Galope muerto."

The paradox of a chaotic symmetry that we find in "Unidad" stems, as we might surmise, from the disquieting method of the visionary mode. As Rimbaud's disordering of the senses was "reasoned," so Neruda's is caused by a tension between cogni-

49

tive opposites of chaos and system. That such Rimbaldian illumination could result only from a previous leap in the dark we learned in "Arte poética," where melancholy marked the prelude to poetic knowledge. The poem illustrates such a method by harmonizing the motley nature of the object with an impassive orderliness, and it goes one step further in relating this tenuous harmony or "unity" to a cyclic pattern common to both subject and object. The final homology intimates, then, a bridging of the gap that separates the two and a way out of irony and alienation.

One would certainly be tempted, from the vantage point afforded by our earlier reading of "Arte poética," to dismiss such unity as a delusion. But such a dismissal would assume a reading order opposite from the one that the book prescribes. That is, to prejudge "Unidad," the fifth poem, in terms of the lessons reaped from "Arte poética," the seventeenth, would be to reverse a dialectical pattern that the reading order suggests. If we now turn back to those first few poems, up to and including "Unidad," we can continue to trace that same sense and unfold an overall pattern.

We may, in fact, think of "Galope muerto" and "Unidad" as the first stages of two sequential sallies, two inquiries into the subject–object dichotomy. The experience of "Galope muerto" marks the origin of the first inquiry, which includes the argument of the next three poems: "Alianza (Sonata)," "Caballo de los sueños," and "Débil del alba." Earlier we learned that this first stage ended by circumscribing the objective limits of visionary experience within a circle—an "anillo del verano." Acknowledging that impasse, "Alianza (Sonata)," the poem that follows "Galope muerto," takes up the same inquiry and refashions it by conceiving the subject–object relationship as intersubjective. The point of contact is the punning title, which, besides heralding an alliance between two people, transforms the earlier "ring of summer" into an explicitly matrimonial symbol (in Spanish *alianza* also means wedding ring). Yet instead of describing a joyous marriage, the poem begins by admitting the union of failed vision and pervasive emptiness:

> De miradas polvorientas caídas al suelo
> o de hojas sin sonido sepultándose.
> De metales sin luz, con el vacío,

con la ausencia del día muerto de golpe.
En lo alto de las manos el deslumbrar de mariposas,
el arrancar de mariposas cuya luz no tiene término. [I, 170]

Of dusty looks fallen on the floor / or of soundless leaves burying themselves. / Of lusterless metals, with emptiness, / with the absence of day suddenly dead. / At the height of hands the dazzling of butterflies, / the taking off of butterflies whose light has no end.

The initial genitive clauses appear to be incomplete only if we fail to infer their grammatical coherence from the title.[28] Thus the "alianza" is *of* failed vision ("miradas polvorientas," "hojas sin sonido") *with* emptiness and absence ("con el vacío, con la ausencia"). The dazzling kaleidoscope of butterflies, looming beyond the speaker's grasp, outlines a visionary horizon and the promise of a brighter union. In the second stanza it is the other person, identified with a familiar second-person pronoun and a female adjective, who appears as the source of that cherished light. The further association of this other person with twilight shows it to be an effulgent though forbiddingly remote landscape. Both a participle and its description as an "objeto de abejas" (object of bees) further expose her passivity, but the third stanza qualifies that passivity as a function of her quiet strength. In contrast to the speaker, who fears the coming of day as preying temporality, she is able to gather those same days in her own "voz de luz" (voice of light), thereby becoming the object on which the speaker hopes to lay the foundation of visionary structure: "Oh, dueña del amor, en tu descanso fundé mi sueño, mi actitud callada" (Oh, mistress of love, in thy tranquillity I founded my dream, my quiet posture) (I, 170). The fourth stanza goes on to underscore their dreamlike relationship, for despite her aid in defining both spatial and temporal dimensions, the subject can feel her presence only "en mi sueño." Finally, in the fifth stanza, the speaker describes the culmination of their alliance as the physical merger of their tears, which, defying the law of gravity, ascend as they are shed by both subjects and meet in the speaker's mind. They "grow" there until they become a turbulent ocean that causes their destruction simply because, we infer, the speaker awakes.

[28] Alonso, *Poesía y estilo*, p. 33.

Pablo Neruda: The Poetics of Prophecy

Thus the second approach to the object ends in failure. In the end the speaker awakes and rejects his experience—a third stage must begin. But the rejection, as we soon discover, will be far from total. The next title, "Caballo de los sueños" (Dream Horse), suggests that the speaker retains the agency of dreams, first introduced in "Alianza," in the quest for unity. Moreover, it becomes evident at this point that the speaker's fall into an explicit dream state, by providing discreet signs of chronological succession, dramatizes a temporal process that increases in importance as we continue reading. Like the first two, this third title will become a sign of the external cyclic sense. Not only does this title signal the recurrence of a dream vision, but it shows the metaphorical source of the earlier "dead gallop." The sequence therefore suggests a dialectical progression toward an increasingly concrete vision (from "galope" to "caballo") despite, or perhaps because of, the greater frequency of dreams.

While in "Alianza (Sonata)" the speaker creates, however fleetingly, the fiction of another desiring subject, now he begins by admitting his sense of isolation and the contingency of bureaucratic drudgery:

> Innecesario, viéndome en los espejos,
> con un gusto a semanas, a biógrafos, a papeles,
> arranco de mi corazón al capitán del infierno,
> establezco cláusulas indefinidamente tristes.
>
> Vago de un punto a otro, absorbo ilusiones,
> converso con los sastres en sus nidos:
> ellos, a menudo, con voz fatal y fría,
> cantan y hacen huir los maleficios.   [I, 171]
>
> Unnecessary, seeing myself in mirrors, / with a taste of weeks, biographers, papers, / I tear from my heart the captain of hell, / I establish indefinitely sad clauses. / I wander from one point to the next, I absorb illusions, / I talk to tailorbirds in their nests: / they often, with a cold and fatal voice, / sing and make curses flee.

Like a degraded Narcissus, the speaker has only himself to desire, peering into faded mirrors in order to nourish the illusion of a union. He thus turns to writing the sad, self-exorcising poems whose power reflects the voice of nature, which he had heard in the course of his quest. The present poem will therefore attempt to sustain the illusion of a continuum beyond the fleeting experience of reflection. As in mirrors and on film screens, in dreams the subject becomes its own object and therefore creates the illusion that irony has been suspended. The poem's first two stanzas constitute the moment of extreme irony that precedes the dream vision. Once asleep, the speaker journeys to "un extenso país en el cielo" (an extensive country in the sky) (I, 171), seeking to recapture the same sense of infinity that he had felt at the end of "Galope muerto." By the end of the fifth stanza he has reached that goal (as the exclamation points suggest), in the form of an effulgent day—the same visionary horizon intimated earlier in "Alianza (Sonata)." The speaker soars victoriously over churches and army barracks astride the day's "rojo caballo" (red horse) (I, 172), a scene that bears an uncanny resemblance to the surrealist landscapes of the early Marc Chagall. The piled-up references to the horse's gallop in so short a space ("*galopo* los cuarteles desiertos de soldados" [I gallop the soldiers' deserted barracks], "su cuerpo de campana *galopa* y golpea" [its bell body gallops and strikes] [I, 172]) call attention to the source of the original sound of "Galope muerto," a discovery that marks the high point of the dream. The latter phrase especially, with its resounding alliteration, renders a total image of the dream horse, while in the last stanza the speaker once again awakes to the contingent world to which his desire binds him. And yet a change has clearly taken place. At first he could desire only his own image, but now he can escape that solipsism and openly vent his wish for illumination beyond his numbered days: "Yo necesito un relámpago de fulgor persistente, / un deudo festival que asuma mis herencias" (I need a lightning of persistent splendor, / a festive relative to receive my inheritance).

So far, then, we have covered three poems that constitute the first three stages of a sequence: first, the initial vision and its impasse ("Galope muerto"); second, a recasting of the subject-object structure as an intersubjective experience that also ends in failure ("Alianza [Sonata]"); third, a plunge into an explicit dream vision that identifies the source of the original vision ("Caballo de los sueños"). "Débil del alba" (Weakling of Dawn),

Pablo Neruda: The Poetics of Prophecy

the fourth and last stage, which fittingly takes place at dawn as the speaker awakes, describes the aftermath:

> El día de los desventurados, el día pálido se asoma
> con un desgarrador olor frío, con sus fuerzas en gris,
> sin cascabeles, goteando el alba por todas partes:
> es un naufragio en el vacío, con un alrededor de llanto.
>
> Porque se fue de tantos sitios la sombra húmeda, callada
> de tantas cavilaciones en vano, de tantos parajes terrestres
> en donde debió ocupar hasta el designio de las raíces,
> de tanta forma aguda que se defendía.   [I, 172]

> The day of the luckless, the pale day peers out / with a tearing cold smell, with its forces in gray, / without neck bells, dropping dawn everywhere: / it's a shipwreck in the void, with a surrounding of tears. / Because the moist, silent shadow left from so many places / from so many cavilings in vain, from so many earthly sites / in which it must have occupied even the design of roots, / from so many a sharp form that defended itself.

The day cannot help belonging to the luckless, among whom the speaker numbers himself. His loss of the preceding dream appears to be written all over the gloomy morning. The description of dawn cites familiar characteristics (paleness, cold, grayness), but includes the more unusual "sin cascabeles," which suggests the subject's nostalgia for the "dream horse." In the glaring absence of the dream horse, dawn sprays its dew over the landscape, as if crying over his loss. And yet, however gloomy, the day is nevertheless present, as opposed to the "sombra húmeda, callada," which eludes the form he would like to provide it:

> Yo lloro en el medio de lo invadido, entre lo confuso,
> entre el sabor creciente, poniendo el oído
> en la pura circulación, en el aumento,
> cediendo sin rumbo el paso a lo que arriba,
> a lo que surge vestido de cadenas y claveles,
> yo sueño, sobrellevando mis vestigios mortales.
>
> Nada hay de precipitado, ni de alegre, ni de forma orgullosa,
> todo aparece haciéndose con evidente pobreza,

Vision and Time

> la luz de la tierra sale de sus párpados
> no como la campanada, sino más bien como las lágrimas:
>
> el tejido del día, su lienzo débil,
> sirve para una venda de enfermos, sirve para hacer señas
> en una despedida, detrás de la ausencia:
> es el color que sólo quiere remplazar,
> cubrir, tragar, vencer, hacer distancias. [I, 172-73]

> I cry in the midst of the invaded, amid the confused, / amid the growing flavor, placing my ear / in pure circulation, in the increase, / yielding without direction the way to what arrives, / to what sprouts dressed up in chains and carnations, / I dream, carrying my mortal remains. / There is nothing precipitous, or joyful, or of proud form, / everything appears making itself with evident poverty, / the light of earth comes out of its eyelids / not like the bell stroke but rather like tears: / the cloth of day, its weak canvas, / is good for a patient's bandage, is good for waving / good-bye, behind absence: / it's the color that only wishes to replace, / to cover, to swallow, to vanquish, to make distances.

In the midst of it all stands the speaker, who, like dawn, is crying and sharpening his ear to the sounds only he can hear, which, together with the memory of past dreams, help him withstand the onslaught of time. Absorbed in poverty, the world now literally pales in contrast to the earlier dream. No "proud form" makes its entrance, and even the dawn's weak light seems to betray its source by slowly peering out of the earth's "eyelids," refracted by the dawn's haze, instead of breaking through the powerful bell stroke, as it once did in "Galope muerto." The day's weakness, like surgical gauze, resides in its ontological lack—it covers, replaces, or hides the wounded world, besides isolating and excluding the subject:

> Estoy solo entre materias desvencijadas,
> la lluvia cae sobre mí, y se me parece,
> se me parece con su desvarío, solitaria en el mundo muerto,
> rechazada al caer, y sin forma obstinada. [I, 173]

> I am alone among rickety matter, / the rain falls over me and resembles me, / resembles me in its derangement, alone in the dead world, / rejected on falling, and without any obstinate form.

Once again, the poem ends with an admission of failure, yet proposing at the same time a negative resemblance, the missing link between subject and object: derangement, isolation, and formlessness.

After tracing this particular sequence we can place in context such a poem as "Unidad" and view its stress on cyclicality as the dialectical result of the texts that immediately precede it. We realize that the emphasis on repetition and sameness—in short, on "unity," as if in reversion to the initial state of siege of "Galope muerto"—is a reaction to the elusiveness of form that we find dramatized in "Débil del alba." Both "Galope muerto" and "Unidad" represent, then, two pauses after scattered movements, regroupings of forces following plundering raids, as it were, during which the speaker takes stock of those structures that guide visionary perception. Indeed, the striking similarity between "Galope muerto" and "Unidad," as well as the position that each poem assumes within the reading order, should persuade us of their analogous roles in the interplay between the two cyclic principles. Within such an interplay internal vision sustains external sequence by providing recurrent pauses during which the speaker is able to regain his sense of direction, an alternation of spasmodic search and withdrawal not unlike the dialectic of melancholy and irony described in "Arte poética."

More important, however, is the temporal process that is implied by such an external cycle. Much has been written about the presence of time as a theme in *Residencia en la tierra*, but the way time actually works in the text has never been explored.[29] The above sequence, I have argued, is built on a dramatic plot or fictional chronology in which the subject attempts several approaches to the object. The unfolding of an intersubjective alliance, its replacement by an explicit dream state, a cruel awakening at dawn are all sequential scenes from a drama of the visionary mind. Within this drama, the poet articulates his displacement through time, which thus becomes a structural principle as well as a major theme. And just as time appears inscribed in the book's title (both in the reference to a "residence"

---

[29]For discussions on the theme of time, see Jaime Concha, "Interpretación de *Residencia en la tierra*," *Mapocho*, 2 (1963), 5-39, and Sicard, *El pensamiento poético*, pp. 112-17.

Vision and Time

and in the use of dates), so temporal progression conditions the entire poetic experience. Time determines the subject's desire to fuse with the object and thereby attain immediate presence. The poem represents the process whereby the speaker's consciousness is gradually transformed from dullness to ecstasy to meditative calm. But the fusion to which consciousness aspires never takes place, and the realization of that experience, which would signal the achievement of total poetic knowledge, is postponed in each case. What generates each text, then, is a fruitless search, a deferment of presence in time and space as determined by memory. That is, experience in the poems is never immediate, but only remembered, seen in retrospect, and thus subject to the distortions of recollection. And as in any composite collection—a tradition begun, perhaps, by Petrarch—the poems appear to be arranged *as if* they were in chronological order, a sequence of disjointed scenes from which the reader can only infer a "psychology" and a writing project.

Bearing in mind such a temporal progression, we can conceive of *Residencia en la tierra* as a poetic diary, a kind of *journal intime*, or what Rodríguez Monegal calls the record of a "season in hell."[30] Neruda's text, like Rimbaud's, is structured according to the subject's experience of time, its writing emerging from, as well as fulfilling, an internal discontinuity that the journal format is meant to repair by unfolding "a kind of ontological respiration, an inward and outward of being, itself punctuated and helping to shape the discontinuous life being lived."[31] It is this

---

[30]Rodríguez Monegal, *Neruda*, p. 270. We should recall that Neruda described *Crepusculario* (1923), his first book, as a "diary of whatever took place in and outside myself, of whatever reached my sensitivity" (III, 712). The slow passage of time is one of Neruda's recurring themes in his correspondence with Eandi. One of those letters, dated October 5, 1929 (though not finished until November 11), was written in diary form; see Neruda and Eandi, *Correspondencia*, pp. 55–63. It would not be farfetched to say that Neruda may have discovered the uses of the journal format while translating, from André Gide's French version, passages from Rainer Maria Rilke's *Notebooks of Malte Laurids Brigge* (1910), which is, significantly enough, the diary of an exiled aspiring poet. Neruda's translation first appeared in *Claridad*, 135 (October–November 1926), and is now reprinted in III, 763-65. For Neruda's subsequent use of his translation, see Chapter 3, n. 26, below. For further discussion of the journal format, in connection with one of Neruda's late books, see my "Afterword" in Pablo Neruda, *Isla Negra*, trans. Alastair Reid (New York: Farrar, Straus & Giroux, 1981), pp. 409-16.

[31]Francis R. Hart, "Notes for an Anatomy of Modern Autobiography," *New Literary History*, 1 (1970), 498.

journal structure that explains, I think, why the poetry of *Residencia en la tierra* is so intent on registering common objects and events (what critics proverbially note as the most definitive trait of Neruda's poetics), as if wishing to fill the vacuum of aimless temporal succession with the dross and regularity of daily experience. Yet writing fills that vacuum not with things, as critics have mistakenly argued, but only with words, the written representation of those things. Instead of allowing the subject to integrate with the object—or, in temporal terms, to attain the experience of infinity—the poem partially temporalizes that object and that goal and removes both from immediate consumption. Writing becomes, instead, an agent of desire: Tantalus' water and fruit. It is the counterpoint of expressive commitment and ironic demystification that causes the dissonance we encounter at every step between the speaker's desire for presence, on the one hand, and his experience of difference—historical or linguistic time—on the other.

IV

To attempt to trace here the entire plot that is reflected by the entries in this poetic diary would be foolhardy, but it seems clear that we can at least draw two provisional conclusions. The first is that, taken as a whole, the poetry of *Residencia* bears a less negative message than the reading of isolated poems has traditionally suggested. What we see, instead, is that the journal structure lends a textual coherence or continuity that rescues the self from time. But precisely because writing is put at the service of the self, it runs the risk of becoming an idolatrous monument in whose sanctuary the self can evade the perils of an authentic temporal destiny, including death. We shall see that this is in fact the outcome of the self in *Residencia en la tierra*.

For the moment, however, we must heed the second conclusion, which addresses the more pragmatic issue of reading these poems. Once we realize that a temporal drama binds them together, seemingly obscure references are seen in a new light. The first line of "Sonata y destrucciones," for example ("Después de mucho, después de vagas leguas..." [After a lot, after vague leagues]) (I, 186–87), refers to the collective reading experience. If we bear in mind the comprehensive dramatic situation, beyond the poem's own, we can better understand the further description of visionary experience ("Amo lo tenaz que sobrevive en mis ojos" [I love the tenacity that survives in my eyes]), as well as the familiar terms of poetic hearing ("Oigo en mi corazón mis pasos de jinete" [In my heart I hear my horseman steps]). Like "Unidad," the poem describes the same visionary method ("Hay entre ciencias de llanto un altar confuso" [Among sciences of weeping there's a confused altar]) as a tension between harmony and disharmony. And the concluding stanza describes yet another familiar experience:

> Acecho, pues, lo inanimado y lo doliente,
> y el testimonio extraño que sostengo,
> con eficiencia cruel y escrito en cenizas,
> es la forma de olvido que prefiero,
> el nombre que doy a la tierra, el valor de mis sueños,
> la cantidad interminable que divido
> con mis ojos de invierno, durante cada día de este mundo. [I, 187]

> Thus, I stalk the inanimate and the mourning, / and the strange testimony I bear, / with cruel efficiency and written in ashes, / is the form of oblivion I prefer, / the name I give to the earth, the value of my dreams, / the endless amount that I divide / with my winter eyes during each day of this world.

The poet's "testimonio extraño" is given with an "eficiencia cruel," another name for the paradoxical unbridled discipline, so to speak, of visionary experience. The disclosure is both self-referential and self-destructive, as writing is here destined for its own oblivion, thereby neutralizing the possibility of effective witnessing.

This is not to say, obviously, that the poems merely repeat the same points or that they differ only in the arrangement of a few common motifs. We have seen, on the contrary, that there is actual dialectical progress within such a cyclical sequence, even if that progress consists mainly of a negative knowledge about the object. What we discover is the unfolding of an all-encompassing dramatic situation that grounds representation, a scene or theater of writing to which the poems refer in order to legitimize visionary discourse. It is this scene of writing that underlies not only the relationship between subject and object but that of the subject with the experience of vision. Such a setting allows, in other words, for an introspection that unveils patterns of selfhood that are as structured as those in the object. Each poem contains, of course, a glimpse of the visionary subject that allows the reader to infer an overall "psychology," and even such poems as "Arte poética" and "Unidad" go so far as to suggest an internal cyclical pattern. Other texts are even more explicit and focus entirely on the subject, as does "Sistema sombrío" (Somber System), for example, which in the reading order immediately follows "Arte poética" and with it shares the center of the book:

> De cada uno de estos días negros como viejos hierros,
> y abiertos por el sol como grandes bueyes rojos,
> y apenas sostenidos por el aire y por los sueños,
> y desaparecidos irremediablemente y de pronto,
> nada ha sustituido mis perturbados orígenes,
> y las desiguales medidas que circulan en mi corazón
> allí se fraguan de día y de noche, solitariamente,
> y abarcan desordenadas y tristes cantidades.   [I, 185]

> Of each of these days, black like old irons / and opened up by the sun like great red oxen / and hardly sustained by air and dreams / and inevitably and suddenly gone, / nothing has replaced my confused origins, / and the unequal cadences that circulate in my heart / are forged there by day and night, solitarily, / and embrace disordered and sad measures.

The title image, itself close to an oxymoron, conveys the proverbial tension that echoes in the image of "días negros." The retrospective scope of the first line is deliberately concise. It assumes the reader's familiarity with such temporal experience as well as with the days' "blackness," which derives from the melancholy imagery of "Arte poética." The series of parallel conjunctive clauses in the first four lines forms a logical sequence whose rhythm conveys that very temporal progression, and together with the retrospective glance it reinforces the impression that the text belongs to a poetic diary. Both the opening and metamorphosis of those same days foster visionary illuminations, but they can hardly be sustained (let alone prolonged or

Vision and Time

enjoyed) because of the passage of time. Temporal sequence is thus unable to penetrate into the deep realm of the self. Like the cognitive tension that fosters vision, the subject's structure fuses opposite poles of chaos and order: "desiguales medidas" embrace "desordenadas y tristes cantidades," images that suggest the finely tuned parts of a clock that keeps time only because its ticking is not synchronous. These images suggest a deep structure, an underlying order of equal cadences, which feed on paradox and antithesis. This structure makes up the visionary subject. The cyclical structure, fittingly, forms part of a "circulatory" system (the heart's systole/dyastole) that works against surface instability:

> Así, pues, como un vigía tornado insensible y ciego,
> incrédulo y condenado a un doloroso acecho,
> frente a la pared en que cada día del tiempo se une,
> mis rostros diferentes se arriman y encadenan
> como grandes flores pálidas y pesadas
> tenazmente sustituidas y difuntas.   [I, 185]

> Thus, then, like a watchman turned unfeeling and blind, / incredulous and condemned to a painful lurking / in front of the wall in which each one of time's days is joined, / my different faces huddle and link themselves / like great pale heavy flowers / tenaciously replaced and dead.

The last stanza proceeds logically in a cause-and-effect sequence despite the first line's ending with the apparently absurd self-designation of "blind watchman," a reference to the Romantic figure of the blind poet-prophet. As in "Sonata y destrucciones," the vigil is an active lurking, though unlike it. Earlier the seer had witnessed "lo inanimado y lo doliente" (the inanimate and the mourning); now he can see only himself. What we have is a visionary cinema on a screen made up of the total recall of temporal experience and a film showing a succession of masks and a parade of former postures. As a watchman, the subject keeps a constant vigil on himself, in an infinite regression: the watchman watches himself in the act of watching a watchman, ad infinitum. The implication is that of a match of temporal succession at the surface with a succession of masks at the core, a synchronization of dailyness and depth identity on behalf of visionary freshness. The image of the chain, first suggested in the earlier "viejos hierros," is the emblem for both this summary identity and the scene of writing, the journal or book of memory that links daily succession.

"Sistema sombrío" aims at a holistic picture of visionary identity by describing a closure, self-contained and self-sustaining, whose formal counterpart is its sonnet form (14 lines). In endowing vision with a "system" of its own, the poem suggests the extent to which visionary discourse has progressed and its articulation improved. So by the time we reach the end of the first book we are able to realize both the extent of that progress and the impasse to which it has led. Indeed, "Significa sombras" (It Means Shadows), the last poem, could be read as an oblique response to "Sistema sombrío," as suggested by the same initials, and as a summary, outlined in the series of rhetorical questions in the first two stanzas, of the issues probed throughout the first book:

> Qué esperanza considerar, qué presagio puro,
> qué definitivo beso enterrar en el corazón,
> someter en los orígenes del desamparo y la inteligencia,
> suave y seguro sobre las aguas eternamente turbadas?
>
> Qué vitales, rápidas alas de un nuevo ángel de sueños
> instalar en mis hombros dormidos para seguridad perpetua,
> de tal manera que el camino entre las estrellas de la muerte
> sea un violento vuelo comenzado desde hace muchos días y
>   meses y siglos?   [I, 203]

> What hope to consider, what pure presage, / what definitive kiss to bury in the heart, / submit in the origins of despair and intelligence, / soft and sure over eternally disturbed waters? / What vital, rapid wings of a new angel of dreams / install on my dormant shoulders for the sake of perpetual security, / in such a way that the road between the stars of death / may be a violent flight begun many days and months and centuries ago.

The catalogue reads like a review of the entire book: while "esperanza" and "presagio" recall the experience of "Galope muerto," the "definitivo beso" echoes the erotic fiction in

Vision and Time

"Alianza (Sonata)"; "orígenes" and "aguas eternamentes turbadas" outline, in turn, interior and surface levels analogous to those in "Sistema sombrío," and they virtually quote from the corresponding passage. Similarly, the "ángel de sueños" recalls the one in "Colección nocturna," and the "violento vuelo" suggests the same dreamlike soaring of "Caballo de los sueños." Lacking an answer of their own, the rhetorical questions carry a tone of retrospective contempt toward all these inquiries. The summary gestures make clear, from the strategic standpoint of the end, that the quest for poetic presence has been a function of the subject's temporal predicament. The "violento vuelo," for example, is but a flight out of time, just as the subject's "orígenes" stand against surface instability. Faced with that uncertainty, the speaker attempts in the third stanza both to rationalize past inquiries and to predict their outcome:

> Tal vez la debilidad natural de los seres recelosos y ansiosos
> busca de súbito permanencia en el tiempo y límites en la tierra,
> tal vez las fatigas y las edades acumuladas implacablemente
> se extiendan como la ola lunar de un océano recién creado
> sobre litorales y tierras angustiosamente desiertas.   [I, 203]

> Maybe the natural weakness of zealous and anxious beings / suddenly searches for permanence in time and limits on earth, / maybe the fatigues and the implacably piled-up ages / will extend like the lunar wave of a newly created ocean / over shores and lands deserted in anguish.

The split into past and future times through present and past subjunctive verbs is subtly concealed by the sentence's parallel structure, as if suggesting an undifferentiated continuum. Whereas during past and present the subject sought comfort from spatial and temporal limits, in the future he will continue to wish for a union between subject and object that would fuse his reserves of temporal anxiety to the equally barren objective reality. That wish translates into several forceful resolutions, the first of which betrays a resignation to the effects of time:

> Ay, que lo que soy siga existiendo y cesando de existir,
> y que mi obediencia se ordene con tales condiciones de hierro

Pablo Neruda: The Poetics of Prophecy

> que el temblor de las muertes y de los nacimientos no
> conmueva
> el profundo sitio que quiero reservar para mí eternamente.
>
> Sea, pues, lo que soy, en alguna parte y en todo tiempo,
> establecido y asegurado y ardiente testigo,
> cuidadosamente destruyéndose y preservándose
> incesantemente,
> evidentemente empeñado en su deber original. [I, 203]

> Oh, may whatever I am keep on existing and ceasing to exist, /
> and may my obedience arrange itself with such iron conditions
> / that the tremor of deaths and births should not move / the
> deep place that I wish to reserve for myself eternally. / May
> whatever I am, then, be someplace and in all time, / established and assured and ardent witness, / carefully destroying
> and incessantly preserving itself, / clearly set on its original
> duty.

The existential doing and undoing disintegrates and in turn reconstitutes the subject according to the cyclical laws that were established in "Sistema sombrío." The "condiciones de hierro," for example, recall the "viejos hierros" of that poem, as does the "profundo sitio" that wrestles against temporal disruption. A note of relieved self-contentment thus sounds through the two references to "lo que soy," as though the speaker had now reconciled himself to the impossibility of total self-definition. He continues to hope for permanence, as we see in the subtle contrast between "alguna parte" and "todo tiempo," but that hope appears mediated by the constraints of visionary identity. The security of visionary witnessing is countered by the risks of a death-in-life cycle that makes that identity possible. The penultimate line, with its chiastic construction, inverting verbs and adverbs, conveys the complexity of that cycle and again links it to the notion of vision as temporal duty. Vision thus becomes "original" in the dual sense of being both new and faithful to origins, the same origins alluded to earlier as an echo of "Sistema sombrío. "

At the end of the first book of *Residencia*, then, the reader is left awaiting an answer because there is none to give, except, of course, the one provided by the last poem. The nebulous affir-

Vision and Time

mation that "it means shadows" does not point to the absence of meaning but rather to the fact that whatever knowledge there is remains shrouded within a mystery that poetic vision has failed to penetrate. The poem describes an impasse, a point beyond which no one can see and where the dialectic of poetry is forced to recoil upon itself. If vision and irony are the two motifs that make up the poetics of *Residencia en la tierra,* then the first book ends by allowing irony to displace vision and returning to the conditions that had produced the scene of writing. The speaker has traced a circuitous journey, since at the end of "Significa sombras" he is no better off than at the beginning of "Galope muerto," the knowledge of having an "original duty" being no clearer than the acknowledgment of a privileged sound. In fact, if we weave together the titles of the first and last poems so as to form a single sentence, we unravel the entire thread of the first book: "Galope muerto significa sombras"—"Dead gallop means shadows." The mystery of vision leads the speaker to inquire into his own nature, but this introspection reaches an impasse as soon as he discovers the negative implications of temporal contingency.

2

Vision and Conversion

> I return so I won't come back,
> I don't want to be wrong again,
> it's dangerous to walk
> backwards because suddenly
> the past becomes a jail.
> —Pablo Neruda, "Return to a City"

I

My treatment of the poems of the first book of *Residencia* may seem overworked, but it is designed to articulate the working details of the visionary mode. In refusing a casual reading, I have emphasized the creation of a visionary speaker whose drama of representation is enacted in every poem and whose specific concerns, which constitute the book's prophetic argument, we can discern by concentrating on the system of cross-references in the poems.

As we move on to the second book, we need to keep that visionary drama in mind as its contrasting key. By focusing again on selected poems, some of which are among Neruda's best known, I attempt to outline the gradual disjunction of the subject from the visionary experience. This does not mean that vision will be forsaken altogether, but that the poems show us different attempts to come to terms with that disjunction. Although I am not so concerned with tracing the cyclical sense of this second book, my argument obviously assumes that such a disjunctive pattern forms part of the reader's experience. We could in fact regard most of these poems as dramatizations of the reading act itself, as they repeatedly expose the limits of the visionary speaker and his capacity for self-delusion. Caught

Vision and Conversion

within an aesthetic enterprise that he understands only in part, the speaker ultimately loses control over the writing project and lapses into the fictions of reification and nostalgia as havens from the experience of time. Besides exposing the monstrous quality of writing, the disjunction between self and vision postulates a radical change from time to history. This change of horizon is not simply thematic but rhetorical, as the experience of conversion splits the subject into two entities whose reconciliation appears elusive. In a final section, devoted to some poems of *Tercera residencia*, I explore the problems attendant on this rhetorical change and attempt an explanation of the failure of these poems as conversion texts.

II

Neruda began to write the poems of the second *Residencia* in Chile, after his return from the Far East. But it was in Spain, where he was sent to head another consulate, that he finally published it in 1935, together with the first book. A year later, when the Spanish Civil War broke out, Neruda showed his adherence to the Republican cause in *España en el corazón* (1938), which became a part of *Tercera residencia (1935-1945)* (1947), the third and final volume of this visionary cycle. It seems important to clarify this particular chronology because the second book has often been thought to prefigure the Civil War experience when in fact it has little to do with it. While its tone and outlook are sufficiently tragic to lend credence to such a reading, it is only in relation to the first book that the second can be understood.[1]

We immediately notice the change in tone in "Un día sobresale" (One Day Stands Out), the first poem, which occupies a leading position similar to that of "Galope muerto." Besides

[1]For further details of Neruda's life during this time, see Emir Rodríguez Monegal, *Neruda: El viajero inmóvil* (Caracas: Monte Avila, 1977), pp. 94-129; René de Costa, *The Poetry of Pablo Neruda* (Cambridge: Harvard University Press, 1979), pp. 73-104; and John Felstiner, *Translating Neruda: The Way to Macchu Picchu* (Stanford: Stanford University Press, 1980), pp. 103-21. For Neruda's role in the literary quarrels of the time, see Juan Cano Ballesta, *La poesía española entre pureza y revolución (1930-1936)* (Madrid: Gredos, 1971), pp. 201-2, and "Pablo Neruda and the Renewal of Spanish Poetry during the Thirties," in *Spanish Writers of 1936*, ed. Jaime Ferrán and Daniel P. Testa (London: Tamesis Books, 1973), pp. 94-106.

indicating the occasion for the poem, the title once again emphasizes the diary format and reminds the reader of the temporal conventions that govern the text. Within the structure of recollection, one particular day stands out:

> De lo sonoro salen números,
> números moribundos y cifras con estiércol,
> rayos humedecidos y relámpagos sucios.
> De lo sonoro, creciendo, cuando
> la noche sale sola, como reciente viuda,
> como paloma o amapola o beso,
> y sus maravillosas estrellas se dilatan.
>
> En lo sonoro la luz se verifica:
> las vocales se inundan, el llanto cae en pétalos,
> un viento de sonidos como una ola retumba,
> brilla y peces de frío y elástico la habitan. [I, 207]
>
> Out of sound come numbers, / dying numbers and ciphers with dung, / moistened lightning and dirty thunderbolts. / Out of sound, growing, when / night comes out alone, like a recent widow, / like a pigeon or a poppy or a kiss, / and its marvelous stars expand. / Within sound light is confirmed: / vowels are flooded, weeping drops in petals, / a wind of sound resounds like a wave, / it shines, and cold and elastic fish live in it.

It takes little effort to recognize here a replay of the revelation we found earlier in "Galope muerto." The poem springs from a similar narrative of aural experience, though the dense ellipses of the title and the self-conscious similes are gone. Now the speaker openly admits that sound is the source of vision, thus releasing his privileged hold on the experience and appealing to a wider reception. The plain, almost confessional title prepares the way for the immediacy of the catalogue of images that replaces the earlier string of similes and thus suggests a rejection of abstraction.

As the aural revelation expands in the third stanza to encompass the invoked objects, we anticipate the longer catalogue of everyday sounds that appear in stanzas 4 through 6. It is as if in listing these sounds and directing our attention toward them the speaker attempted to domesticate their radical otherness and

Vision and Conversion

reduce their potential threat. It is therefore hardly fortuitous that the weird "sound of time" should climax the catalogue in stanza 5, or that silence, described as the "husks of sound" (cáscaras del silencio) (I, 208) should appear "galopando en caballos sin patas" (galloping on hoofless horses) in stanza 9. By the time we reach the twelfth stanza, what began as an innocent and unmediated perception turns into the quiet terror of a visionary nightmare. The reader is asked to see, no longer to listen to, the horrible spectacle of the growth of things in time. Fittingly, the stanza culminates in a simile that casts the entire process as a horse running wildly "in its courts of justice" ("como un caballo el día corre en sus tribunales") (I, 209), thus recalling the original "dead gallop." The last stanza, which repeats the genitive clause of the first two, describes a seemingly calm sunrise. The setting provides a metaphorical context for the title (the sun "standing out" or rising), suggesting that the entire incident took place during a few seconds before dawn and the speaker now returns to the moment in the third stanza when "en lo sonoro la luz se verifica." As the speaker draws a curtain to view the sunrise, he is struck by the pictorial effects of time. Night has yielded to the tinted dawn sky but the scene appears ominously as "sombra recién huyendo / y gotas que del corazón del cielo caen como sangre celeste" (shadow lately fleeing / and drops that fall from the heart of the sky like heavenly blood) (I, 209). A tragic vision of universal bloodshed displaces whatever relief the speaker might have sought in the experience of dawn.

With the aid of "Un día sobresale" we can better measure the distance of these poems from those of the first book in terms of the speaker's rejection of abstraction as a way of reaching the object. The new attempt to dwell on unmediated experience implies the speaker's need to escape the burden of visionary interpretation, and consequently his dissatisfaction as poetic subject. At the end of the poem, for example, we infer the poet's horror at learning that the immediate sounds, which appear in contrast to the rhetorical convolutions of the first poem, have been unable to contain the tragic vision. Because death leaps up in every display of temporal process, the poet will no longer seek, as in the first book, to understand that process but rather will attempt to escape the burden of witnessing it.

Pablo Neruda: The Poetics of Prophecy

It seems important to distinguish this particular self-discontent from the linguistic dissatisfaction that we find in such earlier poems as "Galope muerto." Both experiences arise from a discontinuity within the speaker. But whereas the earlier discontent signaled a dissonance between subject and language, between the speaker and his ability to describe visions, the dissonance is now between two conflicting versions of the same self—one seeking the object through the immediacy of pure naming, the other seeking it through interpretation. In fact, while in earlier poems we infer a lack of confidence in language from the speaker's struggle to find the correct analogy, now a strange overconfidence underlies the sense of visionary burden. While in the first book the speaker takes pains to capture a vision, in the second he takes pains to avoid one. The dissonance that is common to both gestures results in ironic texts. That is, the duplication within consciousness which we see dramatized in "Un día sobresale" is but a more pointed version of the same structure at work in the earlier poems of linguistic mistrust. In both, discontinuity marks a distance through which the subject "comes to know itself by an act of increasing differentiation from what it is not."[2] Irony, then, mediates that split into two entities and signals the rhetorical mode through which the speaker describes his own predicament.

No poem in *Residencia en la tierra* more vividly dramatizes these issues than "Walking around," one of its better-known texts. The suggestive English title by itself captures a sense of wandering and indifference which betrays a radical passivity in the subject. "Walking around" conveys an aimless, circuitous journey in which the speaker is casually, though not unconsciously, engaged in order to retrieve some pleasant experience. Yet the famous first lines complain instead:

> Sucede que me canso de ser hombre.
> Sucede que entro en las sastrerías y en los cines
> marchito, impenetrable, como un cisne de fieltro
> navegando en un agua de origen y ceniza.

---

[2]Paul de Man, "The Rhetoric of Temporality," in *Interpretation: Theory and Practice*, ed. Charles S. Singleton (Baltimore: Johns Hopkins University Press, 1969), p. 195.

Vision and Conversion

El olor de las peluquerías me hace llorar a gritos.
Sólo quiero un descanso de piedras o de lana,
Sólo quiero no ver establecimientos ni jardines,
ni mercaderías, ni anteojos, ni ascensores.

Sucede que me canso de mis pies y mis uñas
y mi pelo y mi sombra.
Sucede que me canso de ser hombre.   [I, 215]

It so happens that I'm tired of being a man. / It so happens that I walk into tailor shops and into movie houses / all withered, impenetrable, like a kind of velour swan / sailing along in a sea of origin and ash. / The smell of barbershops makes me cry and scream. / I only want a respite from stones or wool, / I only want no sight of businesses or gardens, / or marketplaces, or eyeglasses, or elevators. / It so happens that I'm tired of my feet and my nails / and my hair and my shadow. / It so happens that I'm tired of being a man.

The grammatical convergence of an impersonal expression with a subject complement makes for a rare tension of perspectives that is sustained throughout the poem. The opening statement is made from a point outside the subject-object dichotomy, conveying at once objective verification and subjective testimony, as if the speaker had for some time endured his human condition but had only recently become aware of it. Thus an ironic redundancy, echoing that of the book's title, emerges from the ironic statement. Just as one cannot think of a residence anywhere but on earth, a man does not normally tire of being a man. This redundancy has the effect of focusing attention on the conflict between subject and object, between self and world, without placing blame on either one.

The ensuing narrative, which shows instances of that conflict, harks back to the Romantic caricature of "Arte poética," as betrayed by the telling adjective "marchito." Too absorbed in a literary world, the poet feels alienated—like a "cisne de fieltro," emblematic of the *modernistas*—from vulgar commercial establishments. In his commentary on the poem, Amado Alonso argued that at this point the speaker expresses a wish to escape to a pastoral world as a release from the pressures of cultural life. Such may be the meaning, for instance, of the second stanza,

71

which states a preference for "un descanso de piedras o de lana" over "establecimientos" or "jardines."[3] But Alonso's argument, which postulates a Romantic resolution of existential anguish through a marriage of mind and nature, seems to be pointedly denied in the stanza immediately following, which sees an equally intolerable burden in the physical characteristics of human form. Instead of anticipating a resolution through nature, the first three stanzas dramatize an insoluble conflict that is incipient in the first line. More than just being tired of culture, the speaker is tired of being a subject altogether.

It should be evident that the speaker's identity is mostly, if not entirely, literary. Both the earlier self-parody and the reference to the "cisne" make that identity explicit by alluding to texts from private and public canons. The burden of being a "man" actually means the burden of being a visionary poet. Only if we recognize this analogy does the shift in the fourth stanza, which takes exception to the preceding conflict, make any sense. The three acts about which the speaker fantasizes—"asustar a un notario con un lirio cortado" (to frighten a notary with a cut lily), "dar muerte a una monja con un golpe de oreja" (to kill a nun with a box on the ear), "ir por las calles con un cuchillo verde" (to go through the streets with a green knife) (I, 215)—signal a nostalgic flight to a poetic world where such pranks, the few rewards of poetry, would not be censured. But that flight turns out to be brief. In the next two stanzas the speaker has returned to a demystified world that exposes the ills of melancholy as the obverse of those rewards. In addition to setting up a contrast by way of the main verb—the three *no quieros* pointedly offsetting the earlier *sólo quieros*—the stanzas arrange a sequence whose punctuation yields the same panting effect of some passage in the first book. Especially noteworthy are the last lines of stanzas 5 and 6, which conclude the sequence with present participles that emphasize the temporal process. And in a remarkable description of "Monday-morning blues," the following stanza picks up the same theme:

> Por eso el día lunes arde como el petróleo
> cuando me ve llegar con mi cara de cárcel,

[3]Amado Alonso, *Poesía y estilo de Pablo Neruda* (Buenos Aires: Sudamericana, 1968), pp. 240–50.

Vision and Conversion

> y aúlla en su transcurso como una rueda herida,
> y da pasos de sangre caliente hacia la noche. [I, 216]

> That's why Monday morning burns up like oil / each time it sees me arrive with my jail face, / and howls in its course like a wounded wheel, / and takes hot-blooded steps toward the night.

Monday, the first day of the week, marks the beginning of a cycle, whose course is indicated by the "rueda herida." In personifying it as the subject's judge, the speaker demonstrates the degree to which he has objectified time or has at least removed it from internal experience. Not totally an object, time appears suspended in a delicate balance, as if dramatizing a side effect of the ironic tension that runs through the poem.

It is precisely this ironic temporality, the next stanzas suggest, that drives the subject to perform visionary interpretations. Time "pushes" the passive speaker to shoe-repair shops that smell like vinegar and to narrow streets that recall stifling war trenches. Ominous signs spring up everywhere for no apparent reason—"pájaros color de azufre y horribles intestinos" (sulfur-colored birds and horrible intestines) (I, 216) appear out of canaries and link sausages; faded mirrors cloud up with infernal smoke. Only in the last stanza, with the first and only acknowledgment of the speaker's walk, do we note a respite from vision, an intimation that the burden may at last have been lifted:

> Yo paseo con calma, con ojos, con zapatos,
> con furia, con olvido,
> paso, cruzo oficinas y tiendas de ortopedia,
> y patios donde hay ropas colgadas de un alambre:
> calzoncillos, toallas y camisas que lloran
> lentas lágrimas sucias. [I, 216]

> I walk around, calmly, with eyes, with shoes, / with rage, with oblivion, / I pass, cross offices and orthopedic shops, / and backyards where there are clothes hanging from a wire: / undershorts, towels and shirts that cry / slow dirty tears.

Up till the fourth line the speaker appears unperturbed. In fact, the superfluous gesture of acknowledging his own eyes hints at a reconciliation with both physical form and visionary gift, just as he can now bring himself to stroll by the very stores he had avoided earlier. But as in the conclusion to "Un día sobresale," and with similar imagery, the poem's last two lines prove that peace to be illusory. An uncanny spectacle springs up amid the most domestic of scenes: the clothes drying on a line appear like tortured bodies hanging upside down and the dripping washwater resembles dirty tears.

"Walking around," then, is about the failed revolt against vision, a failure that exposes the limits of the speaker and his fall into irony. At the end of the poem the speaker is left helpless before the overwhelming power of vision, as if there were no escape from its curse. One cannot help recalling, apropos of this particular failure, the concluding lines of "Galope muerto," which show the subject stuttering in an attempt at divination with no prospect of success. The analogy may seem forced, but I am trying to adduce a parallel that will also point up a significant difference between the two books. Both the linguistic mistrust of the first poem and the ontological lack treated in the second are shown to serve as the occasion for rather than the obstacle to the achievement of poetry. Both signal, in other words, the kinds of failures on which poetry thrives. But if at first the speaker is shown to accommodate to the limits of language and to submit to a visionary destiny, now he revolts against his own limits and casts his discontent in the form of ironic language. This ironic stance dramatizes a stage halfway between accommodation and the birth of a new self, and it foreshadows an eventual radical change in him.

The implications of this structure for the book's changing concept of time will soon become clear. For the moment, we must recognize that this ironic stance by itself is incapable of effecting any such change. As powerful a mediation as the rhetoric of irony may be, it requires a discontinuity that suspends the possibility of action. Thus, before a moment of crisis is reached, the earlier ironic pathos will recur in a more urgent and tragic mode in other poems, such as "Agua sexual," in which the painful burden of vision is dramatized in the image of "un párpado atrozmente levantado a la fuerza" (an eyelid atrociously lifted by force) (I, 228). This striking image—which recalls a famous scene from Luis Buñuel's *Un chien andalou* (1929), and could well serve as the emblem for the entire second book—marks the climax to

Vision and Conversion

an array of visions that results from a process of abstraction by which the subject gradually empties all content out of the form of rainfall. The eyelid's forced lifting marks a turning point in the poem and gives way to the erotic connotation of the title, a vision that dramatizes the exclusion of the subject from the experience of desire. As the poem ends, the speaker complains that "aunque cierre mis ojos y me cubra el corazón enteramente / veo caer un agua sorda" (though I close my eyes and cover my heart fully / I see a deaf water fall), thus recalling the pathos of earlier poems while paving the way for the gruesome final vision beyond the grave: "Veo pasar sus aguas a través de los huesos" (I see their waters pass through the bones) (I, 288). The transition from the bemused pathos of "Walking Around" to the painful alarm of "Agua sexual" conveys a sense of crisis growing out of the subject's incompatibility with vision. This increasing self-estrangement demonstrates both a recognition of the fatal effects of time and a revolt against that knowledge. For whether the speaker attempts to escape through absorption into immediacy, through ironic detachment, or through abstraction into pure form, the result is always the same—the tragic vision imposes itself to reveal things as the speaker wishes they were not rather than as they really are. Yet it seems equally true that this intensified sense of tragedy no longer leaves any room for irony. There is "no oblivion"—"No hay olvido," warns the title of another poem, as if summarizing the lessons of the second book. If we turn now to this particular poem, and to "Vuelve el otoño" (The Autumn Returns), the text that immediately precedes it, we can explore the limits of the dissonance between speaker and vision that we have so far traced.

"Vuelve el otoño" begins by acknowledging the return of autumn, the season of declining strength and the antechamber of winter death. The title announces a limit that borders on crisis and also heralds cyclical change:

>
> Un enlutado día cae de las campanas
> como una temblorosa tela de vaga viuda,
> es un color, un sueño
> de cerezas hundidas en la tierra,
> es una cola de humo que llega sin descanso
> a cambiar el color del agua y de los besos.

Pablo Neruda: The Poetics of Prophecy

> No sé si se me entiende: cuando desde lo alto
> se avecina la noche, cuando el solitario poeta
> a la ventana oye correr el corcel del otoño
> y las hojas del miedo pisoteado crujen en sus arterias,
> hay algo sobre el cielo, como lengua de buey
> espeso, algo en la duda del cielo y de la atmósfera.   [I, 246]

> A mournful day falls from the bells / like a trembling cloth of vague widow, / it's a color, a dream / of cherries buried underground, / it's a smoke tail that restlessly arrives / to change the color of water and kisses. / I don't know if I'm being understood: when from way up / night starts falling, when the lonely poet / by the window hears the autumn steed running / and the leaves of stamped-upon fear crackle in his arteries, / there's something over the sky, like a thick ox's tongue, / something in the doubt of the sky and the atmosphere.

The alert reader will not fail to note the recurrence of earlier motifs: tolling bells, a noisy gallop, the ox's tongue, even the reflexive remark, all allude to "Galope muerto." The discreet rewriting works as a dramatization of the seasonal return, a retracing that gathers similar past experiences and links memory traces to a new context. Thus along with autumn returns the scene of writing.

In conveying the seasonal experience, the speaker focuses on the moment before sundown and exploits a pun in the colloquial and literal meanings: "día cae" (day is drawing to a close; literally day falls) overlaps with "cae de las campanas" (falls from the bells). The pun emphasizes the verb, to be recalled later on in an important contrast, and sets in motion the declining movement that follows. As in "Galope muerto," the speaker shuffles various similes until he hits on the one that describes autumn as both external season and internal mood. In the second stanza, the clearer and more frequent allusions to "Galope muerto" not only paraphrase the first poem by the use of familiar imagery, but also confirm the internal meaning. By the point in the third stanza where the speaker again invokes the original sound, the discreet rewriting has turned into an explicit quotation:

> pero no es esto, sino el viejo galope,
> el caballo del viejo otoño que tiembla y dura.

Vision and Conversion

> El caballo del viejo otoño tiene la barba roja
> y la espuma del miedo le cubre las mejillas
> y el aire que le sigue tiene forma de océano
> y perfume de vaga podredumbre enterrada. [I, 246]
>
> but it is not that: it's the old gallop, / the horse of the old autumn that trembles and endures. / The horse of the old autumn has a red beard / and the froth of fear covers its cheeks / and the air that follows it has the form of an ocean / and perfume of vague buried putrefaction.

Fittingly, the allusion to the "viejo galope" sets off the return of authentic poetic audition from the recurrence of the inauthentic "cosas a su sitio" (things to their place) and "el abogado indispensable" (the indispensable lawyer) of the third stanza (I, 246). The first line of the fourth stanza ("El caballo del viejo otoño..." which repeats the same motif, makes the allusion more obvious and harder to miss. The remaining alexandrines in the rest of the poem add several forbidding traits to the autumn horse, and their symmetrical, anaphoric series conveys a sense of finality that announces an end to the poem, or at least portends a radical shift.

Indeed, the overt allusiveness of these lines marks a clear juncture. The break becomes noticeable as the fourth stanza repeats the allusion to "the old gallop" with an assertive primacy radically unlike the two previous instances in stanzas 2 and 3. The increasing articulation of this sequence suggests the speaker's gradual recollection of the original poetic experience, as first shown in "Galope muerto," almost as if the poem dramatized his painful remembrance of a suppressed experience. By thus climaxing the allusive sequence, the fourth stanza marks the wholesale return of the textual theater, the scene of writing, as it signals a renewed attempt at the poem of autumn:

> Todos los dias baja del cielo un color ceniciento
> que las palomas deben repartir por la tierra:
> la cuerda que el olvido y las lágrimas tejen,
> el tiempo que ha dormido largos años dentro de las campanas,
> todo,
> los viejos trajes mordidos, las mujeres que ven venir la nieve,
> las amapolas negras que nadie puede contemplar sin morir,
> todo cae a las manos que levanto
> en medio de la lluvia. [I, 246-247]

Pablo Neruda: The Poetics of Prophecy

> Every day an ash color descends from the sky / which pigeons must spread through the earth: / the string woven by oblivion and tears, / the time that has slept long years inside the bells, / everything, / old chewed suits, the women who see the snow coming, / the black poppies that nobody can contemplate without dying, / everything falls into the hands I raise / in the rain.

The new sequence rearranges the old motifs and infuses them with the meaning afforded by the restored sound. More important than the pluralization of "enlutado día" is the shift from *caer* to *bajar* (from "fall" to "descend"), which conveys an intentionality that is radically different from the purposelessness that we see in the first sequence. Just as in the first line "baja" is emphasized by a pun, so in the fifth stanza it is charged by the dual meaning of "cielo" (sky and heaven). Similarly, what had appeared vaguely as "un color" in the first stanza now comes through as "un color ceniciento." Completing the effect of intentionality is the casting of doves in the role of emissary angels, which take up the task of spreading the night.

All of these transpositions suggest that the speaker's perception is structured according to a pattern of oppositional relations, a system of differences that structures and sustains meaning. By the time the speaker finally appears in the last two lines, the entire series has been condensed into an inclusive pronoun ("todo"), ominously anticipated in the one-word fifth line, as the subject of "caer." The recurrence of the initial verb, especially after the important shift, seems to signal a simple regression to the earlier purposelessness, but a careful reading suggests a more complex structure. The complete phrase is "caer a las manos" (to fall into one's hands), which conveys a meaning somewhere between purposelessness and intention and which makes of the fate of the object a mere retrospective illusion. That is, everything *seems* to be destined for the speaker's hands, but the physical context of the falling ("en medio de la lluvia") pointedly undermines that claim. While the recurrent verb does sustain the regressive effect, the complement phrase further qualifies it in order to expose the speaker's final act as a self-delusion. Within the poem's structure, the pair of opposites that governs this particular act refers to his shift in position—whereas in the first sequence he appears sheltered "a la ventana" and passively listening to the run of "el corcel del otoño," now he himself runs outside expecting to act as the world's shelter. What motivates this action is a vision of universal collapse which he attempts to stop, like a latter-day Atlas, by raising his arms, only to realize that he has been deluded by the misty atmosphere ("algo en la duda del cielo") (I, 246) of the autumn rain. The dramatic irony of the last scene becomes all the more poignant because, contrary to the meaning of the inclusive pronoun and the complement phrase, it is the rain that encloses the subject and not the other way around.

We would not be wrong to recognize in this eerie conclusion an echo of "Débil del alba," where the speaker, similarly overwhelmed by the rainy landscape, observed that "la lluvia cae sobre mí, y se me parece / se me parece con su desvarío, solitaria en el mundo muerto" (the rain falls over me, and looks like me / looks like me in its caprice, lonely in the dead world") (I, 173). Yet it should be equally obvious that whatever echo there is serves to underscore further the pathos and despair of the later poem. As bleak a landscape as these quoted lines describe, they nevertheless succeed in locating a saving link between subject and object in the rain's disturbance, a link that goes on to provide, in "Unidad," the minimal elements of a regrouping vision. Here, however, the attempt to rescue a "falling" world already presumes distance, except that it is rendered far worse by the emptying of all value from that distance. Even the tenuous link that was claimed earlier in "Débil del alba" becomes lost. Instead of articulating the present vision, as the reader would expect, the subject chooses (or is compelled) to concentrate on recovering the earlier vision. The poem traces the return, imposition, and ultimate deception (in both its senses of fraud and delusion) of the original poetic sound as a scene of writing. But that inclusive view only serves to reveal the visionary subject at its most limited and abject. The biggest error of all lies, of course, in the poem's title, which invokes the "return" of autumn by attributing such a season to "Galope muerto," when in fact that poem dramatically takes place during the summer and its final lines point to an "anillo del verano." Rather than articulating a successful return, then, "Vuelve el otoño" dramatizes the manner of visionary error, exposing the structure of meaning as the deceptive effect of difference, of meaning as a painful mirage.

The similarity to "Débil del alba" becomes clearer if we regard "No hay olvido (Sonata)" as a counterpart to "Unidad." No two titles could be more different, to be sure, but they both express the same sense of inclusiveness which their structural roles prescribe. For this reason alone perhaps one can detect in both a common retrospective gesture that bridges the arguments immediately preceding each poem, a pointed intertextual play that is a function of their summary message. In "No hay olvido (Sonata)," for example, the musical subtitle surely recalls the earlier "Alianza (Sonata)." More significant still, its admonishing reminder points the moral of the immediately preceding poem. And as if calling attention to that intertextual play, the first few lines go so far as to quote the famous verb from "Walking around":

> Si me preguntáis en dónde he estado
> debo decir "Sucede."
> Debo de hablar del suelo que oscurecen las piedras,
> del río que durando se destruye:
> no sé sino las cosas que los pájaros pierden,
> el mar dejado atrás, o mi hermana llorando.
> Por qué tantas regiones, por qué un día
> se junta con un día? Por qué una negra noche
> se acumula en la boca? Por qué muertos? [I, 247]

> If you ask where I've been / I must say "It happens." / I must speak about the stones that darken the ground, / about the river that enduring destroys itself: / I know only the things the birds lose, / the sea left behind, or my sister crying. / Why so many regions, why does day / join with day? Why does a black night / collect in my mouth? Why the dead?

The quotation has several functions, the most important of which is to set off a present continuum from a past time ("he estado"), the first and most obvious instance of a polarity that will be sustained throughout the poem. Also, because "sucede" refers back to an ironic moment when the speaker was tired "of being a man," the new context implies a rejection of irony and an acceptance of the fallen world. Finally, the verb's literal

Vision and Conversion

meanings (to happen and to succeed in time) reinforce the poem's temporal focus. All of these functions are contained simultaneously in the verb but the ensuing lines emphasize especially the past-present polarity and thereby explicate the title. Since "there is no oblivion" or loss of memory, as the writing project had prescribed, all past events coexist in a present continuum. Past locations become current happenstance. Space, not time, darkens stones. Instead of remembering, one *knows*. And in what amounts to a violent parody, the "río que durando se destruye" inverts the meaning of Heraclitus' exemplary river, thereby denying all significance to process or change. That the speaker should state all this knowledge in the ethical mood suggests that it is the painful lesson drawn from the limits of visionary experience. For to deny the possibility of oblivion amounts to accepting the status quo of things, untouched by poetry, to renounce whatever power vision lays claim to, and to abstain from answering those crucial questions—concerning spatial displacement, temporal succession, melancholy expression, and death—which the subject has posed all along and which now recur at the end of the first stanza.

The rest of the poem merely plays out variations on the same theme, each time rejecting the abstraction of the past for the immediacy of the present. Even as the speaker drifts from the discourse of concrete objects to ponder the consequences of "un día alimentado con nuestra triste sangre" (a day nourished with our sad blood), or waxes nostalgic about "las dulces tarjetas de larga cola" (the sweet postcards of long tail) (I, 247), he catches himself to warn: "Pero no penetremos más allá de esos dientes / no mordamos las cáscaras que el silencio acumula" (But let's not penetrate beyond those teeth / let's not bite the rinds that silence stores) (I, 248). At one level, the self-reprimand is obviously intended to avert, once again, the temptation of vision, to persuade us (and himself, perhaps) that he does not know what to answer ("no sé qué contestar," I know not what to answer). But that the passage should also invoke the same "cáscaras del silencio" (rinds of silence) that earlier had made up the experience of unmediated sound in "Un día sobresale" is enough to demonstrate its corrective scope. Indeed, the poem ends with a rhetorical intensity that is careful to avoid any interpretation save for the subtle arrangement of the last five lines. While their structure recalls the fourth stanza of "Vuelve el otoño," which employed the same procedure to signal a turning point, the absence of an alternative vision serves as a pointed contrast. The repetition of the adverbial "tantos" (so many) renders the sequence even more desperate, but the theme that dominates the conclusion is that these are merely "cosas que quiero olvidar" (things that I wish to forget).

III

I have followed the argument of "Vuelve el otoño" and "No hay olvido" in detail because they conveniently articulate the disjunction between speaker and vision as a two-stage process that we can now summarize as follows: (1) The subject's awareness of the visionary error that results from the deceptive structure of meaning is followed by (2) an avoidance of visionary interpretation, which is manifested as the denial of time as process. The corollary of this denial, as "No hay olvido" demonstrates, is the speaker's self-effacement. One can hardly avoid concluding that the dissonance between speaker and vision is a function of the contradictions inherent in the writing project. While the journal format was originally intended to give shape to the self's internal discontinuities, now the material accumulation of that textual theater, the scene of writing, undermines its own motivation and reduces the past to a spatial simultaneity that obviates the functions of both memory and vision. That is, as the speaker reaches the end of the second book (and it is hardly an accident that these two poems appear where they do), he realizes that the desire to make everything present has subverted the foundations of a rememberable past, has displaced the need for a temporal dimension whose defining characteristic is absence, and has therefore obviated even his own presence. Because everything is written, there is no need for the past.

One may well regard this moment as the revelation of a monstrosity, as the discovery that writing has declared its autonomy and taken over its creator. The consequences of this discovery for the speaker's temporal structure will not become evident until *Tercera residencia*. But already at this juncture the

Vision and Conversion

reader can perceive how the dissonance between speaker and vision involves an ontological limit that forces an eventual change. This change would be no mere modification in order to accommodate to new circumstances, but a literal death and resurrection, a conversion that would create a new person altogether. It could be argued, of course, that not until *Tercera residencia* do we encounter actual conversion poems, in the precise sense of moral accounts "of the experience of a poet who has finally reached the vantage point from which a structure of intelligibility can be imposed on the temporal fragmentation of the self."[4] And yet a striking prefiguration appears in one text in particular, "Entrada a la madera" (Entrance into Wood), the first and most famous of the "Tres cantos materiales" (Three Material Songs). Such a reading may seem surprising, but I find that it is here that the symbolic key to the impasse of the visionary lies. This poem, we shall find, not only explores the speaker's temporal predicament, but along with "Josie Bliss," the nostalgic poem that closes the second book, it dramatizes the consequences of the poet's submission to his monstrous creation.

Because my concern at this point is to trace a symbolic structure that does not necessarily coincide with the reading sequence, it matters little that "Entrada a la madera" precedes "Vuelve el otoño" and "No hay olvido." But even if we did adhere to the reading order, the results would be the same. As this poem follows immediately after "Agua sexual," which ends with a vision beyond the grave, it can be regarded as a response to that particular limit-experience. That response begins with the title, which not only enacts a symbolic shift from water to the more substantial wood, but makes a revealing pun. The Spanish "Entrada a la madera," entrance into wood, echoes *entrar en materia*, to get into a subject or to get down to business, and thus indicates a rejection of the past for the more significant events of the present. In becoming the first *material* of the three songs of this section, *madera* thus draws attention to its root, the Latin *mater* (Spanish *madre*), which is also the root of *materia*.[5]

---

[4]Giuseppe Mazzotta, "The Canzoniere and the Language of the Self," *Studies in Philology*, 75 (1978), 272.
[5]Rodríguez Monegal, *Neruda*, p. 288.

Pablo Neruda: The Poetics of Prophecy

> Con mi razón apenas, con mis dedos,
> con lentas aguas lentas inundadas,
> caigo al imperio de los nomeolvides,
> a una tenaz atmósfera de luto,
> a una olvidada sala decaída,
> a un racimo de tréboles amargos.
>
> Caigo en la sombra, en medio
> de destruídas cosas,
> y miro arañas, y apaciento bosques
> de secretas maderas inconclusas,
> y ando entre húmedas fibras arrancadas
> al vivo ser de substancia y silencio. [I, 229]
>
> With scarcely my reason at all, with my fingers, / with slow waters slow flooded, / I fall to the forget-me-not empire, / to a tenacious mourning atmosphere, / to a forgotten decayed living room, / to a bunch of bitter clover. / I fall in the shadow, in the midst / of destroyed things, / and look at spiders, and graze on forests / of secret inconclusive woods, / and walk along moist fibers torn / from the live being of substance and silence.

The initial adverbial clauses shift the focus of the first stanza from the speaker, who can only be inferred from the possessive and the verb, to the main action. On the other hand, the second clause makes a redundant use of the possessive (since in Spanish it is superfluous in conjunction with parts of the body) for the sake of making the subject explicit. As in "Vuelve el otoño," the action begins with a fall, but the matching of each of the three clauses with a corresponding prepositional phrase couches it in qualifiers that suspend all pathos. Somewhat like Alice in Wonderland, the speaker falls into an enchanted forest that is initially forbidding. It becomes gradually familiar as he wanders in his new surroundings, all the while the forest remains "secreto" and "inconcluso," until he discovers a related substance:

> Dulce materia, oh rosa de alas secas,
> en mi hundimiento tus pétalos subo
> con pies pesados de roja fatiga,
> y en tu catedral dura me arrodillo
> golpeándome los labios con un ángel.

Vision and Conversion

> Es que soy yo ante tu color de mundo,
> ante tus pálidas espadas muertas,
> ante tus corazones reunidos,
> ante tu silenciosa multitud.
> Soy yo ante tu ola de olores muriendo,
> envueltos en otoño y resistencia:
> soy yo emprendiendo un viaje funerario
> entre tus cicatrices amarillas.
> Soy yo con mis lamentos sin origen,
> sin alimentos, desvelado, solo,
> entrando oscurecidos corredores,
> llegando a tu materia misteriosa. [I, 229-30]

> Sweet matter, oh rose of dried wings, / in my sinking I climb up your petals / with heavy feet of red fatigue, / and in your hard cathedral I kneel / beating my lips with an angel. / It's just me before your color of world, / before your pale dead swords, / before your gathered hearts, / before your silent crowd. / It's me before your wave of dying odors, / wrapped in autumn and resistance: / it's me undertaking a funeral journey / among your yellow scars. / It's me with my laments without source, / without food, awake, alone, / entering darkened corridors, / arriving at your mysterious matter.

As the topic of the apostrophe, *materia* comes to replace the *madera* of the title and underscores again the common etymology. Once identified as a feminine subject—not only is the Spanish *materia*, like *madera*, feminine in gender, but so are most of its attributes ("rosa," "catedral," "multitud," "ola," and "cicatrices")—the speaker's attitude shifts from awe to desire. We must imagine him avidly climbing up vertical branches ("tus pétalos"), kneeling before them as if seeking entrance into a sanctuary ("tu dura catedral"), and enacting a ritual that vaguely alludes to the prophetic purging of Isaiah 6:5-7.[6] This new

---

[6] Compare the text of the poem with the biblical passage in Spanish: "Y voló hacia mí uno de los serafines, teniendo en su mano un carbón encendido, tomando del altar con unas tenazas, y tocando con él sobre mi boca, dijo: He aquí que esto tocó tus labios, y es quitada tu culpa, limpio tu pecado." ("Then flew one of the seraphim unto me, having a live coal in his hand, which he had taken with the tongs from off the altar: And he laid it upon my mouth, and said, Lo, this hath touched thy lips; and thine iniquity is taken away, and thy sin purged.")

setting provides a dramatic context for the long fourth stanza, in which he repeatedly calls out and identifies himself as if knocking on a door. The entire passage sounds like a prayer: wood is addressed with the reverent "tú" (thou); narration turns into a litany; and his erotic desire becomes subdued by the solemn occasion, the "viaje funerario" that is channeled between "cicatrices amarillas." These "yellow scars" are but the slits in the bark which provide an entrance, but the pathological content of the image exploits the other meaning of *materia*, pus, for obvious purposes. In narrative terms what takes place is a *peripeteia*, a journey toward death. By the end of the fourth stanza the speaker has arrived at the fringes of the core, where a "materia misteriosa" awaits him. Thus *materia* appears at this end of the journey too, as it did in the initial apostrophe, and suggests its function as a floating signifier that accommodates almost any special meaning. More important, however, the Spanish *materia misteriosa* sounds like the Latin *mater dolorosa,* and thus makes the funeral journey more like a return to the womb, now rendered metaphorically as an integration with the substance of the tree.

Once inside the tree trunk, the speaker witnesses the spectacle of the inner vegetable world; he lists its sights, sounds, and sensations in a sequence that follows the stages of a life cycle. The movement of "corrientes secas" (dry currents) and the growth of "manos interrumpidas" (interrupted hands), for example, suggest an infancy stage; the fury of "vegetales oceánicos" (oceanic plants) simulates adolescence. And as the speaker feels "hojas morir hacia adentro" (leaves die inward) and finally "tu inmovilidad desamparada" (your helpless immobility) (I, 230), the suggestion is that he has experienced a vicarious old age and death. The language is sufficiently ambiguous, of course, to accommodate a reverse sequence, beginning with death and ending in conception, as in a kind of "journey back to the source." Be that as it may, what is clear is that all these actions are meant to imply an internal landscape through which the speaker wanders with curious amazement. The copious inventory that follows in the last stanza suggests a quickening of the pace which soon reaches a state of frenzy:

> Poros, vetas, círculos de dulzura,
> peso, temperatura silenciosa,

Vision and Conversion

> flechas pegadas a tu alma caída,
> seres dormidos en tu boca espesa,
> polvo de dulce pulpa consumida,
> ceniza llena de apagadas almas,
> venid a mí, a mi sueño sin medida,
> caed en mi alcoba en que la noche cae
> y cae sin cesar como agua rota,
> y a vuestra vida, a vuestra muerte asidme,
> y a vuestros materiales sometidos,
> a vuestras muertas palomas neutrales,
> y hagamos fuego, y silencio, y sonido,
> y ardamos, y callemos, y campanas.   [I, 230]

> Pores, veins, circles of sweetness, / weight, silent temperature, / arrows stuck to your fallen soul, / beings asleep in your thick mouth, / dust of sweet consumed pulp, / ash full of spent souls, / come to me, to my measureless dream, / fall into my bedroom where night falls / and falls without stopping like broken water, / and to your life, to your death hold me, / and to your submitted materials, / and to your dead neutral pigeons, / and let us make fire, and silence, and sound, / and let us burn, and hush, and bells.

It is unclear whether the speaker's summoning of the world of wood into his "sueño sin medida" betrays the entire narration as a fiction. What is certain is that the appositive request ("caed en mi alcoba en que la noche cae") alludes to the earlier "noches de sustancia infinita caídas en mi dormitorio" (I, 185) of "Arte poética," and thus identifies it as a metaphor for poetic ecstasy. (The particular significance of the allusion will become evident in light of other details.) Once the wood breaks down into its various components, it is invoked with the formulas of a kind of materialist Franciscanism, a summons that climaxes with the speaker's shift to a passive posture with mystical overtones. This summons constitutes the first of three interconnected series that provide the poem with a highly structured conclusion. The first of these series is the sequence of "caed... cae y cae" (a polyptoton, in rhetorical terms). In turn, the structuring clause in the second series is the conjunctive phrase "y a vuestra/os," save for one line that balances the earlier addition of the conjunction by pointedly omitting it. The symmetrical balance of the two sequences conditions the reader to expect a similar order in the third and final series in the last two lines, a formal intricacy that implies that integration (with matter, mother, or object) can take place only under highly structured conditions.

In the last two lines the conjunctive clauses increase in number and, in contrast with the vertical arrangement of the previous four lines, their horizontal spread suggests a mirror inversion. Both the new format and the steadier rhythm indicate a new stage where subject and object are gradually drawn closer together, as conveyed first by the shift of address from plural *you* to *we*, and the ensuing switch from verbal phrases to verbs. The latter, especially, set up a semantic correspondence that enhances the symmetry of the parallel lines. Yet no sooner have we adapted to this new order than we are jolted by the grammatical disjunction of the last word, which replaces the impending verb (*sonemos*, let us sound) with a noun ("campanas," bells). The bells range in symbolic meaning from death to marriage, of course, but their context suggests that their meaning derives principally from the grammatical difference that is interposed within the series. The change from verb to noun, or from action to substance, obviously signals the union between subject and object. In deriving the final symbol from sound ("sonido"), however, the sequence points to a specifically aural origin that the book consistently identifies with poetic presence. Moreover, the final sequence articulates that presence as the end result of a three-stage process beginning with a purifying conflagration ("hagamos fuego" / "ardamos"), then dying in a quiet stillness ("hagamos silencio" / "callemos"), and finally rising from the ashes as "sonido" and "campanas." Thus what at first seems to be restricted to a material identification is actually the attainment of poetic experience, of presence, even if the cost of attaining that experience is a loss of discursivity and the speaker's dissolution. This loss is what accounts for the grammatical disjunction at the end, as if poetic presence and semantic representation were condemned to be mutually exclusive.

Insofar as the speaker is concerned, then, the poem describes the ultimate fulfillment of his desire, but only through a purgative process, an ascesis, which ends in self-annihilation. In the quest for presence, the speaker has gone so far as to dissolve himself, but because the quest has no reference beyond a poetic or even linguistic object, he is unable to conceive, let alone postulate or represent, his own rebirth. Conversion, or at least its narrative representation, rests on a retrospective structure issuing from a self who, having reached self-understanding and attained ontological coherence, proceeds to give an account of his spiritual progress. The convert narrates his experience from the end, after his spiritual crisis is over, and the plot of his story assumes a rhetorical difference between the self he has become and the self he used to be.[7] But given the dissolution of the self that we find at the end of the poem, how is one to discover any final coherence, let alone a retrospective structure? What "Entrada a la madera" offers, instead, is a narrative of the quest and attainment of idolatrous presence, an itinerary that, far from issuing from the self's retrospection, is frozen in the reified safety of a present time, as the use of the present tense throughout the poem makes clear. What we have is a simulacrum of conversion which merely ritualizes retrospective structure for the sake of achieving poetic presence.

Significantly, the poem shows this simulacrum to be a function of the speaker's temporality. Earlier I remarked that the shift from verb to noun in the last line implied a change from action to substance. We can now complete that description by adding that it implies as well an emptying out of time. Whereas nouns designate an atemporal presence, no verb is conceivable without a tense or temporal definition. (Even the infinitive is temporally defined as the *absence* of tense.) This distinction explains, I think, the end of the poem. The concluding series emphasizes the temporal nature of the speaker's final actions by matching verbal phrases with verbs, thus creating a context within which the intrusion of a noun disrupts temporal flow. The disruptive effect is confirmed in part by the rhythm of the last two lines, which, by alternating conjunctions and imperative constructions, creates the expectation of continuity, only to freeze, abruptly, with the intrusion of the final noun. My interest in this linguistic inference, however, goes beyond formal inspection. For it is as if in displaying a verbal flourish at the end

---

[7] I follow here the useful distinctions on the rhetoric of conversion made by John Freccero in "Dante's Prologue Scene," *Dante Studies,* 84 (1966), especially pp. 20–22, and "Medusa: The Letter and the Spirit," *Yearbook of Italian Studies,* 1 (Florence, 1972), 1–18.

the speaker gathered his temporal predicament in all its intensity before facing extinction in presence. By emptying out all temporal content, he thus transforms himself into an aesthetic object and makes himself immune to time. Far from being, then, the apotheosis of immediacy that is often claimed in isolated readings, the poem provides an ironic commentary. Judged in relation to "Vuelve el otoño," which demonstrates the potential for visionary error, and "No hay olvido," which similarly subverts the writing project, "Entrada a la madera" dramatizes the destructive implications of a poetics that employs the self as the foundation of its quest for knowledge without realizing the consequences of such an enterprise.

It must be stressed that the significance of this aesthetic reification is mostly symbolic, and that as such its influence on the dramatic development of the speaker is oblique. The "entrance into wood" constitutes an internal allegory that exposes the complicity of the visionary quest with the idolatrous effects of writing. Thus in recoiling from an authentic temporal destiny, the speaker unfolds not the retrospective structure of conversion, which would recognize temporal depth from the prospect of an authentic present, but a regressive evasion that slights temporal reality for the illusion of absolute presence. Like the clock in "El reloj caído en el mar" (The Clock That Fell into the Sea), the visionary now runs "desvencijado y herido" (broken and wounded) (I, 246).

It seems necessary, at this juncture, to note that the escape into aesthetic reification is but one among several symptoms of temporal inauthenticity. We have already noted some of them in the course of this chapter, but perhaps the least obvious of all is the speaker's lapse into nostalgia, the retrospective glance with which an authentic temporal destiny is evaded. There are, to be sure, several nostalgic poems in *Residencia*, but it is significant that the second book ends with one, "Josie Bliss," as if in recalling Neruda's famous Burmese mistress the temporal predicament that was advanced earlier were now given concrete dramatic form. We should recall, at this point, that the first *Residencia* includes an earlier poem on the same woman, "Tango del viudo" (Widower's Tango), which expresses the poet's feelings moments after he has abandoned her. Josie Bliss is the woman perhaps most often thought of in connection with Neruda, not

Vision and Conversion

only because of her suggestive assumed name, but because she appears so often in his poetry. In addition to the two texts in *Residencia*, Neruda wrote two other poems about her in the course of his life, and also wrote about their tragic life together in his memoirs.[8] She was, in a very real sense, Neruda's "dark lady," a passionate and jealous lover whose frequent death threats finally drove him away. "Sometimes," he recalled, "a light would wake me up, a ghost brandishing her long, sharpened native knife. It was she, walking around and around my bed for hours at a time, without making up her mind to kill me. When you die, she used to say to me, my fears will end. The next day she would carry out mysterious rituals to make me remain faithful."[9]

Once we know who Josie Bliss is, we are tempted to regard the nostalgic lapse at the end of the book purely from the standpoint of Neruda's biography, as an empirical event in his life whose timely telling would avert an idolatrous ending and rescue the authenticity of the poetry. And yet, however promising, such a reading is not enough to reverse the extent to which the speaker's temporal predicament has been dramatized, nor can it support the priority of biography over poetry. In fact, quite the opposite seems to be the case. To take just one revealing instance, in "Tango del viudo," which is addressed to an anonymous "Maligna," the threatening knife that figures so prominently in the passage from the memoirs quoted above had already appeared "enterrado junto al cocotero" (buried next to the coconut tree), where it is said to be hidden "por temor a que me mataras" (for fear you would kill me) (I, 199). The time sequence here is not only chronological (the poem was obviously published earlier) but dramatic, as the poem recreates a time subsequent to the one described in the memoirs. What I am suggesting, then, is that one need not view nostalgia in an exclusively biographical sense, and that what at first sight appears

---

[8]See "La desdichada," in *Estravagario* (1958), II, 637-39, and "Josie Bliss (I)" and "Josie Bliss (II)" in *Memorial de Isla Negra* (1964), III, 1106-10. Josie Bliss is also alluded to in "Regreso a una ciudad," also of *Estravagario*: "No encuentro la calle ni el techo / de la loca que me quería" (I can't find the street or the house / of the crazy woman who loved me) (II, 607).

[9]*Memoirs,* trans. Hardie St. Martin (New York: Farrar, Straus & Giroux, 1976), p. 87. The passage first appeared in the fourth installment of Neruda's original memoirs: "La calle oriental," *O Cruzeiro Internacional* (March 10, 1962).

to be a casual anecdote actually constitutes a formalized recreation whose textuality provides a crucial comment on the writing project.

Even in "Tango del viudo," which is chronologically closer to its empirical source and therefore more likely to be read in this light, one is forced to recognize, as its title conveys, a formalized lament. The dramatic poignancy of the poem derives in part from an exchange of roles, whereby the speaker conceives himself as the lover's murderer, as well as from his regret, now that he is alone and safely away from her, for having regressed to an earlier stage of lonely dejection:

> He llegado otra vez a los dormitorios solitarios,
> a almorzar en los restaurantes comida fría, y otra vez
> tiro al suelo los pantalones y las camisas,
> no hay perchas en mi habitación, ni retratos de nadie en las paredes. [I, 199]

> I've come once again to lonely bedrooms, / to have a cold lunch in restaurants, and once again / I throw my pants and shirts on the floor, / there are no hangers in my room, or pictures of anyone on the walls.

Caught between the experience of sexual infatuation and the need to survive, the speaker recalls her with a contradictory relieved pathos, and it is only in the last lines that he hints, by means of an elaborate reversal, that staying at her side would have meant having to give up his poetic gift, including the occasion that made this poem possible. The speaker's survival is therefore not just physical but artistic, for in preferring to "kill" the beloved rather than to give up poetry he chooses the lesser of two evils. The choice also reveals, if only in a negative sense, the implicit link between the two: Josie Bliss is the muse gone wrong, too real perhaps to be a source of inspiration.

This chilling conclusion provides the background to the later poem, for in making the haunting memory of Josie Bliss preside over the end of the second book, Neruda seems to be making a similar statement on the link between poetry and desire. In the absence of attendant biographical details, there are no overt signs that suggest the latter poem is a sequel. We shall see, nevertheless, that several clues do exist, and that they disclose

Vision and Conversion

the temporal predicament that is ultimately at stake. For the moment, let us recall that the poem follows immediately after "No hay olvido," where the pervasiveness of memory becomes a function of the monstrous quality of writing. The last words of that poem are "quiero olvidar" (I want to forget); the following statements pointedly contradict that wish:

> Color azul de exterminadas fotografías,
> color azul con pétalos y paseos al mar,
> nombre definitivo que cae en las semanas
> con un golpe de acero que las mata.   [I, 248]
>
>> Blue color of exterminated photographs, / blue color with petals and strolls by the sea, / definitive name that falls on the weeks / with a blow of steel that kills them.

Glancing through faded photographs (the pages of an album, perhaps), the speaker happens upon one in particular which shows him strolling by the sea with a former lover. His lingering remarks about the bluish hue of the pictures convey his fascination with the physical effects of time on the newly discovered scene, a fascination that he immediately translates, as he evokes the woman, into a comment on the aptness of her name. The "bliss" that identifies her has the power to dispel time, much as her memory breaks through after years of oblivion. The effects of that power take hold in the second stanza, where further remarks suggest that her memory has reawakened associations of violent sex. The first two stanzas thus arrange a counterpoint, to be duplicated in the poem's remaining sections, of the speaker's absorption in the photograph and the associations it evokes.

These associations reach a climax of dramatic precision in the fourth stanza, roughly the center of the poem, where the speaker muses about his possible existence in another dimension:

> Tal vez sigo existiendo en una calle que el aire hace llorar
> con un determinado lamento lúgubre de tal manera
> que todas las mujeres visten de sordo azul:
> yo existo en ese día repartido,
> existo allí como una piedra pisada por un buey,
> como un testigo sin duda olvidado.   [I, 248]

Pablo Neruda: The Poetics of Prophecy

> Perhaps I go on existing in a street that the air makes cry / with a determined, lugubrious lament in such a way / that all the women dress in deaf blue: / I exist in that divided day, / I exist there like a stone stepped on by an ox, / like a witness doubtless forgotten.

In the reverie the lover has multiplied into several women for whom time is but an external garment (as its color implies) which covers their desired flesh. This quasi-allegorical representation makes time the obstacle between desire and its fulfillment. And whether we take the participle ("repartido") to modify the speaker or the day, the effect is still one of temporal fragmentation, of a physical scattering among the members of an ascetic harem, so to speak, whose disdain reduces the speaker to a petrified victim—"una piedra pisada por un buey." Petrification, then, would be the end result of the nostalgic lapse into a desire that, being the inauthentic function of time, cannot go beyond infatuation and which relegates the subject to the role of a passive voyeur.

What would thus appear to be limited to a moral admonition, or in biographical terms to a belated expression of Neruda's remorse, is actually a summary comment on the writing project. There is, to begin with, an implied affinity between vision and voyeurism, especially as it appears here within the framework of an erotic nostalgia. Moreover, the above passage invokes the precise word often used to describe the visionary role, notably in "Significa sombras," where the speaker appears as "establecido, asegurado y ardiente *testigo*" (established, assured and burning *witness*) (I, 203; my italics). In fact, on closer inspection the allusion to that poem, which with "Josie Bliss" is one of two closing poems, encompasses a broader context. The line "Tal vez sigo existiendo en una calle que el aire hace llorar" (Perhaps I go on existing in a street which the air makes cry) seems to be a synthesis of both "Sea pues lo que soy *en alguna parte* y en todo tiempo" (May I be what I am *somewhere* and in all time) and "Ay, que lo que soy *siga existiendo*" (Alas, may what I am *keep on existing*) (my italics). The inclusive context suggests, then, not only a degradation of vision to voyeurism, but the ironic fulfillment of the speaker's earlier wish to resolve his temporal predicament. Josie Bliss is but one of those "shadows" that were

Vision and Conversion

conjured up in the title of "Significa sombras" whose meaning is now haltingly revealed.

The interconnections invite the reader in some sense to effect a retrospective closure that would bind together the two books of *Residencia*. But it also prepares us, in the middle of the poem, for the more crucial series of allusions at the end. After enduring the effects of erotic degradation, the speaker once again lingers on the physical aspects of the photographs, only this time he points to the actual presence of the objects rather than to the effects of time:

> Ahí están, ahí están,
> los besos arrastrados por el polvo junto a un triste navío,
> ahí están las sonrisas desaparecidas, los trajes que una mano sacude llamando el alba:
> parece que la boca de la muerta no quiere morder rostros, dedos, palabras, ojos:
> ahí están otra vez como grandes peces que completan el cielo con su azul material vagamente invencible.   [I, 249]

> There they are, there they are, / the kisses dragged through the dust next to a sad boat, / there are the disappeared smiles, the suits that a hand / shakes as if calling dawn: / it seems the dead woman's mouth does not wish to bite faces, / fingers, words, eyes: / there they are again like great fish that complete the sky / with their blue material vaguely invincible.

The clash between a preserved moment of happiness and the memory of erotic degradation makes the picture convey a strange mixture of presence and absence. It is no less than a vision of time itself, to which the speaker points with glee, captured in all its contradictions: as kisses and smiles are both there and "desaparecidas," Josie Bliss is both present and dead, pictured at a rare moment of calm that is at odds with her violent nature. In calling her "la muerta," moreover, the speaker is more than just pointing to the paradox of frozen time—he retroactively supplies the identity of the anonymous heroine of "Tango del viudo." That this is the text he has in mind is confirmed in part by the strategic use of the adverbial term "otra vez" (another time or again), which in the earlier poem appeared twice to underscore the regression to solitude: "he

95

llegado *otra vez* a los dormitorios solitarios, / a almorzar en los restaurantes comida fría, y *otra vez* . . ." (I, 199). This retroactive identification, together with the image of achievement in the next to last line, serves once again to invite the reader to effect a closure. It is as if in noting, however ambiguously, the preservation of the past, the poem offered a metaphor for the idolatrous achievement of the writing project.

Yet the choice of that particular adverbial term ("otra vez") as the link between the two poems suggests a subtle irony that unravels this embracing gesture. Its quotation is designed to comment on the presence of the scene in the photograph, Josie Bliss's invincible return (*nostos*, return) *across* the scene of writing and despite her earlier "death." The very act of quotation, repetition in writing, embodies this recurrence. But, as we recall, in "Tango del viudo" "otra vez" originally signified not presence but absence in the form of solitude and loss as part of a general regression. It is perhaps no accident that the same passage noted also an absence of pictures on the walls.

A radical semantic disjunction thus underlies the quotation. By quoting the earlier poem, the speaker attempts to make the frozen scene coincide with an earlier and ostensibly empirical source. But since in the earlier poem "otra vez" signifies failed repetition, he remains blind not only to their ultimate noncoincidence, but to the inadequacy of the language employed. Far from describing an empirical event that returns the self to an authentic temporal source, the poem confirms the self-enclosure of writing by establishing an endless circuit between itself and an earlier text. In this circuit, the quotation's self-delusive source refers us forward to "Josie Bliss," while the woman's identity turns us back to "Tango del viudo," ad infinitum. Nor is it an accident that a term of time ("otra vez") should ground this delusive link. The circuit is therefore both endless and erring, suspending the self in a limbo between past and present, freezing the lover in the act of meditating on Josie Bliss's assumed English name, her false identity. In the end, that is, the poet becomes petrified by the allure of the former muse, seduced by the letter (the body) of her name.[10]

---

[10]Although there are no overt mythological overtones in the poem, the implication that Josie Bliss is a kind of Medusa is obvious. As Freccero remarks, "It is the power of the Letter to enthrall the beholder that makes of it a Medusa, an

Vision and Conversion

IV

My reading of "Entrada a la madera" and "Josie Bliss" is designed to demonstrate the limits of the poetic speaker within his temporal predicament and to show how those limits determine a death, whether in reification or nostalgia, that forecasts a radical change. In order to locate that change we must now turn, in this brief final section, to those poems of *Tercera residencia* which enact the subject's passage from an obsession with time to a concern with history, or from temporality to historicity. In a sense, all of the poetry of *Tercera residencia*, and especially the poems of *España en el corazón*, delineate this change by their registering of historical events. But by concentrating now on the four conversion texts that appear in the book I hope to locate a pattern in which the passage from time to history determines a palinode of the earlier visionary poetry and this palinode, in turn, prescribes the retrospective structure of conversion narrative. This pattern, which begins with "Entrada a la madera," culminates in *Alturas de Macchu Picchu*.

Ever since Amado Alonso first described *Tercera residencia* as Neruda's "poetic conversion," the term has been widely used to describe the book's marked difference from the earlier volumes.[11] Neruda himself seems to have encouraged the use of the term, of course, since his radical political change after his involvement in the Spanish Civil War suggested nothing less than the workings of a prophetic call. Alonso's reading, nevertheless, was quick to divest the term of any theological implications (for fear perhaps that they would clash with the poetry's political content) while indicating that he meant it in an exclusively "technical-psychological sense." Alonso's qualifier served the purpose of a general description, but in actual practice it only impoverished the term's critical potential.

Critical tradition since Alonso has done no better. It has eschewed a more rigorous analysis in turning to the platitudes of biography to explain the conversion poems. Such an approach does not lower the value of biographical criticism, of course, which in Neruda's case at least is important, but it does point up

---

expression of desire that turns its back to entrap its subject in an immobility which is the very opposite of the dynamism of language and desire" ("Medusa: the Letter and the Spirit," p. 17).

[11] Alonso, *Poesía y estilo*, pp. 339-58.

how strangely elusive the term "conversion" has proved when applied to these poems. From the standpoint of the poet's biography, a conversion derives from a previous existential crisis. But this perspective alone cannot explain the form of a conversion text or its implications for the historical ground from which it springs. The opposite alternative has been a formalist approach that deprives the conversion structure of any contextual meaning. But if allusion, parody, and caricature make up the fabric of "recodification," as Jaime Alazraki suggests, they do so only in consequence of the self-corrective functions of these rhetorical modes.[12]

My own approach falls halfway between these two and follows the road not taken by Alonso. To stress the theological implications of conversion, I submit, prescribes a reading that is as rhetorical as it is religious. Thus by continuing to dwell on context as a source of meaning, we may view the historical allegiance of these poems as a dialectical reaction, within the same visionary cycle, to the earlier grounding in temporality. History becomes time embodied, and the conversion narrative constitutes the dramatic enactment of that embodiment. My contention, finally, is that the retrospective structure of conversion narrative helps us to explain these poems, even if it should prove that they ultimately fail as narratives of conversion.

By itself the title of the third book confirms the need for such contextual reading, even though Neruda gave that title, twelve years after the joint publication of the first two books, to a motley assortment of poems that he had written in the interim. The belated recurrence of a *residencia* conveys the idea of a sequel, of course, but this link is rendered polemical by the replacement of the attendant phrase (and thus the elimination of its irony) in exchange for the closure of a trinity or synthesis. This distinguishing pattern is duplicated in the arrangement of the poems themselves, most of which were inspired by events of the Spanish Civil War, the Russian front of World War II, and

---

[12]"Punto de vista y recodificación en los poemas de auto-exégesis de Pablo Neruda," *Symposium*, 32 (1978), 184-97. Alazraki's use of the term "auto-exégesis" to describe autobiographical poetry is imprecise. The ambiguity seems to originate in Alonso, from whom Alazraki borrows the term (p. 185), and who gave it a different sense in his chapter on poetic conversion. See *Poesía y estilo*, pp. 343-48.

Vision and Conversion

recent Latin American history. The first seven poems, which comprise the first two sections, do not at all share this historical theme and instead resemble closely the style of the first two books. One of them even bears an identical title: "Alianza (Sonata)." The sequence itself thus suggests a conversion structure by juxtaposing earlier and later texts, preserving those that no longer fit the new style as evidence of the subject's gradual change. Underlying this pattern is Neruda's unwillingness to suppress any of his poems, a Romantic bent for comprehensiveness that eventually gathers a surplus of texts only to trigger, in turn, a revisionary poetics, a series of palinodes that rewrite earlier poems. We have already seen some evidence of this revisionary bent in such texts as "Un día sobresale" and "Vuelve el otoño," which discreetly revise earlier motifs, but I am now referring to a more trenchant gesture that goes hand in hand with the retrospective structure of conversion. Dramatically, such revisions expose the speaker's differential crisis. And in the reader's experience, at least, conversion and rewriting become so closely linked that they become one and the same. These poems of conversion are among Neruda's best known, but critical readings often fail to include, let alone explain, the first and most telling sign of conversion in the book—the famous epigraph to Neruda's long erotic poem "Las furias y las penas" (The Furies and the Woes):

> (En 1934 fue escrito este poema. Cuántas cosas han sobrevenido desde entonces! España, donde lo escribí, es una cintura de ruinas. Ay! si con sólo una gota de poesía o de amor pudiéramos aplacar la ira del mundo, pero eso sólo lo pueden la lucha y el corazón resuelto. El mundo ha cambiado y mi poesía ha cambiado. Una gota de sangre caída en estas líneas quedará viviendo sobre ellas, indeleble como el amor. Marzo de 1939.)   [I, 260]

> (This poem was written in 1934. How many things have taken place since then! Spain, where I wrote it, is a waist of ruins. Oh! If with only a drop of poetry or love we could placate the world's anger, but only struggle and the resolute heart can do that. The world has changed and my poetry has changed. A drop of blood fallen on these lines will go on living over them, indelible like love. March 1939.)

Pablo Neruda: The Poetics of Prophecy

What in epigraphs always constitutes an implicit retrospection is here made explicit with the thematics of conversion. The self that is ("marzo de 1939") writes about a self that was ("1934"), who died in a holocaust for which the poem itself, or the act of writing, appears to be partly responsible. Thus "Las furias y las penas," the poem that epitomizes an idolatrous view of sexuality—and whose connection with Josie Bliss may not be too farfetched—appears to have been written in some future time when this view has ostensibly been abandoned. In its stead a link between history and writing is proposed and even dramatized when the present self, by the strategic use of the passive voice, at first disavows any responsibility; the link is made explicit only later in the simultaneous rebirth of history and the writing subject—"El mundo ha cambiado y mi poesía ha cambiado." Before the conversion, the world was impervious to a writing determined solely by poetry and love. After the conversion, world and writing commune so closely that the blood of history turns into the very ink of the text. History becomes the scene of writing, the new textual theater.

The physical constraints of the epigraph, which force an elliptical retrospection, curb the dramatic potential of the conversion narrative. By appearing in the last of the first seven poems, however, and in a text that so closely echoes the erotic degradation of "Josie Bliss," the epigraph does mark a turning point in the sequence with an explicit correction of the earlier poems. Not surprisingly, "Reunión bajo las nuevas banderas" (Meeting under New Flags), the next poem, picks up this correction as if developing in the main body of its text what earlier appeared to be a retrospective appendix:

> Quién ha mentido? El pie de la azucena
> roto, insondable, oscurecido, todo
> lleno de herida y resplandor oscuro!
> Todo, la norma de ola en ola en ola,
> el impreciso túmulo del ámbar
> y las ásperas gotas de la espiga!
> Fundé mi pecho en esto, escuché toda
> la sal funesta: de noche
> fui a plantar mis raíces:
> averigüé lo amargo de la tierra

Vision and Conversion

todo fue para mí noche o relámpago:
cera secreta cupo en mi cabeza
y derramó cenizas en mis huellas.

Y para quién busqué este pulso frío
sino para una muerte?
Y qué instrumento perdí en las tinieblas
desamparadas, donde nadie me oye?
No,
    ya era tiempo, huid,
sombras de sangre,
hielos de estrella, retroceded al paso de los pasos humanos
y alejad de mis pies la negra sombra!   [I, 266]

Who has lied? The lily's foot / broken, inscrutable, all / full of wound and dark splendor! / All, the norm from wave to wave to wave, / the imprecise monument of amber / and the rough drops of the ear! I founded my breast on this, I listened to all / the sad salt. At night / I would go out to plant my roots: / I found out the earth's bitterness. / All for me was night or lightning: / secret wax fitted inside my head / and scattered ashes on my tracks. / And for whom did I seek this cold pulse / if not for a death? / And what instrument did I lose in the forsaken darkness, / where no one hears me? / No, it was high time, begone, / blood shadows, / star ices, retreat to the pace of human steps / and remove the black shadow from my feet!

As in the epigraph, the speaker here appears split into a present self who determines narrative viewpoint and a former self who is identified with the language of the first two books and is charged with the fraud of temporality. This time, however, a polar characterization, facilitated by the rhetorical structure of the poem, signals a split in which the present self uses direct and active language to describe its passive predecessor. This radical shift is complemented by the encompassing gesture conveyed by the insistence on "todo" (which appears no fewer than four times in the first eleven lines).

A radical split between past and present thus determines the narrative viewpoint, and the expressed will to unite refers not simply to the historical unity of the present, but to the need to mend the split subject in a literal re-union: "Y así, reunido, / duramente central, no busco asilo / en los huecos del llanto"

(And thus, reunited, / strongly central, I seek no refuge / in the holes of tears) (I, 270). In Spanish "reunión" can mean either meeting or reunion, but in the poem the latter meaning is obscured by both the patriotic title and the speaker's tone. It is this meaning that permeates the argument of the poem and that underlies the apostrophe in the fourth stanza, where the present self interrogates the former, and the fifth, where he grants peace to the visionary "sol sombrío" (shady sun) and his own "frente ciega" (blind forehead). The allusions to "Sistema sombrío" are not capricious at all, in fact, and they signal the reconciliation of the two selves before the urgency of historical change in a unity that the last four lines suggest with references to an imminent rebirth.

In contrast with the epigraph, then, the poem's expansion of narrative scope accommodates an active prophetic voice whose pointed difference from its passive predecessor, as the rewriting of the earlier poetry attests, forms a dramatic core. But the abiding problem of this as well as the remaining poems lies in their inability to produce a sincere narrative in which the conversion would coincide with the dramatic unfolding of the poem. If, to recall an earlier point, the narrative of conversion accounts retrospectively for the self's progress, this poem dramatizes such a self but fails to report any progress. Such a "progress report" would result from a dialectic between a detached viewpoint, which confers an authentic retrospection, and the autonomous dramatization of the former self. It is this dialectic that allows for the gradual convergence, as the poem unfolds, of present and past, of the speaker as author and the speaker as character, until at the end temporal unity is attained and author and character become one. In this particular poem, however, the radical split imposed at the outset preempts such a dialectic, and in the end the union is merely announced. That is, rather than showing the gradual convergence, the poem simply tells about it, and so an authentic reaction to the past becomes a dramatic failure.

This failure will not be the only one, as "Explico algunas cosas" (I Explain a Few Things) and "Nuevo canto de amor a Stalingrado" (New Love Song to Stalingrad), the remaining conversion poems, make clear for different reasons. In each, Neruda combines the palinode with the chronicle of a historical event, but his penchant for historical immediacy invariably

Vision and Conversion

interferes with the attempt to establish an adequate retrospection. In "Explico algunas cosas," for example, a first-person narrative about the onset of the war supplants all recollection of the visionary past, which is confined to the first five lines and to a couple of brief references. Similarly, most of "Nuevo canto de amor a Stalingrado" deals with the Allied victory in Europe, and only its first five stanzas—scarcely one-fifth of the text—comprise a revision. In fact, given the absence of any authentic retrospection, one wonders whether these poems depict conversions at all.

In these inchoate attempts, however, lie the origins of *Alturas de Macchu Picchu* (1946), Neruda's definitive conversion poem. Its success is due in large measure to a turning away from contemporary events to ancient Latin American history. Moreover, the shift from a general historical solidarity to a cultural cause will add a rhetorical coherence that was present only vaguely, if at all, in earlier attempts. It remains to be seen, however, whether such a historical perspective is able to avert the temptation of immediacy or even to go beyond the limits that language and literature impose. As Neruda begins the imaginative reconstruction of Latin American history, he must first rebuild his own faith as poet by gathering the scattered remains of his work. Yet given the perils of reconstructing history from the vantage point of poetry, and the temptation to use one or the other as the self's idolatrous agent, the revision is bound to extend beyond Neruda's own texts to include the entire Western library. From Neruda's viewpoint, at least, that library is in ruins.

3

Prophecy of Writing

> We ourselves are exotic, descendants of races alien to these naked lands. Exotic is our servitude and exotic is our liberation.
> —Pablo Neruda, "Discurso de Panamá"

> Ma qui la morta poesì resurga.
> —Dante, *Purgatorio* I

> Allegories are, in the realm of thoughts, what ruins are in the realm of things.
> —Walter Benjamin

I

I have argued in the first two chapters that the visionary enterprise of *Residencia en la tierra* forms part of a writing project that initially was designed to arrest temporal dispersion but ultimately is put at the service of the preservation of the self. Both the reified presence of "Entrada a la madera" and the petrified limbo of "Josie Bliss" constitute crystallized moments of this change, in which the self is turned into an icon and writing becomes the self's monument. Neither reification nor self-reference provides an authentic solution, however, for while each provides a haven from time, both require nothing less than the very death from which the speaker attempts to flee. Thus the recurrent conversions in *Tercera residencia* constitute the logical outcome of the desire to flee death, even if they fail to provide a convincing conversion structure.

To speak as I have of the rhetorical implications of conversion assumes the recognition of a common ground for theology and politics. In both, ethical and moral pressures determine a radical change in the self, who thereby views his past as corrupted by

Prophecy of Writing

error and indifference. My approach up to now has been slightly different in that I have viewed conversion less from the point of view of the present than from that of the past, attempting to identify, that is, the temporal errors that would drive the self to seek a new life guided by historical principles and motives. However we may regard conversion, what is ultimately at stake is a description of the text as the dramatic unfolding of the death of a former self, or in Christian terms, the putting off of the old man for the new (Col. 3:9-10). Moreover, to speak of conversion in the context of prophecy is to understand that death as the shedding of a life of self-absorbed silence for one of purposeful speech. The entire *Residencia* cycle is punctuated by the gradual emergence of such a representation. There is no conversion, for example, in "Galope muerto," which deals exclusively with the visionary seizures of the present, while the temporal change dramatized in "Entrada a la madera" is a regressive gesture that, however promising, ends in silence. The very proliferation of conversion texts in *Tercera residencia* attests ultimately to a failure to represent a coherent access to prophecy.

No single poem of Neruda's demands more attention to these issues than *Alturas de Macchu Picchu*. Because conversion constitutes the poem's entire rhetorical fabric and not just an isolated theme, the abiding problem for critics, in the more than thirty years since the work was first published, has been how to understand conversion without reducing it to contemporary politics or to Neruda's life story. As such, critical concern translates into the poem's specificity as literature, its wide resonance of texts from private and public canons, beyond the claims of contemporary politics or confession. Written and published in the mid-1940s, at a time when a climate of cultural nationalism ruled Latin American intellectual circles, the poem has easily become the poetic representation of these issues. Indeed, the ascent to "the lost city of the Incas," the high-flown name that Yale archaeologist Hiram Bingham gave to Machu Picchu when he discovered it in 1911, is often seen as an allegory of Latin America's recovery of its pre-Columbian origins and a coherent statement on the ideology of cultural identity. It could be said, in fact, that the privileged status conferred by this allegory is what has determined the poem's bibliography since its first publication in 1946. Even after being included, four years later, in *Canto General*, it continues to be reprinted by itself both in Spanish and in translation. Thirty

Pablo Neruda: The Poetics of Prophecy

years of additional praise and criticism have tended to reinforce that autonomy.[1]

It is no longer possible, then, to read the poem outside the tangle of intellectual issues that it ostensibly represents. The immediate aim of this chapter is therefore to situate Neruda's writing of the poem in the context of a debate on cultural identity at the heart of which was Neruda's adoption of an "Americanist" mode. Although this debate has been relegated to relative oblivion, it is worth retracing in detail inasmuch as the poem both embodies the debate and elaborates its critique. I shall be equally concerned with the biographical exegesis to which the poem has lent itself and of which Neruda himself, in fact, took advantage on at least two occasions. Twice during his

---

[1]For individual editions of the poem, see Hernán Loyola's bibliography in III, 960-61 and 1068-1106. See also the following: Pablo García, "Interpretación de *Alturas de Macchu Picchu*," *Pro Arte*, 57-58 (1949), 17-22; Alexander Lipschütz, "*Alturas de Macchu Picchu* de Pablo Neruda, visión indiana americana," *Repertorio Americano*, 45 (November 10, 1949), 345-46; Félix Schwartzmann, "El mundo poético de Pablo Neruda como voluntad de vínculo," in *Del sentimiento de lo humano en América* (Santiago de Chile: Universidad de Chile, 1953), pp. 74-80; Mario Rivas González, *Exégesis del poema "Alturas de Macchu Picchu"* (Santiago de Chile, 1955); Mario Rodríguez Fernández, "Exégesis del poema *Alturas de Macchu Picchu* de Pablo Neruda," *Anales de la Universidad de Chile*, 102 (1956), 128-31; Roberto Salama, *Para una crítica a Pablo Neruda* (Buenos Aires: Cartago, 1957), pp. 174-81; Hugo Montes, "Acerca de *Alturas de Macchu Picchu*," *Mapocho*, 2 (1964), 120-34; Mario Rodríguez Fernández, "El tema de la muerte en *Alturas de Macchu Picchu*," *Anales de la Universidad de Chile*, 131 (1964), 23-50; Hernán Loyola, "Los modos de autorreferencia en la obra de Pablo Neruda," *Aurora*, 3-4 (1964), 64-125; Leonidas Morales, "Estructura mítica de *Alturas de Macchu Picchu*," *Estudios Filológicos*, 1 (1965), 167-84; Jürgen von Stackelberg, "Ein Kommentar zur Dichtung," in *Die Höhen von Macchu Picchu*, trans. Rudolf Hagelstange (Hamburg: Hoffmann & Kampe, 1965), pp. 21-26; Hernán Loyola, *Ser y morir en Pablo Neruda (1918-1945)* (Santiago de Chile: Santiago, 1967); Juan Larrea, *Del surrealismo a Machupicchu* (Mexico City: Joaquín Mortiz, 1967), pp. 131-223; Gastón Carrillo, "La lengua poética de Pablo Neruda: Análisis de *Alturas de Macchu Picchu*," *Boletín del Instituto de Filología de la Universidad de Chile*, 21 (1970), 292-332; Cedomil Goić, "*Alturas de Macchu Picchu*: La torre y el abismo," *Anales de la Universidad de Chile*, 157-60 (1971), 153-66; John Felstiner, "La danza inmóvil, el vendaval sostenido: *Four Quartets* de T. S. Eliot y *Alturas de Macchu Picchu*," *Anales de la Universidad de Chile*, 157-60 (1971), 176-96; Françoise Pérus, "Arquitectura poética de *Alturas de Macchu Picchu*," *Atenea*, 425 (1972), 104-30; Robert Pring-Mill, "Preface" to *The Heights of Macchu Picchu*, trans. Nathaniel Tarn (New York: Farrar, Straus & Giroux, 1967), pp. vii-xix; Juan Loveluck, "*Alturas de Macchu Picchu*: Cantos I-V," *Revista Iberoamericana*, 39 (1973), 175-88; Hugo Montes, "Introducción," in *Machu Picchu en la poesía* (sic) (Santiago de Chile: Nueva Universidad, 1972), pp. 47-71; Kay Engler, "Image and Structure in Neruda's *Las Alturas de Macchu Picchu* (sic)," *Symposium*, 27 (1974), 130-45; Françoise Pérus, "*Hauteurs de Macchu Picchu*," *Europe*, 537-53 (1974), 86-110;

Prophecy of Writing

life Neruda published recollections of his 1943 visit to Machu Picchu, recollections that have become, in effect, powerful interpretations of the poem. The rhetorical strategy that these interpretations have in common thus marks an intersection of biography and intellectual history as Neruda attempts, through implicit readings, to inscribe both himself and his poem within the thematics of cultural identity. It is this strategy, I believe, that accounts for the loss of critical distance which, acting more or less implicitly, has prevented a reading of the poem's harrowing meditation on history.

In an attempt to bring together text and context, my reading of the poem will be chiefly concerned with its allusive structure. Far from being ornaments that merely enhance the poem's statement on history, its allusions form its very core in that they form part of a demystified allegorical strategy. The view of the poem as an allegory of cultural recuperation must, I submit, be taken literally because the demystified arbitrariness of allegorical interpretation structures a negative knowledge that infuses the poem's statement about history.[2] Thus in displaying the activi-

---

Roger Caillois, "La cité et le poème," *Europe*, 537-53 (1974), 57-61; Agnes Gullón, "Pablo Neruda at Macchu Picchu," *Chicago Review*, 27 (1974), 138-345; Hugo Montes, *Para leer a Neruda* (Buenos Aires: Francisco de Aguirre, 1974), pp. 63-66; Julieta Gómez Paz, "Aproximación al poema de Neruda '*Alturas de Macchu Pichu*'" (sic), *Sin Nombre*, 7 (1976), 57-70; Perry Christian Higman, "*Alturas de Macchu Picchu* en la obra de Pablo Neruda," (Ph.D. dissertation, University of Iowa, 1976); Noé Jitrik, "*Alturas de Macchu Picchu*: Una marcha piramidal a través de un discurso poético incesante," *Nueva Revista de Filología Hispánica*, 26 (1976), 510-55; Dieter Saalmann, "The Role of Time in Pablo Neruda's *Alturas de Macchu Picchu*," *Romance Notes*, 18 (1977), 169-77; Emir Rodríguez Monegal, "El sistema del poeta," in *Neruda: El viajero inmóvil* (Caracas: Monte Avila, 1977), pp. 447-67; Alain Sicard, *El pensamiento poético de Pablo Neruda*, tr. Pilar Ruiz Va (1977; Madrid: Gredos, 1981), pp. 236-49; Eduardo Camacho Guizado, *Pablo Neruda—Naturaleza, historia y poética* (Madrid: Sociedad General Española de Librería, 1978), pp. 155-59; Salvatore Bizzarro, "Alturas de Machu Picchu" (sic), in his *Pablo Neruda: All Poets the Poet* (Metuchen, N.J.: Scarecrow Press, 1979), pp. 76-87; René de Costa, *The Poetry of Pablo Neruda* (Cambridge: Harvard University Press, 1979), pp. 121-26; John Felstiner, *Translating Neruda: The Way to Macchu Picchu* (Stanford: Stanford University Press, 1980); Manuel Durán and Margery Safir, *Earth Tones: The Poetry of Pablo Neruda* (Bloomington: Indiana University Press, 1981), pp. 88-95; Gastón Soublette, *Pablo Neruda: Profeta de América* (Santiago de Chile: Nueva Universidad, 1980), pp. 57-126.

[2]"Allegory... flaunts the gap we must leap to produce meaning... [it] recognizes the impossibility of fusing the empirical and the eternal and thus demystifies the symbolic relation by stressing the separateness of the two levels.... Only allegory can make the connection in a self-conscious and demystified way" (Jonathan Culler, *Structuralist Poetics* [Ithaca: Cornell University Press, 1975], pp. 229-30).

Pablo Neruda: The Poetics of Prophecy

ties of reading and interpretation in all their conventionality, the poem assures the form of a prophecy of writing, by which I mean an irreducible space in which allegorical interpretation inscribes Latin American historicity.

II

Toward the end of the war in Spain, Neruda returned to Chile, and the government named him special consul for Spanish emigration in 1939. A year later he was sent as Chilean consul to Mexico City, where he lived for the following three years. By then war was raging throughout Europe, and Neruda's antifascism, conditioned as it was by his experience in Spain, was soon exacerbated by the relative impassivity of Mexican intellectuals, and especially of its poets. At least, this was Neruda's perception from the moment he set foot in Mexico, and he hinted, in a well-publicized interview, that Mexican poets were too much concerned with poetic form. Neruda's jab was obviously aimed at the members of the older *Contemporáneos* group, who had been accused of "formalism" during the Cárdenas administration, but his critique was pointed enough to strike a discordant note among the younger intellectuals, to whom Neruda's statement must have seemed anything but diplomatic. The tension increased in 1941, when Neruda refused to allow inclusion of some poems of his in *Laurel*, an anthology of Hispanic poetry that was then being put together by Octavio Paz and others. The explosion came two years later when Neruda interceded with the Brazilian government to allow Luis Carlos Prestes, a jailed Communist leader, to travel to Mexico to attend his mother's funeral. When this request was denied, Neruda publicly criticized the decision before the Brazilian ambassador to Mexico. The Chilean government rebuked him and he submitted his resignation.[3]

---

[3]For additional details on Neruda's life during this time, see Rodríguez Monegal, *Neruda*, pp. 129–41, and Felstiner, *Translating Neruda*, pp. 127–35. Octavio Paz describes the Laurel project in his *Xavier Villaurrutia en persona y en obra* (Mexico City: Fondo de Cultura Económica, 1978), pp. 16–18. See also Wilberto Cantón, "Neruda en México (1940-1943)," in *Posiciones* (Mexico City, 1950), reprinted in *Anales de la Universidad de Chile*, 157–60 (1973), 263–70.

Prophecy of Writing

This diplomatic scandal was the culmination of a series of minor incidents, both political and literary, in which Neruda was involved during his years in Mexico. Shortly after his resignation, a massive banquet was held in Neruda's honor. And in an interview recorded as he was boarding the airplane that would fly him to Panama on the first leg of his return trip to Chile, he remarked that Mexico's poets, unlike its painters and novelists, were totally disoriented and lacking in civic duty.[4]

What seems most worth remembering about Neruda's Mexican sojourn is the theme with which he chose both to open and to conclude it: the apparent failure of contemporary Mexican poets to account for the historical dimension of their times. Whatever the truth of this opinion (and there is sufficient reason to question it), one must view Neruda's complaint as an offshoot of the historical consciousness that stemmed from his experience during the Spanish Civil War. From Neruda's viewpoint, contemporary Mexican poets were pursuing the same visionary quest that he had already found fruitless. The historical failure he denounced was due not so much to the distance from which Mexicans viewed the war in Europe as to their relative indifference toward native American reality, or their apparent refusal to account for a mode of consciousness peculiar to it. This particular complaint, as we shall see, was part of the broader intellectual climate in Latin America during the 1940s. But it seems equally plausible that Neruda's reaction may have resulted from his fresh contact with Mexican culture, which openly displays, on the surface at least, indigenous traits that are either missing or camouflaged in other Latin American countries. Thus the glaring absence of Mexico's indigenous culture in its contemporary poetry msut have disturbed Neruda, whose own work was beginning to develop within a specifically Latin American context.

Neruda's change seems especially relevant when we consider that all of the poetry he wrote and published in Mexico had an "Americanist" thematics, by which I mean a poetry that attempts to register an immediate impression of Latin American

---

[4]Rodríguez Monegal, *Neruda*, p. 135. For a partial response on the part of Mexican intellectuals, see Octavio Paz, "Respuesta a un cónsul," *Letras de México*, 4 (August 15, 1943), 5.

Pablo Neruda: The Poetics of Prophecy

reality, whether through its landscape or through its history.[5] Implicit in this thematics was Neruda's deliberate adoption, as another version of the new historical mode, of the cultural immediacy that he believed Mexican poets were eschewing or at least taking for granted. But Neruda's Americanist bent was so deliberate and so unexpected that the change could not help raising questions among his less compliant readers. "He was not always so nativist [lo indíjena] as he now pretends to be," wrote Juan Ramón Jiménez in the August 1943 issue of *Repertorio Americano*.[6] Jiménez' strained relationship with Neruda dated back to the pre-Spanish Civil War years in Madrid, when the literary battles of the time pitted one against the other, and to an earlier lyrical caricature in which Jiménez had presented a less than flattering image of the Chilean poet and his work.[7] This time, however, Jiménez was replying to an essay by José Revueltas, a Mexican novelist who had criticized Jiménez' apparent condescension toward Neruda's Americanist sensibility in an "Open Letter." Whereas Revueltas saw in Jiménez' long look "the problem of Europe itself... as it faces a new fact," for Jiménez Neruda's new turn seemed "too much like an Indigenism learned in an international travel experience."[8]

This debate is important because it stemmed from a series of mutual misreadings that reveal more about the question of Americanism as an intellectual enterprise than about the facts concerning Neruda's work. Jiménez' "Open Letter" was partly a revision of his earlier statements about Neruda, partly an apology in view of his own recent acquaintance with Latin America, where he had spent some of the early years of his exile from Spain. "This new acquaintance," Jiménez wrote, "has made me

---

[5]Neruda's first "Americanist" collection was "América, no invoco tu nombre en vano," in *América*, 19 (July 1943), followed by publication of such poems as "Botánica" and "Atacama" as part of *Canto General de Chile*, privately published in Mexico in 1943. For a complete list see Loyola's bibliography, III, 954-63.

[6]"¿América sombría?" *Repertorio Americano*, 24 (August 14, 1943), 209-11.

[7]See Juan Ramón Jiménez, *Españoles de tres mundos* (Buenos Aires: Losada, 1942), pp. 121-26; the essay dates originally from 1939. For an overview of Neruda's early quarrel with Jiménez, see Juan Cano Ballesta, "Pablo Neruda y los ideales de la poesía impura," in *La poesía española entre pureza y revolución (1930-1936)* (Madrid: Gredos, 1971), pp. 201-12.

[8]José Revueltas, "América sombría," *Repertorio Americano*, 23 (May 9, 1942), 141; "¿América sombría?" p. 210. Revueltas' essay was first published in Mexico in *El Popular*, March 13, 1942, while Neruda was still living there.

see many things relating to Latin America and Spain in another way." Jiménez was convinced that Neruda expressed "with measured exuberance a general authentic Spanish-American poetry, with all the natural revolution and this continent's metamorphosis of life and death." After admitting that he "deplored," though nevertheless accepted, such a poetic state, Jiménez concluded, addressing Neruda in his own words, that "chaotic piling up is antecedent to necessary definitive clearing, as is the prehistoric to the posthistoric, the turbulent and closed shadow to the better open light. You are antecedent, prehistoric, closed, and dark."[9] What at first may seem to be harsh value judgments or the vestiges of personal rancor are actually more of a sense of Castilian awkwardness on Jiménez' part. Throughout his letter, Jiménez was admiring and conciliatory, rare qualities in the Spaniard's often vitriolic prose. Yet the most important, and perhaps ironic, feature of this reevaluation is that it referred to *Residencia en la tierra* and not to the more recent Americanist poems. Although the "Open Letter" was dated January 1942, it clearly refers, for instance, to earlier "very sad events in Madrid." Moreover, Jiménez' view of the poetry as "a chaotic piling up" essentially restated his earlier disparagement of Neruda's poetry as "a dumping ground, at times a sewer."[10] Had Jiménez meant to refer to the new Americanist poems, his description would have been different, as indeed it turned out to be in his subsequent response, since the "chaos" and "darkness" he was then deploring were metaphors for the visionary mode that Neruda himself had already deplored. What was new in Jiménez' reevaluation, then, was not his opinion of *Residencia en la tierra*, for that remained consistently negative, but his discovery of a Latin American context in light of which he could understand, though not necessarily approve of, both Neruda and his poetry.

In his response, Revueltas showed no sign of understanding Jiménez' belated contextualization and instead objected to the latter's patronizing reading of Latin America as a "turbulent and closed shadow" beneath Europe's "better open

---

[9]Juan Ramón Jiménez, "Carta a Pablo Neruda," *Repertorio Americano*, 23 (January 17, 1942), 12.
[10]Jiménez, *Españoles de tres mundos*, p. 123.

light."[11] And because his own defense of Neruda was tied to this objection, it linked Jiménez' disparagement of the broader "poetic state" with Neruda's poetry. In his "Open Letter" Jiménez had kept the two distinctly separate—however much he deplored chaos, he still praised *Residencia*. But Revueltas was blind to this retrospection and he viewed the letter as an attack on the Americanist poems. This view is implicit throughout his article, but it emerges with special force in a passage that opposes Neruda's Americanist sensibility to Rubén Darío's and compares Neruda's poetry with Mexican muralist painting.

That little more than a year later Jiménez would indeed wage an attack in his rejoinder, and that his critique should then have extended to the entire Indigenist trend in contemporary Latin American art, was the ironic outcome of this heady exchange. It was all the more ironic since Jiménez had in fact praised Neruda's work as "authentic Spanish-American poetry," even if by then the object of his praise had little to do with the kind of Americanism that Neruda was espousing. Jiménez' own shift was exacerbated by Revueltas' response, of course, but it had more to do, as Jiménez himself suggested, with Neruda's sudden change. Whereas Jiménez believed the visions of *Residencia en la tierra* were authentic renditions of Latin American "chaos," he viewed the more recent poems as "artificial Indigenism," which portrayed "the Indian, the black ... from the outside, as forced literature, not direct poetry."[12] By thus contrasting Indian poetry with indigenous literature (in accordance with the symbolist distinction between *poésie* and *littérature*), Jiménez was not only clarifying his view of Neruda but putting his finger on the rhetorical impasse of the modern Latin American writer. Once direct claims to the pre-Columbian, non-Western past are no longer possible, it would seem that the writer can no longer assume cultural difference without succumbing to bad faith. A bit like modesty, Americanism seems to share the fate of an aporia: the moment you say you have it, you've lost it.

Jiménez' prescription for breaking this impasse was "to incorporate experience ... into an embracing totality."[13] Like Borges,

---

[11]Revueltas, "América sombría," p. 140.
[12]"¿América sombría?" p. 210.
[13]Ibid.

he believed that the problem was essentially rhetorical and that it would disappear as soon as the Latin American artist relinquished his claim to cultural difference and acknowledged his kinship with the West. Still, one cannot help viewing Jiménez' belated solution as itself part of the same issue. For what earlier he had regarded as chaos, which for him attested to an authentic "poetic state," was but the effect of the coincidence of his own estranged perception with Neruda's, the former in Latin America and the latter in the Far East; the kinship across time, that is, of two radically different and yet uncannily similar "residences on earth." But if so, then chaos as an ostensible ground for cultural difference has no validity, chaos being no more peculiar to Latin America than to any place else. Difference would seem to depend, instead, on a tension between subject and object, as Jiménez himself suggests in his "Open Letter." All this shows, therefore, that Jiménez, no less than Revueltas, was caught in the need to invoke cultural peculiarity as a way of domesticating Neruda, as if there were something about the poetry that forced such a reading. Only Jiménez' symbolist aesthetics, which pointedly avoided mimetic representation, prescribed a view of Americanism that was radically unlike Revueltas' or Neruda's.

I have lingered on the details of this particular debate in order to illustrate the kinds of equivocations that accompanied Neruda's assumption of an Americanist mode. To be sure, the debate was no simple spillover from the diplomatic scandal that had driven Neruda from his consular post, but a symptom of the intellectual climate that pervaded Latin American intellectual life during those years. "The forties," according to Roberto González Echevarría, "was a period of search for Latin American consciousness and for the formation of a literature of its own, distinct from Europe."[14] Aware of the cultural rupture that both the Spanish Civil War and World War II entailed, Latin American writers now looked to themselves and their own culture to perform the self-inquiry that earlier had been denied them as an effect of colonial displacement. The idea of an autochthonous Latin American culture was of course not new, dating back as it

[14]In *Alejo Carpentier: The Pilgrim at Home* (Ithaca: Cornell University Press, 1977), p. 99.

does to the early-nineteenth-century movement toward political independence and its Romantic ideology—the creation of national cultures and literatures. It was in the 1940s, however, that the issue became an obsession with leading essayists and a topic for writers of fiction: Pedro Henríquez Ureña, Mariano Picón Salas, Leopoldo Zea, and Alejo Capentier, to mention only a few.

It would be misleading, however, to regard these efforts at cultural self-awareness solely as a reaction to an intellectual vacuum left in Latin America after the war in Spain, as a self-generated discourse that would signal the assumption of an unmediated Latin American consciousness. González Echevarría has shown, on the contrary, that this particular intellectual trend is but a belated echo of a certain strand of German philosophy, the works of Hegel and Spengler in particular, which was disseminated throughout the continent in the 1920s with the writings of Ortega y Gasset and his *Revista de Occidente*. The vision of a world different from Western culture which earlier in the century had been proposed in the various offshoots of European modernism (and an echo of which we can still hear in Jiménez) had its counterpart in Spengler's philosophy of history, which postulated the decline of ethnocentrism and predicted a polycentric world. Spengler's critique of the West's departure from a naive stage of culture, in which faith in their own abilities allowed people to build a world of possibility, for a fallen stage of civilization, in which self-conscious culture becomes a function of outward domination, struck a familiar note to Hispanic intellectuals, who saw in such concepts some justification for their own marginality.[15] Yet the contradictions inherent in the adoption of Spengler's view, as Jiménez' critique of Indigenism demonstrates, soon led to a logical quandary. For in choosing both the Spenglerian concept of culture and the aspirations of the uncultured masses to escape the unhealthy self-consciousness of the West, Latin American writers attempted to synthesize two radically incompatible postures into a cultural ideal that was compromised by their own act of self-reflection,

---

[15]Ibid., pp. 116-29. For a synthetic discussion of Spengler's role in modern intellectual history, see Wilson H. Coates and Hayden V. White, *The Ordeal of Liberal Humanism* (New York: McGraw-Hill, 1970), pp. 378-84.

by the very same writing with which they attempted to justify cultural innocence. The bad faith that pervades this rhetorical gesture would seem to constitute the elusive essence that defines Latin America, or a peculiarly "Latin American" intellectual practice.

While Jiménez' view of Americanism as a rhetorical mirage provides an accurate description of the impasse created by this intellectual climate, one cannot so easily dismiss the use to which both writers and critics put this mirage as a working context. Nor can one simply brush aside the Latin American artists' full awareness of the potential bad faith inherent in the Americanist enterprise. Neruda, at least, seems to have suggested as much in a little-known speech he delivered in Panama. Barely three weeks after the publication of Jiménez' rejoinder, he urged Latin American intellectuals to join in a united front against fascism. He remarked then that by doing so they would be following in the footsteps of their longsuffering European counterparts, and added, almost as if wishing to avert any accusation of blind ethnocentrism, that this particular choice "would but continue the American tradition," since even "the most distant plants, the most difficult seeds, can reproduce here. We are therefore," he concluded, "not frightened by the old singsong of exotic ideas. We ourselves are exotic, descendants of races alien to these naked lands, exotic was our servitude and exotic is our liberation."[16] Such a statement betrays, at the very least, an anxiety that stemmed from the tension between the reality of European precedence and the moral imperative of Latin American origins. Yet Neruda's use of this tension goes beyond rhetorical juggling and subverts, in effect, the very notion of cultural identity. For to assert cultural sameness through exoticism, to define what lies inside the self (personal or cultural identity) in terms of what falls outside (the *ex*otic) amounts to exchanging the idealistic core of a cultural thematics for a historical consciousness that assumes the otherness of every cultural enterprise. The question then becomes not whether the Latin Ameri-

---

[16]"Palabras de Pablo Neruda (Al dar las gracias por el homenaje que el pueblo panameño le hizo la noche del 3 de septiembre de 1943 por invitación de la Sociedad Española de Beneficencia)," in *Repertorio Americano*, 24 (October 13, 1943), 274.

can writer succumbs to bad faith in asserting cultural difference, but which rhetorical strategy best suits this particular enterprise.

Whether or not Neruda meant his remarks in Panama to serve as an oblique response to Jiménez is perhaps impossible to determine. But there is little doubt that the issues that gave rise to his remarks were in his mind by the time he reached Peru (following a brief visit to Colombia) and visited the pre-Inca ruins of Machu Picchu.[17] From most reports, it seems to have been an uneventful visit; yet few events in Neruda's life have attracted so much interest. It is even said that Neruda, as if wishing to deflate the potential solemnity of the occasion, remarked to a friend that the ruins were a great place for a barbecue. One does not find such flippancy, however, in either the solemn poem that emerged from the visit or Neruda's later recollections, in which he described it as a soul-stirring experience. Given such biographical richness, in fact, it should not be surprising that this frequent retelling has contributed to the poem's fame. Not only have these accounts provided a handy code of biographical interpretation, but they have linked the experience at the ruins to the thematics of cultural identity. A brief look into the language of these recollections and the interpretive power it exerts will allow us to place the problem in proper focus and bring us closer to our own reading of the poem.[18]

Neruda's first account was given in a 1954 lecture at the University of Chile on the occasion of his fiftieth birthday, in which he discussed the origins of *Canto General* (1950). The ascent to

---

[17]In a letter dated October 15, 1942, notifying Jiménez of the death of Miguel Hernández, Neruda acknowledged his "Open Letter." But this was before Jiménez' rejoinder to Revueltas. The text of the letter appears, along with other pertinent comments, in Ricardo Gullón, "Relaciones Pablo Neruda-Juan Ramón Jiménez," *Hispanic Review*, 39 (1971), 141-66. There are at least two other extant documents of Neruda's itinerary: a journalistic account of three lecture/recitals in Colombia (Andrés Holguín, "Tres conferencias de Pablo Neruda," *Revista de las Indias* [Bogotá], 56 [August 1943], 267-70) and Neruda's speech before a group of Peruvian intellectuals ("Las lámparas deben continuar encendidas," first published in *La Noche* [Lima], October 22, 1943, and now reprinted in III, 651-54) barely ten days before his visit to Machu Picchu.

[18]Although Neruda's first published words about Machu Picchu appeared in an interview, two months after his visit, for a Chilean newspaper ("Pablo Neruda habla," *El Siglo*, December 5, 1943, p. 12), neither its limited circulation nor the spontaneous quality of its language amount to the kind of autobiographical elaboration that is the focus of my argument.

Prophecy of Writing

Machu Picchu, he explained, had the effect of broadening the scope of the book he was writing, then limited to Chile, to encompass the entire Latin American continent. Corresponding to this spatial breadth, which thus dictated a book of longer proportions, was a new historical perspective that recognized the significance of pre-Columbian culture. I quote at some length:

> Cuando pasé por el Alto Perú fui al Cuzco, ascendí a Macchu Picchu.
> Hacía tiempo que yo había regresado de la India, de la China, pero Macchu Picchu es aun más grandioso.
> Todas las civilizaciones de los manuales de Historia nos hablaban de Asiria, de los arios y de los persas y de sus colosales construcciones.
> Despúes de ver las ruinas de Macchu Picchu, las culturas fabulosas de la antigüedad me parecieron de cartón piedra, de papier maché.
> La India misma me pareció minúscula, pintarrajeada, banal, feria popular de dioses, frente a la solemnidad altanera de las abandonadas torres incásicas.
> Ya no pude segregarme de aquellas construcciones. Comprendí que si pisábamos la misma tierra hereditaria, teníamos algo que ver con aquellos altos esfuerzos de la comunidad americana, que no podíamos ignorarlos, que nuestro desconocimiento o silencio era no sólo un crimen, sino la continuación de una derrota.
> El cosmopolitismo aristocrático nos había llevado a reverenciar el pasado de los pueblos más lejanos y nos había puesto una venda en los ojos para no descubrir nuestro propios tesoros.
> Pensé muchas veces a partir de mi visita al Cuzco. Pensé en el antiguo hombre americano. Vi sus antiguas luchas enlazadas con las luchas actuales.
> Allí comenzó a germinar mi idea de un Canto General americano. Antes había persistido en mí la idea de un canto general de Chile, a manera de crónica. Aquella visita cambió la perspectiva. Ahora veía a América entera desde las alturas de Macchu Picchu. Este fue el título del primer poema con mi nueva concepción.
> Fui precisando lo que era necesario. Tenía que ser un poema extraordinariamente local, parcial. Debía tener una coordinación entrecortada, como nuestra geografía. La tierra debía estar invariablemente presente.

Pablo Neruda: The Poetics of Prophecy

Escribí mucho tiempo más tarde este poema de Macchu Picchu. Como es la preparación de una nueva etapa de mi estilo y de una nueva preocupación en mis propósitos, este poema salió demasiado impregnado de mí mismo. El comienzo es una serie de recuerdos autobiográficos. También quise tocar allí por última vez el tema de la muerte. En la soledad de las ruinas la muerte no puede apartarse de los sentimientos.
Escribí Macchu Picchu en la Isla Negra, frente al mar.[19]

When I passed by High Peru I went to Cuzco, I climbed Macchu Picchu. Some time earlier I had returned from India, from China, but Macchu Picchu is even more magnificent. All the civilizations in the history books spoke to us about Assyria, about the Aryans and the Persians and their fabulous constructions. After seeing the ruins of Macchu Picchu, the fabulous cultures of antiquity seemed made of papier maché. India itself seemed minuscule, gaudy, banal, a popular fair of gods, compared to the proud solemnity of the abandoned Inca towers. I could no longer set myself apart from these constructions. I understood that if we trod the same hereditary ground, we had something to do with these high efforts of the American community, that we could no longer ignore them, that our ignorance or silence was not only a crime but the continuity of a defeat. Aristocratic cosmopolitism had made us revere the past of the most distant peoples and had blinded us to our own treasures. Ever since my visit to Cuzco I have thought many times. I thought about ancient American man. I saw his ancient struggles linked to our own. That's where my idea of an American General Canto began to germinate. Before that, I had had the idea of a general canto of Chile, in the manner of a chronicle. That visit changed my perspective altogether. Now I could see the whole of America from the heights of Macchu Picchu. That was the title of the first poem with my new conception. I began to see what was necessary. It had to be an extraordinarily local, partial poem. It had to have a broken coordination, like our geography. The earth had to be constantly present. Much later I wrote this poem of Macchu Picchu. Because it was preliminary to a new stage in my style and a new concern in my purpose, the poem came out too drenched with my own self. The beginning is a series of autobiographical recollections. I also wanted to touch there on

[19]"Algo sobre mi poesía y mi vida," *Aurora*, 1 (1954), 12–13.

the theme of death for the last time. In the solitude of ruins death cannot be far from one's thoughts. I wrote Macchu Picchu at Isla Negra, facing the sea.

From Neruda's viewpoint the ascent to Machu Picchu was the turning point of his career as a poet because the experience dispelled his cultural alienation and tempered his sense of identity as a Latin American. This fusion of poetry and culture runs parallel here to the union of poet and ruins, a union that is dramatized, as it would be in the second account, by a recurrent use of organic imagery. Woven through both recollections, this imagery suggests the realization during the visit of a natural circuit in which ruins, poet, and poem are bound together. The poem, for example, "comenzó a germinar" during the visit as a result of a "nueva concepción"; the metaphor of conception (in the dual sense of idea and procreation) suggests the fruit of a marriage between poet and ruins, an instance of the Romantic theme of the marriage between mind and nature in poetic perception. It is this natural circuit that toward the end of the passage guarantees the mimetic quality of the poem, which, being the offspring of poet and ruins, bears the traits of both parents. It is "como nuestra geografía" and at the same time issues from the poet, in a weird reversal of the same kinship imagery, "impregnado de mí mismo." The strategic use of this organic imagery thus sets up an implied contrast between the pre-Inca ruins and those of other civilizations, which, as Neruda notes, now seem bookish and unreal. The suggestion is that, unlike other ruins, which normally remind one of death, these are able to engender life, even if they serve, as the passage ultimately admits, as the occasion to meditate upon that fact. Machu Picchu's life-giving quality is closely tied to its ability to symbolize the immediacy of a Latin American consciousness. The same assertion reappears eight years later in the second account, contained in the fourth installment of Neruda's *O Cruziero* memoirs, which recasts the visit as a "journey back to the source":

> Yo no puedo vivir sino en mi propia tierra, sin poner los pies, las manos y el oído en ella, sin sentir la circulación de sus aguas y de sus sombras, sin sentir cómo mis raíces buscan en ella las sustancias maternas.

Pablo Neruda: The Poetics of Prophecy

> Pero antes de llegar a Chile hice otro descubrimiento que agregaría una nueva estrata al desarrollo de mi poesía.
> Me detuve en el Perú y subí hasta las ruinas de Macchu Picchu. Ascendimos a caballo, pero entonces no había carretera, y desde lo alto vi las antiguas construcciones de piedra rodeadas por las altísimas cumbres de los Andes verdes. Desde la ciudadela carcomida y roída por el paso de los siglos se despeñaban torrentes y masas de neblina blanca, se levantaban desde el río Wilcamayo. Me sentí infinitamente pequeño en el centro de aquel ombligo de piedra, ombligo de un mundo deshabitado, mundo orgulloso y eminente, al que de algún modo yo pertenecía. Sentí que yo mismo había trabajado allí en alguna etapa lejana cavando surcos, alisando peñascos.
> Me sentí chileno, peruano, americano. Había encontrado en aquellas alturas difíciles, entre aquellas ruinas gloriosas y dispersas, una profesión de fe para la continuación de mi canto.
> Allí nació mi poema "Alturas de Macchu Picchu."

> I can live only in my own country. I cannot live without having my feet and my hands on it and my ear against it, without feeling the movements of its waters and its shadows, without feeling my roots reach down into its soil for maternal nourishment. But before getting back to Chile, I made another discovery that was to add another layer of growth in my poetry. I stopped in Peru and made a trip to the ruins of Macchu Picchu. There was no highway then and we rode up on horseback. At the top I saw the ancient stone structures hedged in by the tall peaks on the verdant Andes. Torrents hurtled down from the citadel eaten away and weathered by the passage of the centuries. White fog drifted up in masses from the Wilkamayu River. I felt infinitely small in the center of that navel of rocks, the navel of a deserted world, proud, towering high, to which I somehow belonged. I felt that my own hands had labored there at some remote point in time, digging furrows, polishing the rocks. I felt Chilean, Peruvian, American. On those difficult heights, among those glorious, scattered ruins, I had found the principles of faith I needed to continue my poetry. My poem *Alturas de Macchu Picchu* was born there.[20]

---

[20]*Confieso que he vivido: Memorias* (Barcelona, 1974), pp. 249–50; *Memoirs*, trans. Hardie St. Martin (New York: Farrar, Straus & Giroux, 1977), pp. 165–66.

Prophecy of Writing

As part of the memoirs, the passage places additional emphasis on the poet's role in the experience. The final maternal metaphor, which recalls the imagery used in the first account, concludes its central motif. Chile's native soil provides "sustancias maternas" from which the poet, like a latter-day Atlas, cannot bear to be uprooted. Whereas in the first account Machu Picchu had appeared as the spouse who engendered the poem-offspring, now it becomes an ancient womb welcoming back its long-lost son. Besides alluding to the name of Cuzco (which in Quechua means navel), the maternal motif signals an intimacy between poet and ruins as the key to the sense of totality that we feel at the end of the recollection. In short, what eight years earlier had been a detached and somewhat abstract vision now appears as a rapturous discovery of the poet's cultural being.

Had Neruda's two biographical accounts not served so often as interpretive screens for the poem, perhaps we could refrain from recalling them here, less in deference to the tradition they initiate than in an attempt to avoid its pitfalls. Despite their documentary value, these texts cannot yield any positive critical insight because they deliberately confuse Neruda's recollections of the visit with the actual poem. What is more, critical readings that invoke these accounts while failing to discriminate between text and experience end up conferring authority on both an autobiographical source and the thematics of cultural identity. And while it would be difficult to deny the importance of these two interpretive threads, one must be equally alert to the danger of reducing the poem to authorial directives that would blind us to its complexity. It could be shown that, as in the history of the criticism of *Residencia en la tierra*, most readings of the poem blindly follow Neruda's prose accounts and propose similar, if not identical, interpretations.[21] Indeed, it would be interesting, and perhaps even useful, to undertake a systematic analysis of such readings. But precisely because the principal obstacle to a balanced criticism has been the loss of distance, it might be less instructive to dwell on them than to examine the opposite critical tendency, namely, the kind of reading that goes so far as to

---

[21]See especially Hernán Loyola, "Los modos de autorreferencia" and *Ser y morir*, passim.

question, and perhaps even to discredit, Neruda's views on his own text.

It is this kind of exercise that Juan Larrea's "Machupicchu, piedra de toque," one of the most violent attacks to which Neruda was ever subjected, is designed to offer.[22] By invoking it now I do not mean to endorse its violence or even most of its conclusions. Yet, despite its misguided motivation, Larrea's essay performs a valuable reading that helps to situate my own and in addition exposes some of the problems of a text such as *Alturas de Macchu Picchu*. Long an enemy of Neruda's, Larrea was a Spanish surrealist turned critic who wrote at length on a variety of Latin American topics. In 1944, a few months after Neruda's departure from Mexico, Larrea published his first attack, one that owed much to Jiménez (and may have been, in fact, an offshoot of Jiménez' quarrel with Revueltas), and in which he undertook a radical questioning of Neruda's Americanist sensibility.[23] Larrea accused Neruda then of espousing what he called a "materialist subpoetics" that ran contrary to Latin America's ideal destiny, a destiny that only such true poets as Rubén Darío had been able to express. The argument, as we can see, runs along the same lines as Jiménez' and implicitly refers to *Residencia en la tierra*. Their common target was the belated Americanism of Neruda's book. But, as we also saw earlier, such a reading is not possible unless one first postulates a cultural ideal that Larrea—like Jiménez, a Spanish exile living in Latin America—similarly felt the need to uphold. Thus in 1967, more than twenty years after his first attack, Larrea took up the same cause with a reading of *Alturas de Macchu Picchu* which was calculated to prove the poem's betrayal of that ideal.

Alleging that Neruda had not written any Americanist poetry before the publication of his first essay, Larrea begins by claiming that his critique was responsible for the course Neruda took in *Canto General*. But this claim is merely an isolated instance in Larrea's misreading. Though Larrea at no time mentions any of Neruda's published recollections, his comments on Neruda's

---

[22]In Larrea, *Del surrealismo a Machupicchu*, pp. 132-223; all translations are mine.

[23]"El surrealismo entre viejo y nuevo mundo," *Cuadernos Americanos*, 3-5 (1944), 216-35, 210-28, and 235-56, respectively; reprinted in *Del surrealismo a Machupicchu*, pp. 17-100.

role in the poem amount to an indirect response to them. His ambitious and at times tortuous arguments make two main objections. First, Larrea criticizes the existence of a prophetic voice in the poem, which he considers to be a sign of Neruda's arrogance. "He places himself, with authority, at the head of America's love, as if presuming to direct it, rather as Yaweh shows himself through the voice of his ministers."[24] Second, he objects to details of the poem's language and specifically to the ninth canto of the poem, which consists solely of a catalogue of eighty-one metaphors that together create a lyrical image of the ruins. Larrea adduces Neruda's bad faith from his failure to include a greater number of native American words. "Among the 161 adjectives and nouns that make up this gabble, one finds only two poor American words: *puma* and *andino.*"[25] And after arguing the inappropriateness of most of Neruda's metaphors and proposing several native substitutes, Larrea offers his own turgid version of the same catalogue, replete with *Americanisms,* which he claims to be a more authentic rendition. Although Larrea ultimately admits that, given the catalogue's paratactic structure, the permutations of the metaphors are virtually infinite, one leaves this violent misreading with the clear impression that Larrea is convinced that his version is an improvement.

One might well be inclined to dismiss Larrea's reading on the grounds that it merely reflects the extremes to which a resentful poet-critic can go in reading a rival text. But even in his wrongheadedness, Larrea offers us a crucial insight. Indeed, the clumsy accuracy with which he identifies a prophetic voice in the poem, even though he takes it to be a sign of Neruda's arrogance, should be enough to persuade us of his interpretive power. It is perhaps ironic that so crucial an insight should have appeared in the context of an attack against Neruda when it has been absent from many a bland panegyric. It is Larrea's unwitting distance from Neruda's authorial prejudice that allows him to succeed, though for the wrong reasons, where other readers have failed. And for this reason alone, despite the violence of his argument, one is compelled to give a fair hearing to his second objection, which in effect questions the efficiency, if not the very

[24]*Del surrealismo a Machupicchu,* p. 141.
[25]Ibid., p. 149.

existence, of the kinship between author and text which Neruda takes pains to establish in his two retrospective accounts. Larrea's belief in a cultural ideal that the language of the poem ostensibly betrays leads him to attempt what is in effect a rewriting of the ninth canto by means of native American words, and thus to close the gap that he feels Neruda's excessively Western rendition has opened between text and experience. Farther on in the same essay, and as part of the same strategy of discrediting Neruda, Larrea identifies several Western literary traditions in the poem, including Dante and the poetry of ruins, which for him suggests the possibility of plagiarism. And yet, once again, one need not share Larrea's extreme conclusion to recognize the philological accuracy of his insight.

On witnessing this battle of interpretations, one may be tempted to assume a broad relativism and regard Neruda's two accounts as no less violent than Larrea's reading. But as useful as critical distance may be, one must ultimately suspect any critical exercise that disparages a given text in the name of an ideal norm without regard for either the potential nihilism of literary language or the critic's own inevitable margin for error. More important, what in Larrea becomes the pretext to wage a personal attack should instead be viewed as the peculiar tension that pervades the poem and, by extension, all of Latin American literary history—the paradox of having to create an original literature while one is still dependent on Western culture. *Alturas de Macchu Picchu* suspends the very idea of Latin American identity not so much through Neruda's lack of authenticity as through the contradictions inherent in his subject—namely, the impossibility of knowing origins by naming them or of speaking the myth of immediacy without being thrown into a historical act of mediation. The poem, in this sense, is far from being the only text beset by this tension, for the problem lies at the core of any body of writing that is in quest of cultural identity.

As we begin now to identify this tension in the poem, we must continue to distinguish between Larrea's conclusions, some of which we can share, and his motivations, which we must reject. But we must also be no less aware of the kinds of misreadings that stem from Neruda's own politics of poetics, so to speak, from the author's attempt to achieve interpretive supremacy over his poetry by conditioning critical assumptions

Prophecy of Writing

about it through his own prose texts. We must not only wonder what self-interest motivates strategic recollections such as Neruda's but also identify those aspects of the poem that lend credence to the critical assumptions that these recollections have influenced.

III

It is generally acknowledged that *Alturas de Macchu Picchu* begins by alluding to the poetry of *Residencia en la tierra*. The allusions appear throughout the first five cantos and they retrace the earlier book in mood and style. In Neruda's account of his first visit to the site, when he disclosed that the beginning of the poem was "a series of biographical recollections," he may have been referring to his experience in the Far East. Be that as it may, critics agree that the allusions resound strongly enough to make a difference, though such agreement has never gone beyond viewing them as a formal index that separates the two halves of the poem.[26] It would seem, however, that an explicit allusion to one of Neruda's better-known works should have a greater structural significance, for what appears to be a passive rereading of *Residencia* becomes an active rewriting as soon as we notice its explicitness. The allusions in the first half of the poem not only differentiate it from the second half but determine the allusive character of the entire poem. The allusions to *Residencia* thus set the stage for a broader allusive strategy.

One need not recognize the allusions to *Residencia*, however, to sense the poem's prefigurative thrust. That thrust begins with the first canto, a prologue that summarizes the argument of the poem. Most readings ignore the presence, not to mention the importance, of this prologue and mistake it for the first stage of the speaker's dramatic itinerary. The mistake persists even though the canto clearly includes a condensed version of that

---

[26]"The first five sections are a rereading of *Residencia en la tierra*. The other seven are a kind of protest against the questions that arise from the speaker's retrospective reflection in the initial series" (my translation from Hernán Loyola, "Itinerario de Pablo Neruda," *Anales de la Universidad de Chile*, 157-60 [1971], 16). "The first five sections hark right back to the moods and even the techniques of *Residencia en la tierra*" ("Introduction," *Pablo Neruda: A Basic Anthology*, ed. Robert Pring-Mill [Oxford: Dolphin, 1975], p. xxxvii). See also Loveluck, "*Alturas de Macchu Picchu*."

itinerary. While the first two stanzas, for example, anticipate the existential lethargy and syntactical ambiguity of cantos II through V, the last two depict the resolution of that state as dramatized in the rest of the poem. The sole purpose of a prologue seems at first sight to be to guide the reader through the poem's tortuous and at times confusing argument. But if this were so, one would expect a more direct and less metaphorical prologue. As a canto written from the end of the poem, as if the experience that sustains it had already taken place, the prologue has a prefigurative rather than a descriptive function. In the first canto, that is, the speaker provides a retrospective summary of his experience.

Instability and material dispersion make up the thematic nodes of the first two stanzas, in which the speaker wanders without progress ("Del aire al aire," From air to air) and appears to be devoid of any content or purpose ("como una red vacía," like an empty net) (I, 331). The use of the imperfect tense conveys the sense of a wavering and uncertain movement, as in a journey without origin or cause, while the lack of syntactical object in the rest of the first stanza conveys the same uncertainty. Farther into the second stanza, where parentheses add a sense of confinement and the punctuation suggests the stages of an impersonal assembly line, this movement suggests a grinding that ends in dispersion. By contrast, the third and fourth stanzas dispel the previous uncertainty with a meeting with a third person and with the speaker's return to a point of origin:

> Alguien que me esperó entre los violines
> encontró un mundo como una torre enterrada
> hundiendo su espiral más abajo de todas
> las hojas de color de ronco azufre:
> más abajo, en el oro de la geología,
> como una espada envuelta en meteoros,
> hundí la mano turbulenta y dulce
> en lo más genital de lo terrestre.
>
> Puse la frente entre las olas profundas,
> descendí como gota entre la paz sulfúrica,
> y, como un ciego, regresé al jazmín
> de la gastada primavera humana.   [I, 331]

Prophecy of Writing

> Someone who waited for me among the violins / found a world like a buried tower / plunging its spiral lower than all / the leaves the color of hoarse sulphur; / lower still, in the gold of geology, / like a sword wrapped in meteors, / I plunged my hand turbulent and sweet / into the most genital part of the earth. / I placed my forehead among the deep waves, / I descended as a drop among the sulphur peace, / and, like a blind man, I returned to the jasmine / of the spent human spring.

Between the two events, between the meeting with "alguien" and the return, the speaker discovers a "mundo"—what later will turn out to be Machu Picchu—which provides the axis for pivotal change. More precisely, it is the third person, the "alguien," who discovers this world. This anonymous person is in fact none other than the speaker himself, seen in retrospect and unfolded by narrative time. Because the "alguien" is that other whom the speaker will eventually become, the effect of unfolding or *dédoublement* anticipates the radical conversion he will undergo in the course of the poem.

As we saw in the last chapter, the narrative representation of conversion splits the speaker into two entities—the one before the conversion experience and the one after it, the speaker as character and the speaker as author of the poem. The dialectical interplay between these two entities, as unfolded from the privileged and true perspective of the end, structures the successful conversion text. The anticipated split in the prologue startles us at first in its apparent incoherence, but it constitutes the rhetorical counterpart of the poem's prefigurative movement. By thus attributing the discovery of the "world" to a third person, the text dramatizes a direct link between the encounter with Machu Picchu and the conversion experience. Equally important is the change of implicit landscape that the prologue anticipates. Whereas in the first two stanzas we find a series of disturbing images that suggest an urban wasteland, the latter two present a succession of allegorical figures that make up a kind of *paysage moralisé*: "torre enterrada," "espiral," "olas profundas." The dramatic counterpart to this change of landscape is the speaker's shift from a state of wandering, in the first two stanzas, to a definite downward movement. What is implied, at

127

any rate, is a descent of infernal connotations ("ronco azufre," "paz sulfúrica") followed by an ascent or return to a point of origin. These two opposite directions, it is implied, will structure the narrative of a journey or quest.

By dwelling on the prologue we can thus see that the rhetoric of conversion underlies the poem's structure, in which the allusions to *Residencia en la tierra* play a central role. The very presence of a prologue demonstrates that a restrospective viewpoint governs the poem. This retrospection encompasses both the experience of the poem and, at a biographical level, a rewriting of Neruda's own past, for which the poetry of *Residencia* stands. It could be claimed, in fact, that unless we recognize the implied affinity between conversion and rewriting, we fail to understand the poem's central argument.

Beginning with canto II, the actual dramatic starting point, the homeless pilgrim attests to a radical difference between human beings and the rest of nature. Whereas flowers spread their pollen disinterestedly and stones preserve their own physical integrity, human beings are intent on transforming their environment and causing their own spiritual pollution. The first stanza ends with imperative constructions that both dramatize this self-destruction and denounce it through ruinous imagery. The theme of that tragic breach continues in the second and third stanzas as part of a rhetorical thrust toward the speaker's personal statement. Both stanzas open with rhetorical questions. But whereas the second stanza dwells on the relative inferiority of human beings ("quién guarda su puñal [como las encarnadas / amapolas] su sangre?" [who holds his knife (like the deep red / poppies) its blood?]) (I, 132), the third and fourth stanzas render the same idea as a personal testimony:

> Cuántas veces en las calles de invierno de una ciudad o en
> un autobús o un barco en el crepúsculo o en la soledad
> más espesa, la de la noche de fiesta, bajo el sonido
> de sombras y campanas, en la misma gruta del placer humano,
> me quise detener a buscar la eterna veta insondable
> que antes toqué en la piedra o en el relámpago que el beso
>   desprendía.
>
> (Lo que en el cereal como una historia amarilla
> de pequeños pechos preñados va repitiendo un número

Prophecy of Writing

que sin cesar es ternura en las capas germinales,
y que, idéntica siempre, se desgrana en marfil
y lo que en el agua es patria transparente, campana
desde la nieve aislada hasta las olas sangrientas.) [I, 332]

How many times in the winter streets of a city or in / a bus or a ship at twilight or in the solitude / most dense, that of the feast night, under the sound / of shadows and bells, in the very cave of human pleasure, / did I wish to stop to look for the eternal unfathomable vein / that earlier I touched in the stone or in the lighting that the kiss gave off. / (What in grain like a yellow history / of small pregnant breasts goes on repeating a number / that is ceaselessly tender in the germinating layers, / and which, always the same, scatters itself in ivory, / and what in water is transparent fatherland, a bell / from the isolated snow down to the bloody waves.)

More than just a rhetorical question, the first stanza is a lament that exposes the speaker's failure to find the stable meaning that he calls "la eterna veta insondable." Both the urban landscape that hinders this quest and the attendant parentheses recall details from the prologue scene. We should note, also, that the quest is described in the terms of vision and hearing, familiar from *Residencia en la tierra* ("bajo el sonido de sombras y campanas"). Whether in fact this particular meaning is evident in the experience of erotic love, as is also suggested, is perhaps of no less consequence. What seems crucial, at any rate, is that the fourth stanza restates the speaker's plaint in terms of an allusion to *Residencia*. The lines "va repitiendo un número / que sin cesar es ternura en las capas germinales, / y que, idéntica siempre, se desgrana en marfil" conceal a subtle rewriting of a line from "Unidad": "repitiendo su número, su señal idéntica" (repeating its number, its identical sign) (I, 173). As earlier, the poem invokes repetition and sameness in reaction to the object's dispersion. Only their immediate context (the parenthetical stanza) suggests that repetitions and similarities constitute merely provisional solutions to the isolation that plagues the subject. The allusion, we should note, is not at all gratuitous because semantically it helps to pinpoint, as it were, the speaker's quest. And as if reinforcing this allusive thrust, the fifth and last stanza opens with the same gesture:

Pablo Neruda: The Poetics of Prophecy

No pude asir sino un racimo de rostros o de máscaras
precipitadas, como anillos de oro vacío,
como ropas dispersas hijas de un otoño rabioso
que hiciera temblar el miserable árbol de las razas asustadas.

No tuve sitio donde descansar la mano
y que, corriente como agua de manantial encadenado
o firme como grumo de antracita o cristal,
hubiera devuelto el calor o el frío de mi mano extendida.
Qué era el hombre? En qué parte de su conversación abierta
entre los almacenes y los silbidos, en cuál de sus movimientos
   metálicos
vivía lo indestructible, lo imperecedero, la vida? [I, 333]

> I was able to grasp only a cluster of faces or precipitate / masks, like rings of empty gold, / like dispersed clothing, daughters of a furious autumn / that would make the miserable tree of frightened races tremble. / I had no place in which to rest my hand / and which, running like water from a chained spring / or firm like a chunk of anthracite or glass, / would have returned the warmth or cold of my extended hand. / What was man? In what part of his open conversation, / among warehouses and whistles, / in which of his metallic movements / lived the indestructible, the immortal, life itself?

This time the text alluded to is "Sistema sombrío," whose image of clustered faces ("rostros diferentes se arriman y encadenan / como grandes flores pálidas y pesadas" [different faces huddle and link themselves / like great pale heavy flowers]) (I, 185) reappears in the first line. Unlike the first allusion, which preserves its source, this one rewrites the image as a negative moment. The revision of what earlier had been a healthy sign of retrospection allows for a dialectical positing of permanence and constancy as a corollary of the quest. This much is implied at least in the metaphors "manantial encadenado" and "grumo de antracita o cristal," which reestablish a missing link between humanity and nature. The new context thus recasts the image as a limit that is exceeded by the new quest, the summary of which (in the last three lines) invokes indestructibility as part of human nature. Perhaps the most crucial aspect of the quest, as now summarized, is its inclusion of the gift of language, which appears to hold the key to the human enigma.

Prophecy of Writing

These allusions to *Residencia,* along with their various degrees of revision, invite the reader to begin to measure the distance that now separates Neruda's past from his present, what in terms of the poem's discourse is the difference between the author's "now" and the character's "then," between the narrative "I" and the "alguien" he will eventually become. But while the allusions provide the underpinning of this retrospective movement, one need not identify them in order to detect the dramatic change that they describe. As the prologue anticipates, cantos III through V reveal a descent to death. Dramatically, canto III attributes the consequences of the failed quest to the effects of temporality. The image of a shaking ear of corn provides the metaphorical basis for the extended discussion on death. As the kernels drop one by one, so death occurs separately and individually:

> y no una muerte, sino muchas muertes llegaba a cada uno:
> cada día una muerte pequeña, polvo, gusano, lámpara
> que se apaga en el lodo del suburbio, una pequeña muerte de
>   alas gruesas
> entraba en cada hombre como una corta lanza
>
>   . . .
>
> todos desfallecieron esperando su muerte, su corta muerte
>   diaria:
> y su quebranto aciago de cada día era
> como una copa negra que bebían temblando.   (I, 333)
>
> and not one death, but many deaths came to each one: / each day a little death, dust, worm, lamp / that flickers out in the mud of the suburb, a little death with thick wings / entered inside each man like a short lance / . . . all of them died waiting for their death, their short daily death; / and their daily broken damage was / like a black cup that they drank trembling.

The insistence on the individual and dispersive character of death could almost certainly be read as a lyrical version of the Marxist critique of bourgeois individualism. That this individual death fails to offer any transcendence is at least clear from the passage. What may not be so clear is that the obsessively repeated "pequeña muerte" (little death) is borrowed from the text that has come to symbolize this brand of individualism: Rilke's *Notebooks of Malte Laurids Brigge*. The presence of Rilke in

Pablo Neruda: The Poetics of Prophecy

Neruda may seem, at first sight, forced and far-fetched. But only if we fail to recall that in his youth Neruda translated, from André Gide's French version, the precise passage from Rilke's *Notebooks* in which the young Danish poet recalls his grandfather's impressive death: "Antaño se sabía—o tal vez se sospechaba—que uno contenía su propia muerte como el fruto de su hueso. Los niños tenían una pequeña, los adultos una grande. Las mujeres la llevaban en el seno, los hombres en el pecho. Uno tenía su muerte, y esta conciencia os daba una dignidad singular, un silencioso orgullo." (Formerly one knew—or perhaps one suspected—that one had one's death within one, as a fruit its kernel. The children had a little death within them and the grown-ups a big one. The women had it in their breasts and men in their chests. One *had* one's death, and that gave one a singular dignity and a quiet pride).[27] Rilke's ironic tone conveys the critique that later was to be accented in Neruda: death as a hyperbole of isolated individuality.

I am less concerned with the nature of Rilke's conception than with Neruda's use of it. The graft of the translation onto the poem not only points up the distance that separates him from the image of a "pequeña muerte" (little death), but in effect implies, by climaxing the series of allusions to *Residencia,* a complicity between the earlier poems and Rilkean death. Whether or not such a complicity in fact exists is of little consequence. What matters is that the poem interprets the complicity so, as an attempt, that is, to turn away from a past whose representation is everywhere permeated by error. Fittingly, the association between *Residencia* and Rilke is confirmed in part by the fact that Rilke's *Notebooks* is the diary of an exiled poet. More important, however, is the broader rhetorical gesture described by all these

---

[27]First published in *Claridad,* 135 (October–November, 1926); reprinted in III, 763–65. Translation slightly modified from *The Notebooks of Malte Laurids Brigge,* tr. M. D. Herter Norton (1949; New York: Norton, 1964), p. 18. On Rilke see William Rose, "Rilke and the Conception of Death," in *Rainer Maria Rilke: Aspects of his Mind and Poetry,* ed. William Rose and G. Craig Houston (New York: Gordian Press, 1970), pp. 41–84. Some of the affinities between Neruda and Rilke are discussed in Dieter Saalmann, "Der Tod als Sinnbild Aesthetischer Affinität zwischen Rainer Maria Rilke und Pablo Neruda," *Deutsche Vierteljahrsschrift für Literaturwissenschaft und Geistesgeschichte,* 48 (1974), 197–227, and Nancy Willard, *Testimony of the Invisible Man: William Carlos Williams, Francis Ponge, Rainer Maria Rilke, Pablo Neruda* (Columbia, Mo.: University of Missouri Press, 1969), pp. 83–115.

Prophecy of Writing

allusions, including the one to Rilke. For the encounter with the fragments of earlier texts, alluded to or grafted onto the poem, demonstrates the extent to which the rewriting of Neruda's earlier work permeates the speaker's descent. Rilke's "little death" thus comes to stand for both physical death and the poetic demise to which the poetry of *Residencia,* now interpreted as an individual enterprise, had led.

It is this overpowering death ("La poderosa muerte") (I, 334), understood in both its physical and its poetic senses, that cantos IV and V invoke directly in order to dramatize its effects on the speaker. The most immediate of these effects, in canto IV, appears in the speaker's encounter with an abyss, a point of no return whose description prefigures the actual encounter with Machu Picchu:

> Yo al férreo filo vine, a la angostura
> del aire, a la mortaja de agricultura y piedra
> al estelar vacío de los pasos finales
> y a la vertiginosa carretera espiral:
> pero, ancho mar, oh muerte!, de ola en ola no vienes,
> sino como un galope de claridad nocturna
> o como los totales números de la noche.   [I, 334]

> I came to the stony edge, to the narrowness / of air, to the death shroud of agriculture and stone, / to the empty abyss of final steps / and to the vertiginous spiral highway: / but, wide sea, oh death! you come not in waves, / but like a gallop of nocturnal clarity, / or like the total numbers of the night.

The shift to an apostrophe to death in the last three lines creates a sense of immediacy that is sustained throughout both cantos. In addition, the images of "férreo filo," "estelar vacío," and "vertiginosa espiral," call up the same allegorical landscape that we first saw in the prologue. Along with the reference to a "mortaja de agricultura y piedra," they suggest a moral association with death, though they stop short of identifying the site.[28]

---

[28]For a subtle review of these allegorical emblems see Paul Piehler, *The Visionary Landscape* (London: Edward Arnold, 1971); Goić stresses the "torre enterrada" as an emblem for poetic revelation in his *"Alturas de macchu Picchu,"* p. 155. For further bibliography, see Stephen Gilman, *The Tower as Emblem* (Frankfurt am Main: Vittorio Klostermann, 1967), especially pp. 46-57.

Pablo Neruda: The Poetics of Prophecy

The particular significance of this anonymity will become evident further on. For the moment, it is enough to note that here the speaker takes up his meditation on death, beginning with the recognition of its inaccessibility to human knowledge. Far from coming in waves that would allow for comfortable research, as the Rilkean conception posits, death breaks through in destructive onslaughts that exclude the very possibility of knowledge as the temporal accumulation of experience. The passage, we should note, encompasses a poetic as well as a physical meaning by way of the discreet allusion to "Galope muerto" in the image of "galope de claridad nocturna." And we perceive the radical nihilism of the canto in its concluding lines, which show the speaker sliding toward a vertiginous descent:

> entonces fui por calle y calle y río y río
> y ciudad y ciudad y cama y cama
> y atravesó el desierto mi máscara salobre,
> y en las últimas casas humilladas, sin lámpara, sin fuego,
> sin pan, sin piedra, sin silencio, solo,
> rodé muriendo de mi propia muerte.   [I, 334]

> And then I went through street and street and river and river / and city and city and bed and bed / and my salty mask crossed the desert, / and in the last humiliated houses, without lamp, without fire, / without bread, without stone, without silence, alone, / I rolled down dying of my own death.

The end of the canto is notable for the unmistakable ring of its last line. As Neruda had earlier rendered the end of Rilke's passage with the definitive "murió de su dura muerte" (he died of his hard death) (III, 765), so this canto ends with "rodé muriendo de mi propia muerte." By altering the Rilkean formula with *rodar*, which introduces the action of rolling or tossing about, Neruda conveys an image of the speaker as a rolling stone. The image of self-petrification suggests both the degree of the speaker's death and an ironic resemblance to the immediate landscape. More important, the image of petrification recalls the precise metaphor for poetic death that appears at the end of the second *Residencia*. The end of the canto amounts, then, to an allegorical restatement of the temporal inauthenticity with which the earlier book concluded.

Prophecy of Writing

Thus in the fifth canto, which concludes the first half of the poem, the speaker addresses death from the nadir of his itinerary:

> No eras tú, muerte grave, ave de plumas férreas,
> la que el pobre heredero de las habitaciones
> llevaba entre alimentos apresurados bajo la piel vacía.   (I, 335]

> It wasn't you, grave death, bird of stone feathers, / whom the wretched heir of rooms / carried among gulped-down food under his empty skin.

In the new apostrophe death becomes a bird, as was first suggested in canto III ("una pequeña muerte de alas gruesas," a little death with thick wings). "Heredero de las habitaciones" is but an elliptical reference to the "resident on earth." Such a projection of the past onto an outside object allows the speaker to denounce the earlier obsession with death as a mirage of temporal anxiety. For if death is nothingness, then Rilkean death succeeds in making something out of that nothing, turning it into a mere fetish. Knowledge of death, that is, can be acquired only negatively, as the images in the canto suggest. When death is understood in its absolute nothingness, the only remaining step is its own annihilation and the discovery of its bare nothingness:

> ... hundí las manos
> en los pobres dolores que mataban la muerte,
> y no encontré en la herida sino una racha fría
> que entraba por los vagos intersticios del alma.   [I, 335]

> I plunged my hands / into the poor pains that were killing death, / and I found nothing in the wound but a cold wind / that was coming in through the vague interstices of the soul.

The representation of the death of Death marks an end point in the speaker's itinerary and signals a turn that corresponds to the end of the third stanza in the prologue. Indeed, we must read the canto as the simultaneous end and beginning that are seen in the prologue (I, 331), where the plunging of the "hand turbulent and sweet / into the most genital part of the earth" coincides with the discovery of the ruins. Fittingly, canto VI underscores from the start the ruins' earthen quality:

> Entonces en la escala de la tierra he subido
> entre la atroz maraña de las selvas perdidas
> hasta ti, Macchu Picchu. [I, 335]

> Then on the earth's ladder I have climbed / amid the cruel thicket of the lost forests / up to thee, Macchu Picchu.

Thus the dramatic sequence of cantos V and VI, in which an encounter with the ruins follows a long meditation on death, fulfills the conceptual affinity between death and ruins which the prologue anticipates in metaphorical terms.

One is readily persuaded, upon reading canto VI, that the pilgrim has in fact reached a new stage in his journey. Dramatically, besides locating the action in a concrete geographical site, the encounter signals the end of the descent and the beginning of an upward movement. The poem further conveys the temporal underpinning of this shift by balancing the moments before and after the encounter with the same adverb: "*entonces* fui por calle y calle" (*then* I went through street and street), "*entonces* en la escala de la tierra" (*then* in the ladder of the earth) (my italics). Both the ceremonial tone of the apostrophe and the new diction signal a clear change. All of the shifts introduced in canto VI are part of a narrative strategy to show progress in the pilgrim's journey, the signs that convey a sense of duration and which constitute the "kinesis" of allegorical discourse.[29] But, as the conceptual affinity between death and ruins suggests, these shifts are not so radical or definitive as the narrative indicates. The metaphorical structuring of this passage, on which the entire poem pivots, betrays a disruption of narrative illusion.

---

[29]I borrow this term from Gay Clifford, *The Transformations of Allegory* (London: Routledge & Kegan Paul, 1974), pp. 14-15: "In allegory the concern is always with process." For a far-ranging discussion of "the fundamental structure of allegory... in the tendency of the language toward narrative," see Paul de Man, "The Rhetoric of Temporality," in *Interpretation: Theory and Practice*, ed. Charles S. Singleton (Baltimore: Johns Hopkins University Press, 1969), p. 206. For general discussions of allegory and narrative, see Angus Fletcher, *Allegory: The Theory of a Symbolic Mode* (Ithaca: Cornell University Press, 1964), and the special issue of *Genre*, 3 (1973).

Prophecy of Writing

Whereas for the poet as character the ruins do signal progress because they embody the earlier abstraction of "the indestructible," for the poet as author there is no change because the ruins also embody death. Narrative coherence, in the passage from abstraction to concrete symbol, is preserved by the common referent of death along with the apostrophe that is common to Cantos IV and VI. Moreover, the "escala de la tierra" with which the ruins become identified bears an uncanny resemblance to the "carretera espiral" that earlier formed part of the anonymous landscape. Even the adverbial balance in cantos IV and VI can be regarded as another instance of repetition. All of these analogies can be equally viewed, then, as a subversion of narrative illusion, and together they suggest that what appears to be sequential progress may be but a single event that takes place wholly within the self. As the conceptual affinity of death and ruins was shown to be the narrative version of a metaphor, so the encounter with the ruins in canto VI turns out to be the temporal unfolding of an internal change. It is in fact this temporal unfolding of signification, this deferred identification of the site, that explains the earlier anonymous landscape. It should be clear, however, that paradoxical as it may seem, the rhetorical gesture we are describing requires the coincidence of both narrative duration and metaphorical analogy, not the exclusion of one by the other.

The implications of this structure cannot be fully grasped until we read the sixth canto, where the speaker addresses the ruins and explains their significance:

> Alta ciudad de piedras escalares,
> por fin morada del que lo terrestre
> no escondió en las dormidas vestiduras.
> En ti, como dos líneas paralelas,
> la cuna del relámpago y del hombre
> se mecían en un viento de espinas.
>
> Madre de piedra, espuma de los cóndores.
>
> Alto arrecife de la aurora humana.
>
> Pala perdida en la primera arena.

Pablo Neruda: The Poetics of Prophecy

Esta fue la morada, este es el sitio:

aquí los anchos granos del maíz ascendieron

y bajaron de nuevo como granizo rojo.

Aquí la hebra dorada salió de la vicuña
a vestir los amores, los túmulos, las madres,
el rey, las oraciones, los guerreros. [I, 335-36]

> High city of scaling stones, / at last dwelling place of which the earth-bound / did not hide among the sleeping vestments. / In you, like two parallel lines, / the cradle of lightning and of man / were rocking in a wind of thorns. / Mother of stone, froth of the condors. / High reef of the human dawn. / Lost shovel in the first sand. / This was the dwelling, this is the place: / here the wide grains of corn ascended / and came down again like red hail. / Here the golden thread came out of the vicuña / to dress up the loves, the tombstones, the mothers, / the king, the prayers, the warriors.

The canto celebrates the ruins' ability to reconcile man and nature. Like the "encarnadas amapolas" of the first canto, which bore their inmost nature on the surface, the ruins' earthen quality blurs all inside-outside distinctions. All of the remaining praise derives logically from this central quality, which shows the site to be the source of a synthesis of nature and culture. Critics agree, moreover, that the language of the canto recalls the poetry of ruins of the Spanish Golden Age, a recollection most evident in the repeated demonstrative pronouns, the eulogy of fame (here turned into a eulogy of synthesis), and the adverbs of place that convey a sense of spatial immediacy.[30] Unlike the pre-Romantic German or English poetry of ruins, the Romance tradition to which the Spanish strain belongs harks back to Petrarch and the Renaissance discovery of antiquarian knowledge. Garcilaso de la Vega and the other imitators of Petrarch in Spain begin the tradition, which extends through the baroque and culminates in Rodrigo Caro's "Canción a las ruinas de Itálica," its *locus classicus*. The ruins, in this classical poetry,

---

[30] See especially Goić, "*Alturas de Macchu Picchu*," pp. 159-63.

constitute the objective correlative of moral topics. Besides reminding the spectator of death (*memento mori*), their decay raises questions about the fate of their inhabitants (*ubi sunt*). Above all, the poetry of ruins occasions meditations on the fortunes of history and on the contingency of human will.[31]

This was not the first time that Neruda had paid homage to this particular tradition. In *España en el corazón*, his eulogy on the Spanish Civil War, he included a poem about the bombing of Madrid, "Canto sobre unas ruinas," whose echo of Caro's "Canción" was strong enough to make Amado Alonso remark upon its influence and proclaim "Canto" the best poem in the volume.[32] Alonso's judgment was for the most part correct, though he failed to notice the differences between the two poems. Aside from those of style, which are numerous, the most important among these differences are the nature of the ruins and the events that occasioned them. Whereas Caro's poem provides a moral argument on the vanity of history through ruins decayed by the weathering of time, Neruda's is a lament for human fate through the spectacle of ruins destroyed by human intervention. Unlike Caro, Neruda pointedly omitted a historical object in the earlier poem, either because the immediacy of the ruins preempted any such meditations or because the poem's context was felt to suffice. In Neruda's bombed wasteland the destruction was so complete that little if any trace of human intention was left standing and therefore the "ruins" of the poem's title hardly existed.

That the meditation on Machu Picchu obliquely corrects the earlier "Canto" hardly needs to be stressed. Except for the

---

[31] For a reading of the tradition, see Bruce W. Wardropper, "The Poetry of Ruins in the Golden Age," *Revista Hispánica Moderna*, 35 (1969), 295-304. On Caro see E. M. Wilson, "Sobre la 'Canción a las ruinas de Itálica,'" *Revista de Filología Española*, 23 (1936), 20-31. Predictably, Larrea objected to this particular echo: "In order to write in our century a poem worthy of what Machupicchu was, is, and will be in the future, it is not enough to adopt the rhetorical grandiloquence of *A las ruinas de Itálica*" (*Del surrealismo*, p. 160). For readings of the motif in European literary history, see Jean Starobinski, "Melancholy among the Ruins," in *The Invention of Liberty, 1700-1789*, trans. Bernard C. Swift (Geneva: Albert Skira, 1964), pp. 179-81; Laurence Goldstein, *Ruins and Empire* (Pittsburgh: University of Pittsburgh Press, 1977); and Thomas McFarland, *Romanticism and the Forms of Ruin* (Princeton: Princeton University Press, 1980).

[32] *Poesía y estilo de Pablo Neruda* (1940; Buenos Aires: Sudamericana, 1968), p. 355. The poem appears in *Tercera residencia* (1947), I, 284.

Pablo Neruda: The Poetics of Prophecy

common subject, there are no identifiable allusions to the earlier poem, of course, but the difference between the two texts, like the difference between the "Canto" and Caro's "Canción," emphasizes the implied link between the figure of ruins and historical consciousness. Ruins are not simply the wasteland that occasions nostalgic laments but historical signs that, being marks of transience, render their presence paradoxical and their meaning far from certain. "In the ruin," Walter Benjamin notes, "history has physically merged into the setting. And in this guise history does not assume the form of the process of an eternal life so much as that of irresistible decay."[33] Benjamin's definition of ruins as the union of history and nature clarifies for us the speaker's feelings of synthesis when he first sees Machu Picchu. But Benjamin's further comment serves to remind us as well that such permanent meaningfulness is merely an initial impression, and that whatever significance the synthesis of nature and culture may portend is threatened by the simultaneous sense of "irresistible decay." The last two stanzas are instructive in this regard. Whereas the canto begins with the recognition of the site as the source of a privileged synthesis, it ends by acknowledging the irretrievable loss of that source:

> Miro las vestiduras y las manos,
> el vestigio del agua en la oquedad sonora,
> la pared suavizada por el tacto de un rostro
> que miró con mis ojos las lámparas terrestres,
> que aceitó con mis manos las desaparecidas
> maderas: porque todo, ropaje, piel, vasijas,
> palabras, vino, panes,
> se fue, cayó a la tierra.
>
> Y el aire entró con dedos
> de azahar sobre todos los dormidos:
> mil años de aire, meses, semanas de aire,
> de viento azul, de cordillera férrea,
> que fueron como suaves huracanes de pasos
> lustrando el solitario recinto de la piedra. [I, 336]

---

[33] *The Origin of German Tragic Drama*, trans. John Osborne (1928; London: NLB, 1977), pp. 177–78. Benjamin's chapter "Allegory and Trauerspiel" (pp. 159–235) discusses the ruin as part of baroque poetics.

Prophecy of Writing

> I look at the vestments and the hands, / the vestiges of water in the sonorous emptiness, / the wall softened by the touch of a face / that looked with my eyes at the terrestrial lamps, / that oiled with my hands the disappeared / wood: because everything, apparel, skin, vessels, / words, wine, bread, / was gone, fallen to earth. / And the air entered with fingers / of orange blossom over all the sleeping ones: / a thousand years of wind, months, weeks of air, / of blue wind, of ferreous mountain chain, / which were like soft hurricanes of steps / polishing the solitary precinct of the stone.

The first of these stanzas in particular is often cited as proof of the speaker's empathy with the ruins, an empathy said to be revealed, for example, by the speaker's exchange of his own eyes and hands for those of an ancient dweller's. It is this exchange that ostensibly grounds the poem's sense of cultural kinship and participation in history and assigns this particular meaning to the speaker's encounter with the ruins. That this interpretation should be applied to a meditation on the loss signified by the ruins is all the more surprising when we consider the precise terms of the encounter. For it is not so much that the speaker sees and touches through the dweller as the reverse: it is the dweller that sees and touches through the speaker. Far from describing a moment of empathy that locates the act of perception within the subject, the poem displaces this act onto a fictional entity whose only attribute is pure anteriority. What seems to convey a sense of immediacy actually constitutes an acknowledgment of the past as the loss of presence. This negative reversal seems to be confirmed in part by both the end of the first stanza, whose catalogue includes the loss of language ("palabras"), and the end of the last, which hints at the same meaning by personifying the wind with the image of "dedos / de azahar." If the ruins' historical meaning rests entirely on this moment of "empathy," then it appears to be condemned to self-delusion. But it is not so much that the poem excludes the possibility of such identification as that its historical sense is based on a more tangible structure.

The seventh canto develops this overwhelming sense of loss by dwelling on the historical oblivion into which the ruins have fallen. As canto VI hinted at this oblivion in the fall of cultural objects, so historical death now appears as a total collapse:

Pablo Neruda: The Poetics of Prophecy

Muertos de un solo abismo, sombras de una hondonada,
la profunda, es así como al tamaño
de vuestra magnitud
vino la verdadera, la más abrasadora
muerte y desde las rocas taladradas,
desde los capiteles escarlata,
desde los acueductos escalares
os desplomásteis como en un otoño
en una sola muerte.
Hoy el aire vacío ya no llora,
ya no conoce vuestros pies de arcilla,
ya olvidó vuestros cántaros que filtraban el cielo
cuando lo derramaban los cuchillos del rayo,
y el árbol poderoso fue comido
por la niebla y cortado por la racha.   [I, 336]

Dead of a single abyss, shadows of a chasm, / the deep, thus it is as if to the size / of your magnitude / came the true, the most burning / death, and from the pierced rocks, / from the scarlet pilasters, / from the laddered aqueducts / you collapsed as in an autumn / in a single death. / Today the empty air no longer weeps, / no longer knows your feet of clay, / has forgotten your jugs that filtered the sky / when the lightning knives spilled it, / and the powerful tree was devoured / by fog and cut down by the wind.

The collective nature of this oblivion—variously stressed in the series "*solo* abismo," "*una* hondonada," "*sola* muerte," and the climactic "árbol poderoso"—is as important as the description of "la verdadera, la más abrasadora / muerte," which appears here in pointed contrast to the earlier Rilkean "pequeña muerte." Indeed, the contrast is pointed enough to suggest a moral hierarchy that makes individual mortality, as portrayed in the first half of the poem, appear insignificant in comparison with the magnitude of cultural annihilation. Nor should we miss the highly suggestive terms in which the metaphor of structural collapse is couched—the crescendo of prepositional phrases and the pertinent architectural terminology. The beginning of the canto constitutes, in dramatic terms, the speaker's imaginative reconstruction of the process by which the culture was destroyed. It enacts, in other words, the *re*construction of a *de*struction. One may thus be tempted, upon realizing the

Prophecy of Writing

metaphorical implications of this image, to view this moment as the first stage of a healing process in which the poet's imaginative conjuring reverses the effects of physical decay. No such reversal is evident, however, and we must regard this confluence of opposite forces as another instance of simultaneous presence and absence in the speaker's perception of the ruined landscape. As the initial impression of synthesis yielded an acknowledgment of loss, so this moment betrays a positive insight that refuses to surrender any negative knowledge.

Once again the poem recognizes the "irresistible decay," the inscription of death that plagues historical meaning and that ruins embody in an exemplary sense. That the passage constitutes a comment on history is conveyed in part by the architectural metaphor, which implies the presence of the city, the site of historical commerce. However positive the later invocation of the city may be, we must identify this particular instance as part of the theme of downfall or collapse which dominates the first two stanzas. It appears in the images of "abismo" and "hondonada," for example, along with the definitive main verb, the cutting down of the "árbol poderoso," and the recurrent variations on *caer*. These variations on the idea of collapse emphasize, of course, the tragedy of cultural loss, but in addition they serve to dramatize further the etymology of the word "ruin" (from Latin *ruere*, to fall, to rush down, to break into fragments) as a summary of the downward movement that begins in the sixth canto. In fact, as we identify the ascending and descending movements that are described by cantos VI and VII, we discover that they are mirror images. The ascent in the first half of canto VI matches the descent in the corresponding stanzas in canto VII, while the descent in the second half of canto VI matches the ascent (or at least the leveling off) in the remaining stanzas of canto VII. The formal parallel serves more than just a gratuitous symmetry. It conveys the precise significance that the speaker attaches to the ruins. That is, the metaphor of structural collapse provides a scale model of the descent that the speaker endures in the first half of the poem. The ruins embody, in a sense, a miniature mirror in which the speaker sees himself— only he never mistakes this reflection for a sign of self-presence, as we saw earlier, but understands it as a negative representation.

Pablo Neruda: The Poetics of Prophecy

This particular analogy holds broader implications for the poem's narrative strategy. As the analogies in the earlier cantos disrupt narrative illusion, so the parallel between dramatic descent and structural collapse upsets the sense of duration. The pilgrim does not simply arrive at the ruins: he himself is the ruin of a man. Indeed, the recurrence of narrative disruption cannot be simply dismissed as one of the necessary inconveniences of allegorical discourse. Nor can we assume, when we consider its further rhetorical implications, that they merely locate a couple of blind spots in the text—moments, that is, of undecidability which unravel the poem's ontological pretensions. The disruptions we have so far encountered appear, on the contrary, within two radically negative passages whose own discursive logic and mutual correspondence rest on the acknowledgment of nothingness. The encounter with the ruins does not neutralize the speaker's descent, as one might wish, but rather confirms its radically negative meaning. Nor is it enough to interpret these passages as evidence of the unfolding of an internal allegory, a kind of "anatomy" of the self's spiritual change. We must, in addition, consider the contextual effect of these disruptions and view what would otherwise seem restricted to a dramatic enactment as an extended commentary on literary history.

It seems hardly coincidental that both moments should climax densely allusive passages. The earlier shift from abstract meditation to concrete symbol, for example, invoked the poetry of ruins while bringing to a close the series of allusions to *Residencia* and their complicity with Rilkean death. The second instance, whose wider range derives from the analogy between ruins and descent, alludes to the same tradition, with specific reference to Caro's poem. Indeed, Neruda's "hoy el aire vacío ya no llora" seems to be a subtle rewriting of Caro's "¿Cómo en el cerco vago / de su desierta arena / el gran pueblo no suena?" (How is it that in the vague arena / of its deserted sand / the great populace no longer is heard?).[34] Both passages also occur within contexts of architectural ecphrasis; both represent, that is, attempts to identify a voice in the otherwise mute ruins. In fact,

---

[34]Quoted from *Renaissance and Baroque Poetry of Spain*, ed. Elias L. Rivers (New York: Dell, 1965), p. 248.

Prophecy of Writing

Neruda's displacement of the ecphrasis motif onto canto VIII seems to echo the strategy used by Caro, who deferred the motif until his own fifth stanza and there developed a macabre dramatization of *vox populi*.[35] Finally, the inclusion of "sílabas raídas" (effaced syllables, reminiscent of the "palabras" of canto VI) among the fallen objects reinforces the allusion through the same motif. This dense textual reminiscence prepares us for its development in cantos VIII and IX and also sets the stage for the more immediate revisionary twist in the last two stanzas:

> Pero una permanencia de piedra y de palabra:
> la ciudad como un vaso se levantó en las manos
> de todos, vivos, muertos, callados, sostenidos
> de tanta muerte, un muro, de tanta vida un golpe
> de pétalo de piedra: la rosa permanente, la morada:
> este arrecife andino de colonias glaciales.
>
> Cuando la mano de color de arcilla
> se convirtió en arcilla, y cuando los pequeños párpados se
>   cerraron
> llenos de ásperos muros, poblados de castillos,
> y cuando todo el hombre se enredó en su agujero,
> quedó la exactitud enarbolada:
> el alto sitio de la aurora humana:
> la más alta vasija que contuvo el silencio:
> una vida de piedra después de tantas vidas.   [I, 337]

But a permanence of stone and of word: / the city like a cup was lifted in the hands / of everyone, the living, the dead, the silent, all held up / by so much death, a wall, from so much life a blow / from a stone petal: the permanent rose, the dwelling place: / this Andean reef of glacial colonies. / When the clay-colored hand / became clay, and when the small eyelids closed / full of rough walls, peopled with castles, / and when all of humanity became entangled in its hole, / exactness was lifted up: / the high place of the human dawn: / the highest vessel that contained silence: / a life of stone after so many lives.

---

[35]For discussions of ecphrasis, see Jean H. Hagstrum, *The Sister Arts* (Chicago: University of Chicago Press, 1958), pp. 18 and 49–50, and Emilie L. Bergmann, *Art Inscribed: Essays on Ecphrasis in Spanish Golden Age Poetry* (Cambridge: Harvard University Press, 1979).

Rhetorically, the passage shifts from the imaginative reconstruction of decay to that of physical endurance. The entire canto (indeed, the entire poem) pivots on the opening conjunction, which, more than the earlier "entonces" of canto VI, infuses the rhetorical shift with the thrust of a moral choice. By valorizing the ruins' physical endurance, the speaker implicitly rejects the fallen quality that earlier had attracted him. As the ruins' decay provided a metaphor for his own spiritual descent, so now their endurance gives value to spiritual lapse as the cost of a redeeming knowledge.

We shall see shortly that this revisionary tendency, which overflows into the next canto, has an even wider range. For the moment, however, we must beware of mistaking this stage of illusionless awareness for self-delusion. The revision of the motifs that underpin the poetry of ruins does not simply reverse its pervasive nihilism but rather identifies a glimmer of redemption in the dark acknowledgment of "irresistible decay." The passage carefully alternates units of life and death: offsetting the positive series "palabra," "vaso," "vivos," "sostenidos," and "permanente" are the negative "piedra," "muertos," "callados," "glaciales," and "silencio." This complex rendering is more than just a playful balance of words associated with life and death. It conveys the sense that the burden of a historical consciousness and its authentic moral choice rest on the acknowledgment of death itself as a sign of possibility—the "word" despite and because of the "stone." Thus it is the city, the traditional metaphor for history, that the hands of the living and the dead raise like a vessel. This "vaso," which counterbalances the earlier "copa negra" (I, 333) of Rilkean death, becomes the symbol for collective historical meaning. Whatever the Christian connotations of the image, its difference from the earlier figure rests on the erasure of a negative adjective and its reduction to pure instrumentality.[36] As collective death lays the bricks of a wall, so does its infusing life provide the petals of a "rosa permanente," traditionally the symbol of authenticity.[37] Both this image and the following "morada" fuse the life–death

---

[36]For a discussion of the Christian resonance of this image, see Pring-Mill, "Preface," *Heights of Macchu Picchu*, pp. xiv–xv.

[37]For an interesting survey, see Barbara Seward, *The Symbolic Rose* (New York: Columbia University Press, 1960).

Prophecy of Writing

balance into single metaphors. While "rosa permanente" fuses two opposites, "morada" brings together the etymological cognates of dwelling and death—*morare* and *morire*.

The second stanza describes this balance at its moment of crystallization. Just as the death of the ancient dweller appears, in a slight variation of the biblical commonplace (Gen. 3:19), as the fulfillment of a metaphorical cycle, Machu Picchu's "fall" fits a pattern of poetic justice in that it affords an "exactitud enarbolada." The latter term, which recalls the earlier "árbol poderoso" and thus implies a reversal of the "otoño" in the prologue, conveys Machu Picchu's synthesis of height and ruins, rise and fall. And as the canto ends, it is the altitude of the site, in the images of "alto sitio" and "alta vasija," that remains with us. Indeed, it is assumed in the first line of the next canto: "Sube conmigo, amor americano" (Climb up with me, American love) (I, 337).

To be sure, the metaphor of height appears in the poem's title and dominates the apostrophe to the ruins. In addition, the anonymous landscape of canto IV had itself prefigured an elevated topography ("vertiginosa carretera espiral," "escala de la tierra"). Not until the end of this particular canto, however, where height offsets the ruins' fall, do we get a dramatic sense of the theme. It could be said, in any case, that the motif of altitude is what distinguishes the poem from beginning to end. And while one could easily dismiss it as an empirical description of Machu Picchu, we must recall that in the poem landscape acquires an allegorical function to the point of constituting the metaphor for the speaker's internal state. By the time the eighth canto acknowledges this heightened state, then, the landscape has already become a dramatic vehicle for the speaker's conversion and thus acquires a precise allusive function that recalls the *locus classicus* of ascent: Dante's *Purgatorio*.

Critics have often noted the strong Dantean echo in *Alturas* and throughout *Canto General*, but the exact implications of this relationship still await a reading that does not betray its complexity.[38] We should note, as a first step, that the echo of *Pur-*

---

[38]See Goić, "*Alturas de Macchu Picchu*," p. 155. Roberto Fernández Retamar noted the Dantean echo in his "Prologue" to Pablo Neruda, *Poesías* (Havana: Casa de las Américas, 1965). Perhaps the earliest to notice the presence of Dante was Sarandy Cabrera, "Primera teoría del *Canto General*," *Número*, 13-14 (1951), 189-95.

gatorio, the *cantica* of the celebration of art and of poetry, serves as a bridge for the poem's revision of literary history and alters retrospectively our perception of the first half of the poem. The events there, in which the speaker wanders through a dark forest of alienation and falls into a total descent, amount in effect to an analogue of the *Inferno*. In his famous prologue scene, we should recall, Dante dramatizes the bankruptcy of Neoplatonic philosophical ascents in the pilgrim's failure to climb, in a first attempt, "il dilettoso monte" (the delectable mountain). In Plato's *Republic*, for example, the philosopher is the one who knows, and his knowledge consists of realizing the deceptiveness of the flickering shadows on the sides of the cave. It is this knowledge that, for Plato, redeems the philosopher and defines his ascent as the unchaining of the mind from the fetters of the body. By having the pilgrim fail at this purely intellectual ascent, Dante in effect rewrites Plato's metaphoric or philosophical itinerary of the mind, thus requiring that it become an internal spiritual process, cleansed of all pride, as a descent or turning upside down of the earlier philosophical scheme.[39] The pilgrim's failed attempt is a fall into the wilderness or spiritual ruin, akin to Adam's, which Dante describes with the metaphorical scheme that Neruda exploits in his own poem: "mentre ch'i *ruinavo* in basso loco" (while I fell back to the lower place) (l. 61; my italics). In the *Purgatorio,* only after descending through the depths of Hell and emerging from its bottom, does the pilgrim ascend. The ascent, at this point in the allegory, signifies a moral purgation of the cardinal sins, which are inscribed, with seven P's (for *peccatum,* offense) on the pilgrim's forehead. Each of these letters, in turn, is erased as the pilgrim climbs, with the aid of several agents, the seven terraces of Mount Purgatory and at last gains the summit where the earthly paradise is lodged: "Qui fu inocente l'umana radice / qui primavera sempre ed ogni fruto" (Here the human root was innocent / here was always spring and always fruit) (*Purgatorio,* XXVIII, ll. 142–43). It could

---

[39]For this background see John Freccero, "Dante's Prologue Scene," *Dante Studies,* 84 (1966), 1–25. Giuseppe Mazzotta argues that Dante's detour from the abstractions of Neoplatonism must in addition be read in relation to the turn to history that is signaled by the pilgrim's encounter with Vergil and the historical world of the Aeneid. See *Dante, Poet of the Desert: History and Allegory in the Divine Comedy* (Princeton: Princeton University Press, 1979), pp. 152–57.

be said that the two ascents, the abortive journey of the prologue and the successful climb of the *Purgatorio,* provide the dramatic underpinning of the entire *Commedia.* For, as Charles Singleton has shown, much of the poem's significance rests on the difference between the two attempts: one simply an ascent, the other an ascent that succeeds.[40]

We could regard Neruda's use of Dante as a condensed rearrangement of the *Commedia*'s three *cantiche.* Excluding the prologue, cantos II through V correspond to the descent of the *Inferno,* VI through IX to the ascent of the *Purgatorio,* and X through XII to the *Paradiso.* One need not press this general correspondence, of course, to realize that Neruda's poem principally refers to the *Purgatorio.* Besides being suggested in the reference to altitude in Neruda's title, the second *cantica* is suggested in the seven cantos that make up the latter half of the poem (cantos VI through XII), which evoke the seven terraces of Mount Purgatory. In both poems, Dante's and Neruda's, the ascent signifies the central experience of purgation; but the motives for the ascent differ. Whereas in the *Commedia* the pilgrim expiates the sins of moral blindness, in *Alturas* he atones for the errors of cultural alienation, a blindness that has kept him from seeing the true way of pre-Columbian origins. This difference explains each pilgrim's vision: Dante discovers, at the summit of Mount Purgatory, the Garden of Eden, while Neruda, high atop the Andes, looks upon a garden made of ruins, the spectacle of historical signs. Dante adopted the scheme of prophetic ascent both in reaction to earlier philosophical tradition and in borrowing from pertinent biblical passages and patristic tradition.[41] After Dante, of course, the tradition of ascent is so widespread that one need not refer to its original model. It includes, among others, the Renaissance ascents of Petrarch, St. John of the Cross, and Camões, the Romantic prospects in Rousseau, Wordsworth, Schiller, and Nietzsche, and the modern and postmodern versions by Thomas Mann and Jack Kerouac. It is clear, in any case, that

---

[40]"*De exitu Israel de Aegypto,*" in *Dante: A Collection of Critical Essays,* ed. John Freccero (Englewood Cliffs, N.J.: Prentice-Hall, 1970), p. 110.

[41]For Dante's biblical sources see Carol V. Kaske, "Mount Sinai and Dante's Mount Purgatory," *Dante Studies,* 89 (1971), 1-18.

Alturas belongs to this tradition and that it constitutes a modern, secular version of the *peregrinatio,* the parable of the Prodigal Son's long journey toward home, which M. H. Abrams describes as "an education in experience which culminates on the level of intellectual maturity . . . [and] in which the protagonist finally learns who he is, what he was born for and the implicit purpose of all he has endured on the way."[42]

Still, it is in reference to the *Purgatorio* that Neruda's revision achieves its greatest significance. The least obvious meaning, perhaps, is related to the rewriting of *Residencia en la tierra,* whose temporal argument now is amended by the pressures of purgatorial experience. Whereas time in *Residencia* dispersed the self into fragments that could be rescued only by an aesthetic project, the purgatorial scheme of *Alturas* posits a teleological thrust that lends time a moral urgency. Besides providing a "realm of possibility, where the spiral topography summarizes spiritual motives,"[43] purgatorial time translates the speaker into the human community, turning his aesthetic gratification to ethical care and his temporal fear to historical trust. Moreover, Neruda's use of Dante's topography obliquely makes Machu Picchu a site of earthly redemption. If we recall further details of Dante's imaginary geography, Mount Purgatory was an island at the farthest remove from Jerusalem, the city located at the center of the world according to the description of Ezekiel 5:5. In the medieval conception, the antipodes formed the diametrical obverse of the Northern Hemisphere and occupied a fourth, condemned space, separated from Adam and Christ by an impassable ocean, which did not fit the trinitary geography that was upheld by the church fathers. *Inferno* XXXIV, in particular, provides the geological allegory of the Southern Hemisphere's origin as the hollow made by the earth's flight as it sought to avoid contact with Satan during his fall. A mountain island was thus formed as the earth's bowels rushed upward toward the south, and there deposited, atop the only land in the lower hemisphere, the earthly paradise. Thus in a gesture ultimately

---

[42] *Natural Supernaturalism: Tradition and Revolution in Romantic Literature* (New York: Norton, 1971), pp. 193-94. For a partial reading of the tradition of ascent, see Marjorie H. Nicolson, *Mountain Gloom and Mountain Glory* (Ithaca: Cornell University Press, 1959).

[43] Ricardo J. Quiñones, *The Renaissance Discovery of Time* (Cambridge: Harvard University Press, 1972), p. 72.

Prophecy of Writing

intended as a metaphorical redemption of the antipodes, Dante locates Eden, the scene of man's fall, at a point directly opposite Jerusalem, the scene of man's redemption: "contraposto a quel che la gran secca / coverchia e sotto 'l cui colmo consunto / fu l'uom che nacque e visse senze pecca" (Opposite that where spreads the continent / of land, underneath whose meridian perished / The man who sinless came and sinless went).[44]

It takes no particularly scientific mind to deduce that what medieval geography called the antipodes is what today we know as the Western Hemisphere. As Edmundo O'Gorman has shown, in a definitive contribution to historiography, the antipodes were the mythical prefiguration of the New World, an *orbis alterius* whose existence was "invented" before it was actually discovered.[45] A trenchant revisionary pattern thus emerges with Neruda's metaphorical association of Machu Picchu with Purgatory. By locating in concrete space what in Dante is but a figure derived from theological tradition, Neruda confronts the West with its own otherness and makes it stumble upon the fiction it once expelled. Not only does this gesture have the effect of bringing paradise down to earth in order to show us, through a meditation on ruins, its necessarily historical meaning, but it rescues the very concept of "New World" from the stigma to which the antipodes doctrine condemned it. Machu Picchu's physical permanence goes beyond the redemption of an American space from theological fallenness to dissolve the figurative opposition between Jerusalem and the earthly paradise within a scheme of concrete human history.[46]

Neruda's recourse to Dante, then, is intended both to exalt

---

[44]I quote from *La Divina Commedia*, ed. C. H. Grandgent and rev. Charles S. Singleton (Cambridge: Harvard University Press, 1972), p. 307. For the sources of Dante's geographical/logical allegory, see John G. Demaray, *The Invention of Dante's Commedia* (New Haven: Yale University Press, 1974), pp. 154-68; Rodolfo Bernini, "Origine, sito, forma e dimensioni del Monte del Purgatorio e dell'Inferno dantesco," *Rendiconti della Reale Accademia di Lincei*, 5th ser., 25 (1916), 1015-1129; and Edward R. Moore, "The Geography of Dante," in *Studies of Dante*, 3d ser., *Miscellaneous Essays* (1903; rpt. New York: Greenwood Press, 1968), pp. 109-43.

[45]*The Invention of America: An Inquiry into the Historical Nature of the New World* (Bloomington: Indiana University Press, 1961).

[46]It could be shown, of course, that Neruda's text remains partially blind to Dante's own historical interpretation of Eden, which in *Purgatorio* appears as "a place of radical ambiguity... that shatters its seemingly idyllic quality" (Mazzotta, *Dante*, p. 114).

Pablo Neruda: The Poetics of Prophecy

Machu Picchu and to emphasize the poem's redemptive act. This redemption takes place, as we have seen, within and through a dense network of texts that duplicates, at the level of reading, the historical revision proposed by the poem. For this reason it becomes all the more significant that critics who noted this strong Dantean echo should have suggested the influence of Rubén Darío's "Visión" (1907), an overtly Dantean poem that describes the symbolist poet's ascent to a realm of pure poetry.[47] In adducing this influence, Neruda's critics assumed Darío's mediation of Dante almost as if to suggest that one must justify the *Commedia*'s passage through Latin American literary history before taking note of Neruda's own statement. Juan Larrea, for example, thought Darío's echo so strong that he collated the two poems and denounced Neruda's virtual quotations as further proof of his betrayal of an Americanist sensibility.[48] Yet the link between the two poems, I submit, is part of a revisionary strategy that includes Darío's Romantic tradition as well as Dante. For contrary to Larrea's defense, Darío's poem eschews all geographical reference for a world of pure poetry in which the *Paradiso* represents the symbolist ideal of nonrepresentation. Larrea's defense of Darío on the precise grounds that his poem rejected becomes, in fact, all the more puzzling in view of the fact that Neruda's revision challenges Darío's nonmimetic reading by opposing the importance of the *Purgatorio* (the only one of the three *cantiche* that takes place in time) to the ostensible superiority of the *Paradiso*.[49]

It is not in reference to Darío, however, that we can best detect Neruda's challenge to Romanticism, but in reference to José María Heredia and his "En el teocalli de Cholula" (On the Pyramid of Cholula) (1820), whose synthesis of visionary perspective and lamentation over a ruin make it even more clearly an antecedent. The setting for Heredia's ode, a *locus classicus* of Americanist poetry, is a ruined pre-Columbian

---

[47]The echo of Darío is mentioned by Goić, "*Alturas de Maćchu Picchu,*" p. 155, and Larrea, *Del surrealismo,* pp. 176–79. The text of the poem appears in Rubén Darío, *Poesías Completas,* ed. Alfonso Méndez Plancarte and Antonio Oliver Belmás (Madrid: Aguilar, 1968), pp. 720–22.

[48]Larrea, *Del surrealismo a Machupicchu,* pp. 179.

[49]Ibid., p. 178. Larrea, moreover, grants Darío the revision of Dante which he denies Neruda (see p. 176). But in doing so he reveals that his reading of Darío is colored by his reading of Neruda.

Prophecy of Writing

pyramid on which the poet sits in meditation. What begins as a pre-Romantic argument on the analogy of self and landscape soon turns into the typical Neoclassical tirade against tyranny and superstition. However much Heredia may have intended this poem as an allegory of contemporary Mexican politics, its focus on Indian ruins as the vehicle for abuse stigmatized them as the vestiges of a barbarous civilization whose time was past. Underlying Heredia's poem is a providential ideology that views the ruins as a lesson on pagan instincts and implicitly justifies the virtual annihilation of Indian culture that occurred during the Conquest. Even the most cursory comparison between the two poems reveals how Neruda inverts Heredia's prejudice in order to defend that culture's historical significance: "permanencia de piedra y de palabra" seems to be a distant response to Heredia's "Muda y desierta / ahora te ves, pirámide" (Silent and deserted / you find yourself now, pyramid) with which the ruins are condemned.[50]

Heredia's Christian argument is also heir to the providential vision that permeates much of the earlier poetry of ruins, in which the fall of Rome was seen as a sign of divine justice. Rodrigo Caro's "Canción," for example, ends with an invocation of San Geroncio, Itálica's prelate and martyr, a poignant ending that suggests that the ruins attest to God's wrathful vengeance. The same theme recurs in at least one other famous ruins poem, Juan de Arguijo's "A Cartago," which adduces a temporal parallel between the ruins' lesson on antiquity and their future witnessing of Christ's Second Coming.[51] This mixture of praise and moral condemnation generally reflects the Renaissance ambivalence toward the ancient past: its physical accomplishments were revered while its pagan values were condemned. But what on the surface appears to be mere thematic coincidence is actually the appearance of a major biblical topos, *occidit urbis*, the fall of the city, which not only clarifies

---

[50]José María Heredia, *Poesías completas,* ed. Angel Aparicio Laurencio (Miami: Universal, 1970), p. 195.

[51]See *Renaissance and Baroque Poetry of Spain*, pp. 350-51; and Juan de Arguijo's sonnet: "Ejemplo cierto fue en la edad pasada, / y será fiel testigo a la futura, / del fin que ha de tener la más segura / Pujanza vanamente confiada" (True example it was in times gone by, / and will be faithful witness in future times, / to the end that awaits the surest / ambition, vainly self-confident) (p. 143).

Heredia's argument but provides a rhetorical clue to the prophetic message of *Alturas*. Ruins, in the Old Testament, symbolize God's retribution for Israel's transgression of its covenant as a chosen people. The prophets repeatedly interpret the physical devastation of Jerusalem, whether by military or natural disaster, as God's wrathful response to Israel's apostasy, to the spiritual waywardness that is manifest in its recurrent fall into idolatry. As the architectural metaphor stands throughout the Bible for confidence in God and obedience to his commands, so ruins symbolize Israel's waywardness and disobedience.[52] One can hardly exaggerate, then, the rhetorical importance of this imagery for the redemptive scheme of Neruda's poem. The ruins motif provides a discreet contrast between this biblical metaphor for apostasy and Machu Picchu's cultural faithfulness. Indeed, Machu Picchu's historical meaning lies precisely in the fact that it symbolizes cultural sameness, another meaning of the "permanence" invoked in canto VII. Though discreet, the difference is pointed enough to convey, within the poem's redemptive argument, both the undeserved punishment to which Machu Picchu was subjected and the profound injustice to which its inhabitants fell victim.

From the poetry of ruins, to Dante, to Heredia and Darío, to the Old Testament, the poem's revisionary scope thus coincides with the speaker's access to cultural self-awareness as a Latin American. One cannot miss the paradox inherent in this strategy as the Western library is called upon to represent, with

[52]For a striking contrast see Isaiah 28:16 ("Behold, I lay in Zion for a foundation, a stone, a tried stone, a precious corner stone, a sure foundation: he that believeth shall not make haste"), in contrast to Isaiah 25:2 ("For thou hast made of a city an heap; of a defenced city a ruin, a palace of strangers to be no city"). "The foundation stone," according to J. Lindblom, "means confidence in Yaweh, the walls mean justice and confidence and righteousness.... Those who understood and practised this religion would be saved from ruin, while the "scoffers,' those who made lies their refuge, would perish" (*Prophecy in Ancient Israel* [Philadelphia: Fortress Press, 1962], pp. 342–43). For a different reading in terms of the theme of *fiat justitia, pereat mundus*, see Abraham J. Heschel, *The Prophets* (New York: Harper & Row, 1955), pp. 279–306. The motif appears in both St. Augustine (*The City of God*, XV, 4) and Orosius (*History against the Pagans*, V, i) as a scheme of salvation history. More recently it reappears as a political metaphor. See especially C. F. Volney, *Les ruines, ou Méditations sur les révolutions des empires* (1791), and the examples cited in Goldstein, *Ruins and Empire*.

all its authority, the unspoiled signs of pre-Columbian culture. How valid, one might ask, is the claim to Latin American self-awareness if it can be voiced only through Western literary traditions? Would not the adoption of these texts, as rhetorical strategies, signal instead a literary self-consciousness that preempts any such claim? If the pilgrim truly atones for cultural error, and if the literary revisions indeed constitute a conversion, how can such a densely allusive text become the vehicle for authentic change? None of these questions can be answered with the handy dialectical formulas of the "tradition and originality" type, for the poem poses nothing less than the possibility of subverting the imperialism of Western literary history. Nor can one ignore the truly problematic nature of these allusions. For if gaining access to Machu Picchu's meaning allows Latin America to wipe the slate clean of all Western prejudice and make a new beginning, then it would seem that the speaker's conversion ought to deny all Western signs, including the very allusions that form (and subvert) his own writing. When Neruda recalls his first visit to Machu Picchu and says that all other ruins seemed bookish in comparison, he implies that neither Machu Picchu nor his poem were bookish. But then why write an allegory, the most bookish or overtly fictional of literary texts?

Paradox, then, may well be the figure that describes the poem's rhetorical tension, its seemingly outrageous claim for cultural immediacy, but it is paradox, nevertheless, that lends coherence to its argument and forms the core of its statement on history. The answer (although not the solution) to this apparent impasse is provided by the next two cantos, in which the speaker, now converted to his new allegiance, takes up the task of translating the ruins' silent message. Indeed, translation seems to be the best description not only for the dramatic movement of the next two cantos, but for the speaker's insistence on seeing beyond the reified matter of the ruins and achieving a redemptive interpretation. The first step in this poetics of translation[53] is the summoning of "amor americano," Machu Picchu's genius of place. Neruda's alliterative name, we

---

[53] I borrow the term from John Freccero, "Medusa: The Letter and the Spirit," *Yearbook of Italian Studies*, 1 (Florence, 1962), 17, who uses it in contrast to a "poetics of reification."

should note, poetically motivates the two words and valorizes *americano* through *amor*. More important, the series of imperatives throughout the canto, of which "sube" is the first, shifts the tone from passive description to restrained urgency. Whether the invitation to climb addresses only the genius of place or includes the speaker as well is left unclear. The ambiguity, at any rate, is significant. By using the present tense of the same verb that in canto VI was used in the present perfect ("Entonces en la escala de la tierra *he subido*") (I, 335), another instance of narrative disruption is suggested. This time, however, the shift in tense conveys the specifically temporal nature of the disruption, a distinction that in context emphasizes its link to the poem's cultural allegory. As the ruined landscape proved earlier to be a projection of the speaker's internal state, so now his pilgrimage turns out to be a necessary illusion—he has been there all along. That is, as an allegory the poem has unfolded an atemporal awareness of cultural values as a "successive mode capable of engendering duration."[54] The recurrent disruptions, of which this latest one is perhaps the most revealing, expose the illusionary quality of duration. And while such exposure may redefine the manner of the conversion, it does not invalidate what is ultimately an epistemological adjustment in the speaker. What it does threaten is the status of the cultural allegory, which is thereby implied to be just as illusionary. That is, the notion of process is retained symbolically despite the disappearance of the hierarchy of values and objectives.

Whatever the further implications of these disruptions may be, they occur as the speaker evokes, in the word's precise etymological sense of calling forth, the genius of place. And his second plea, "Besa conmigo las piedras secretas" (Kiss with me the secret stones) (I, 337), conveys the desire to decipher the ruins jointly. Similarly, the Urubamba River, the apostrophe to which dominates the canto, embodies the genius itself as it magically flies pollen back to its point of origin. The topos of *genius loci*, as Geoffrey Hartman has shown, is intrinsically related to "vision and prophecy: to determining the destiny of an individual or nation." Moreover, to invoke the genius of landscape prepares us, as we shall see, for "a deeper, ceremonial merging

---

[54]De Man, "Rhetoric of Temporality," p. 207.

Prophecy of Writing

of the poet's spirit and the spirit of place."[55] The Urubamba is presented as a guardian genius and also, therefore, as a historian who, like the Muse of epic poetry, will disclose to the poet the history of the site. To this end the canto suggests the river's eloquence by setting up a contrast between its thunderous "plata torrencial" (torrential silver) and "sonoro pedernal andino" (sonorous Andean flint), on the one hand, and the "silencio del cajón serrano" (silence of the mountain strongbox), on the other (I, 337-38). Language, indeed the motivated language of poetry itself (as the lingering recurrence of "Amor, amor" suggests), constitutes the genius' infusing spirit, whose "minúscula vida," a pointed antidote to the earlier "pequeña muerte," the speaker summons for the first of two times in the canto. And as the apostrophe to the river—called Wilkamayu, its Indian name—is about to begin in the fifth stanza, he has already become the blind man ("el hijo ciego de la nieve" [the blind son of the snow]) (I, 338) anticipated in the prologue.

The apostrophe, in the next five stanzas, assumes this linguistic motif as part of the speaker's investigation into the causes of Machu Picchu's ruin:

> Oh, Wilkamayu de sonoros hilos,
> cuando rompes tus truenos lineales
> en blanca espuma, como herida nieve,
> cuando tu vendaval acantilado
> canta y castiga despertando al cielo,
> qué idioma traes a la oreja apenas
> desarraigada de tu espuma andina?
>
> Quién apresó el relámpago del frío
> y lo dejó en la altura encadenado,
> repartido en sus lágrimas glaciales,
> sacudido en sus rápidas espadas,
> golpeando sus estambres aguerridos,
> conducido en su cama de guerrero,
> sobresaltado en su final de roca?
>
> Qué dicen tus destellos acosados?
> Tu secreto relámpago rebelde

---

[55]"Romantic Poetry and the Genius Loci," in *Beyond Formalism: Literary Essays, 1958-1970* (New Haven: Yale University Press, 1970), pp. 314-22.

Pablo Neruda: The Poetics of Prophecy

antes viajó poblado de palabras?
Quién va rompiendo sílabas heladas,
idiomas negros, estandartes de oro,
bocas profundas, gritos sometidos,
en tus delgadas aguas arteriales?

Quién va cortando párpados florales
que vienen a mirar desde la tierra?
Quién precipita los racimos muertos
que bajan en tus manos de cascada
a desgranar su noche desgranada
en el carbón de la geología?   [I, 338-39]

O Wilkamayu of sonorous threads, / when you break your linear thunders / in white froth, like wounded snow, / when your steep storm / sings and punishes awaking the sky, / what language do you bring to the ear hardly / uprooted of your Andean froth? / Who imprisoned the lightning of the cool air / and left it chained on the height, / scattered about in its glacial tears, / shaken in its rapid swords, / striking its battle-scarred fabric, / led out in its warrior's bed, / assailed in its rock's end? / What do your vexed glimmers say? / Your secret, rebellious lightning, / did it once travel full of words? / Who's breaking frozen syllables, / black languages, gold standards, / deep mouths, subdued screams, / in your thin arterial waters? / Who's cutting down floral eyelids / that come to look from the ground? / Who rushes the dead clusters / that descend in your cascade's hands / to scatter their scattered night / in the coal of geology?

We must read this apostrophe in connection with the earlier references to silence as the speaker turns to the river in an effort to gather information that the ruins themselves cannot yield. By thus alternating inquiries into the river's eloquence with those into the site's violent past, the canto suggests a crucial link between language and historical reconstruction. And yet the Urubamba's embodiment of eloquence constitutes an analogy between language and the river's flow, which, like the movement of history itself, will not be arrested and must be understood in its ability to unsettle all stable meanings. For this reason the speaker gives up the goal of finding a specific culprit when he realizes that any attempt at historical reconstruction must face up to the precarious nature of such knowledge. More point-

Politics of the Book

edly, he avoids the temptation of nostalgic idolatry ("no toques la frontera / ni adores la cabeza sumergida" [don't touch the facade / or revere the drowned head]), which would turn the Indian past into a mere fetish, and argues instead for an authentic temporality that faces up to the risks of historicity:

> deja que el tiempo cumpla su estatura
> en su salón de manantiales rotos,
> y, entre el agua veloz y las murallas,
> recoge el aire del desfiladero,
> las paralelas láminas del viento,
> el canal ciego de las cordilleras,
> el áspero saludo del rocío,
> y sube, flor a flor, por la espesura,
> pisando la serpiente despeñada. [I, 339]

> let time accomplish its height / in its room of broken water, / and, between rapid water and the walls, / gather the canyon's air, / the wind's parallel layers, / the blind channel of the mountain range, / the dew's rough greeting, / and arise, flower by flower, through the thickness, / trampling the flung serpent.

To time's erosion the speaker opposes time's own sediment, the cumulative layering that yields, metaphorically at least, Machu Picchu's "stature." Physical decay, that is, cannot be divorced from historical significance because ruins are the place where matter and morality interact. It is therefore to the narrow space somewhere between the river's eloquence and the walls' silence ("entre el agua veloz y las murallas") that the speaker directs the genius of place in a second summons to climb. This second summoning parallels the later imperative in the penultimate stanza,

> Ven a mi propio ser, al alba mía,
> hasta las soledades coronadas.
> El reino muerto vive todavía. [I, 339]

> Come to my own being, to the dawn of me, / up to the crowned solitudes. / The dead kingdom still lives,

which urges the genius of place to join in the poet's rebirth. One cannot simply gloss over this climax. Poetic renewal is shown here to coincide with the last stage in the poetics of translation, a self-investiture that can be described only as a linguistic access to prophecy. Like the singer amid mute objects in "Galope muerto," the prophet sets out to speak on behalf of the ruins, even as the specter of death, symbolized by the condor, threatens to cut that project short: "Y en el Reloj la sombra sanguinaria / del cóndor cruza como una nave negra" (And in the Clock the bloody shadow / of the condor crosses like a black ship) (I, 339). The symbolic bird was prefigured in cantos III and V, but its ominous reappearance against the background of the allegorical "Reloj" harks farther back, to the temporal anxieties of *Residencia en la tierra*. Besides giving a sense of urgency to the prophet's task, the bird's appearance at this juncture serves to demystify any illusions of immortality that might have been implanted by the preceding self-investiture.

It is at this point, then, that canto IX, the intriguing catalogue that Larrea disliked, completes the ecphrastic sequence of cantos VII and VIII. If we have in fact identified in this sequence the various stages of a poetics of translation, then canto IX must be its resulting text. The paratactic catalogue of nominal phrases, especially following a prophetic summoning, suggests a kind of mantic song flowing from a state of ecstasy. Moreover, as Felstiner notes, many of the words in the canto—*ciega, escala, párpado, polen, serpiente, rosa, manantial, muralla*, and so on—are taken from the earlier narrative, as if in an attempt to gather scattered fragments.[56] The catalogue thus translates silence onto poetic presence in the form of a series of descriptions which amounts to a metaphorical reconstruction of the city. The compacting of eighty-one metaphors into one single column, as if it were a stone block, creates a spatial illusion that attests to the translation's success. We cannot miss the specifically visual effect of this ecphrastic mimesis, the result of writing or script (as opposed to the effect of a voice) which in turn depends on the experience of reading. It is the writing/reading metaphor that ultimately guarantees the indelibility of the ruins' message. Instead of merely speaking for them, the prophet now *writes* on their behalf: *verba volant, scripta manent* (words fly, writings remain).

The implications of this metaphor are crucial. In terms of the

[56]Felstiner, *Translating Neruda*, p. 180.

Politics of the Book

poem's statement on history, it signals Machu Picchu's access to Western consciousness as embodied in the institution of writing and its role in the production of historical record. Such access reverses in effect the historical obliteration of Inca culture, which, unlike its Mesoamerican counterparts, had no system of writing. Moreover, the poem shows this historical access to be linked to a process of translation by which the past is transformed, with all its attendant revisions, into the present. It is the act of translation, in fact, that provides the culmination to the earlier revision of literary history by becoming the figure that adopts Western signs as part of a new beginning. And yet it would be naive simply to assume this metaphor as a recuperative process—a healing agency, that is—whose access to historical consciousness would render the ruins present. On the contrary, writing and history appear to be linked in the poem in their common erosion of unmediated presence. Canto IX, in this sense, constitutes a turn against referentiality, against the reality of the ruins, which signals textual autonomy. Not only does the language of the canto violate (as Larrea aptly complained) both empirical reality and cultural propriety, but it offers a verbal analogue whose formal qualities compete with the real Machu Picchu. Besides providing an impeccable ecphrasis, for example, the canto occupies a position in the poem which corresponds to the midpoint of the ascent, halfway between the initial encounter in canto VI and the end of the poem in canto XII. In addition, were we to pursue the specific echo of Dante we would find that, besides alluding to the magical number associated with Beatrice in *La vita nuova*, the ninth canto corresponds to the midpoint of Dante's own ascent, the fourth terrace of Purgatory, where the cardinal sin of acedia or spiritual sloth is cleansed. Acedia, which in Dante means spiritual sloth due to insufficiency of love, is the medieval name for melancholy, which was the "fuel" of prophetic vision in the poetics of *Residencia en la tierra*.[57] Thus the oblique allusion to *Residencia*

---

[57]See Fritz Saxl, Erwin Panofsky, and Raymond Klibansky, *Saturn and Melancholy* (London: Thomas Nelson, 1964), pp. 75-81, for a discussion of the medieval view of melancholy, based primarily on St. Thomas (*Summa Theologiae*, Prima, q. lxiii, art. 2). In *Purgatorio*, the fourth terrace corresponds to Canto XVIII, where the slothful are made to run continually around the terrace. For the mystic significance that Dante attaches to the number 9 (the square of 3, or the Trinity), see *La vita nuova*, especially sections 2 and 3: *The Portable Dante*, ed. Paolo Milano (New York: Viking Press, 1947), pp. 547-51.

Pablo Neruda: The Poetics of Prophecy

within the context of the new poetics of translation itself involves a discreet rewriting that raises the canto above its empirical source.

It is on writing as spacing, then, on the irruptive and irreducible marks that displace presence and significance, that the poem's writing metaphor rests. The poem's translation of silence into language, of historical obliteration into consciousness, itself deconstructs those Western metaphysical assumptions that underlie such concepts as translation and consciousness. Writing as spatial difference, that is, exposes the sign's inherent lack and its need to be supplemented by an endless chain of other signs. And far from being confined to the ecphrasis of canto IX, spacing is everywhere implied by the poem's allegory, which observes a code *outside* the text, as well as by its dense allusive texture, as if supplementing its own ontological lack through other literary texts.[58] It is the difference implied, finally, by the very title of the poem, which not only changes *ruinas* to *alturas*, but also changes *Machu* to *Macchu*, Neruda's own spelling for the Quechua word for "old."

Starting with the poem's publication in 1946 and throughout all four editions of his *Obras Completas*, Neruda ignored the traditional spelling and wrote the name of the site with four *c*'s instead of three. Critics have noticed, though never explained, the unorthodox spelling, and recently it so disturbed one Chilean scholar in particular that, in an edited anthology of poems about Machu Picchu, he changed it to make it conform to the traditional spelling employed by the other authors.[59] No

---

[58] For this view of writing as spacing see Jacques Derrida, *Positions*, trans. Alan Bass (1972; Chicago: University of Chicago Press, 1981): "This interweaving, this textile, is the *text* produced only in the transformation of another text.... Spacing designates *nothing*, nothing that is, no presence at a distance; it is the index of an irreducible exterior, and at the same time of a *movement*, a displacement that indicates an irreducible alterity" (pp. 26, 81). The term "allegory" itself designates a discourse of otherness (from Greek *allos*, other, and *agouerein*, to say), as defined by Isidore of Seville: "Nam allegoria dicitur ab *alleon* graece, quod in latinum dicitur *alienum*" (Allegory comes from the Greek *alleon*, what in Latin is said as *alienum*, other) (*Etymologiarum sive Originem Libri XX*, ed. W. M. Lindsay [Oxford: Clarendon, 1966], I, xxxviii, 220. For a brilliant discussion of the affinity of writing and allegory in terms of a "play of otherness," see Benjamin, *Origin of German Tragic Drama*, pp. 159-67.

[59] See *Machu Picchu en la poesía*, ed. Hugo Montes (Santiago de Chile: Nueva Universidad, 1972). Pring-Mill adds: "The proper spelling of the place name is

Politics of the Book

Quechua dictionary, to be sure, recognizes Neruda's spelling. And while anthropologists report that there are several variants for the orthography of *picchu*, they note a single and consistent one for *machu*.[60]

My point has less to do with the need to observe a "correct" spelling than with this error, so to speak, as an index of the poem's writing metaphor. Neruda's rewriting, we should note, improves visually an otherwise unsymmetrical name. The extra letter in the first word (Machu) supplies a typographical symmetry which, besides conveying a cognate link, points to a numerical correspondence between the twelve letters of the new title and the poem's twelve cantos. As such, the altered name reflects a cosmic balance similar to that of an hourly or monthly cycle and thereby attempts to correct the imbalance of the traditional spelling. In so doing, the new spelling unwittingly mirrors and magnifies the arbitrariness that subverts all attempts to transcribe the sounds of any Amerindian language. In fact, it would be a mistake to speak of a "misspelling," for what is involved here is the very basis of determining Machu Picchu's "proper" name and, beyond that, of the "proper" in general. Indeed, Neruda's disrupting orthography may be but one more turn in the ongoing controversy surrounding the name "Machu Picchu," which anthropologists have long suspected to be a misnomer.[61] By thus suspending semantic depth, by becoming

---

'Machu Picchu,' since the first word does not contain the Quechua guttural represented by the second *c* of Picchu" (*Pablo Neruda: A Basic Anthology*, [Oxford: Dolphin, 1975], p. xxxiii).

[60]Luis E. Valcárcel, *Machu Picchu* (Buenos Aires: EUDEBA, 1964), p. 7. The name in Quechua means the fully grown or old peak, in distinction to Huayna Picchu, the half-grown or young peak, which stands alongside the site of the ruins. In current use *machu* and *huayna* mean grandfather and young man, respectively, and are also used figuratively as comparative terms to distinguish visually the height of Andean peaks.

[61]For a meditation on the "proper name" as the sign of deceptive self-presence, see Jacques Derrida, *Of Grammatology*, trans. Gayatri Chakravorty Spivak (1967; Baltimore: Johns Hopkins University Press, 1976), pp. 101-18. According to Hiram Bingham, the ruins took the name of the mountain "because when we found them no one knew what to call them" (*The Lost City of the Incas* [New York: Duell, Sloan, 1948], p. viii). This "misnomer theory," so to speak, has been challenged by José Uriel García [see "Machu-Picchu" *Cuadernos Americanos*, 106 (1961), 161-251], who cites both the testimony of French archaeologist Charles Wiener (in his *Pérou et Bolivie* [Paris: Hachette, 1880]) and an eighteenth-century notarial record to uphold the ancient name. Still, neither

163

a nonsign of the impossibility of significance, the supplementary letter short-circuits referentiality and points to a *different* place. More crucial still, the extra *c* can be nothing but a written sign, an inaudible mark (at least in Spanish pronunciation) which must be read, experienced visually, in writing, not unlike the column of metaphors in the ninth canto. The extra letter constitutes the pure movement of differentiation with which writing displaces presence, empirical experience, and which results in a disjunction, a *décalage* of referentiality, the gap that Larrea attempted to close in his violent rewriting.

We may regard the final three cantos as enacting the consequences of this writing metaphor. In the tenth canto, for example, after the subversion of Machu Picchu's presence, the speaker undertakes a radical demystification of the ruins. In language that recalls the first half of the poem, he questions whether the original inhabitants could have escaped the alienation he endured then:

> Fuiste también el pedacito roto
> de hombre inconcluso, de águila vacía
> que por las calles de hoy, que por las huellas,
> que por las hojas de otoño muerto
> va machacando el alma hasta la tumba?
> La pobre mano, el pie, la pobre vida...
> Los días de luz deshilachada
> en ti, como la lluvia

---

document settles the crucial issue of whether the name refers to the ruins or the mountain, and Uriel García is forced to admit, in reference to the motley group of witnesses who figure in the latter document: "One wonders whether all these people truly knew about the marvelous, hidden, dead city" (p. 180). It is interesting to note that Neruda visited Machu Picchu in the company of Uriel García, then a senator from Cuzco, as he states in the interview "Pablo Neruda habla," *El Siglo* (Santiago de Chile), December 5, 1943, p. 12. The two must have known each other at least since 1939, when Neruda spoke at a dinner in his honor: "Discurso en homenaje a Uriel García," *Qué Hubo* (Santiago de Chile) 30 (January 2, 1940). For a revealing discussion of Uriel García's possible influence on Neruda, see Felstiner, *Translating Neruda*, pp. 143-44. Uriel García's essay seems to have been part of a series that included "Sumas para la historia de Cuzco I-III," in *Cuadernos Americanos*, 104 (1959), 133-51, 140-61, and 152-86. The challenge to this "misnomer theory" has been taken up anew by Simone Waisbard, *Machu Picchu: Cité perdue des Incas* (Paris: Robert Laffont, 1974), pp. 155-64, published in English as *The Mysteries of Machu Picchu* (New York: Avon, 1974), pp. 121-29.

Politics of the Book

> sobre las banderillas de la fiesta,
> dieron pétalo a pétalo de su alimento oscuro
> en la boca vacía?
>   Hambre, coral del hombre,
> hambre, planta secreta, raíz de los leñadores,
> hambre, subió tu raya de arrecife
> hasta esta altas torres desprendidas?   [I, 341]

> Were you also the little broken piece / of inconclusive man, of empty eagle / which through today's streets, through the tracks, / through dead autumn's leaves / goes on crushing the soul to the grave? / The poor hand, the foot, the poor life . . . / Did the days of tattered light / in you, like rain / over feast-day banners, / give petal by petal of its dark food / in the empty mouth? / Hunger, human coral, / hunger, secret plant, woodcutters' root, / hunger, did your line of reefs climb up / to these high disjointed towers?

The apostrophe marks a stage of unillusioned awareness of human limits beyond the promises of history, as if the speaker attempted to ward off the delusions of cultural discovery that are sustained by the allegory. Besides posing Machu Picchu's significance in terms of death, the profuse self-quotations in the first stanza therefore amount to yet another exposure that unmasks the successive illusions of allegorical discourse. While the adjectives in "águila vacía" and "luz deshilachada," for example, recall salient images of the prologue, other phrases—"calles de hoy," "hojas del otoño muerto," "machacando el alma" virtually quote from the descriptions of an urban wasteland in the second canto. This unmasking of temporal duration culminates in "Hambre, coral del hombre," a line whose pun exposes the uncanny closeness of human nature to human lack beyond historical redemption. The self-quotations thus dramatize, at the level of reading, the speaker's demystified awareness of history. As the allegory is once again shown to be of fictive duration, history is exposed as the (albeit necessary) illusion of progress. For this reason, "hambre," human lack and desire, becomes the recurrent metaphor for demystified knowledge throughout the speaker's interrogation, which seeks to acquire factual knowledge beyond the distorting laws of archaeology.

Whether in fact the ruins harbor this knowledge remains an

open question, as demonstrated by the suspension of an answer at the end of canto X and the opening lines of canto XI, which abandon the issue altogether:

> A través del confuso esplendor,
> a través de la noche de piedra, déjame hundir la mano
> y deja que en mí palpite, como un ave mil años prisionera,
> el viejo corazón del olvidado!
> Déjame olvidar hoy esta dicha, que es más ancha que el mar,
> porque el hombre es más ancho que el mar y que sus islas,
> y hay que caer en él como en un pozo para salir del fondo
> con un ramo de agua secreta y de verdades sumergidas.
> Déjame olvidar, ancha piedra, la proporción ponderosa,
> la trascendente medida, las piedras del panal
> y de la escuadra, déjame hoy resbalar
> la mano sobre la hipotenusa de áspera sangre y cilico.
>
> [I, 342]

> Through the confused splendor, / through the night of stone, let me plunge my hand / and let beat in me, like a bird a thousand years imprisoned, / the old heart of the forgotten! / Today let me forget this happiness, which is wider than the sea, / because man himself is wider than the sea and its islands, / and one must fall in it as in a well in order to emerge from the bottom / with a branch of secret water and submerged truths. / Let me forget, wide stone, the powerful proportion, / the transcendent measure, the honeycomb stones / and those cut square, today let me slip / my hand over the hypotenuse of rough blood and silicon.

The speaker plunges his hand, thus repeating the prologue ("hundí la mano turbulenta y dulce"), into "confuso esplendor," the metaphor for his own perplexity, as if leaping over the conceptual problems that are entailed in the preceding demystification for the sake of identifying with the ancient past. Except that by this point in the allegory that past has been acknowledged to be death itself, a meaning hinted at in the simile "como un *ave* mil años prisionera." Further details in the canto emphasize the subtle use of the symbol here, but we must for the moment read this acknowledgment within the context of a renunciation. The tone of the passage is one of imperative pleading, as if the speaker were struggling to wrench himself from the

Politics of the Book

opposite extremes of skepticism and self-deception. The imperatives, for example, signal in succession his renunciation of both a demystified questioning and the ruins' aesthetic lure, while their respective objects ("*hundir* la mano," "*resbalar* la mano") mark the identity and difference between the two gestures. Halfway between, as if pointing to the space of the allegory, an overt allusion to Dante's inverted route from the bottom of Hell to the entrance of Mount Purgatory accounts for both.[62] Its strategic placement, within the context of renunciation, conveys the intermediate position that the poem assumes in regard to both mythical faith and demystified knowledge.

The poem opts, instead, in a profoundly dialectical move, for the alternative of a vision:

> Cuando como una herradura de élitros rojos, el cóndor
>   furibundo
> me golpea las sienes en el orden del vuelo
> y el huracán de plumas carniceras barre el polvo sombrío
> de las escalinatas diagonales, no veo a la bestia veloz,
> no veo el ciego ciclo de sus garras,
> veo el antiguo ser, servidor, el dormido
> en los campos, veo un cuerpo, mil cuerpos, un hombre, mil
>   mujeres
> bajo la racha negra, negros de lluvia y noche,
> con la piedra pesada de la estatua:
> Juan Cortapiedras, hijo de Wiracocha,
> Juan Comefrío, hijo de estrella verde,
> Juan Piesdescalzos, nieto de la turquesa,
> sube a nacer conmigo, hermano.   [I, 342-43]

When, like a horseshoe of red wing cases, the furious condor / batters my temples in his flight / and the hurricane of butcher feathers sweeps the somber dust / of the diagonal stairways, I don't see the nimble bird, / I don't see the blind cycle of its talons, / I see the ancient being, servant, the sleeper / in the fields, I see a body, a thousand bodies, one man, a thousand women, / under the black gust, black with rain and night, / with the statue's heavy stone: / Juan Stonecutter, son of

---

[62]See especially *Inferno* XXXIV. For a discussion of inversion as a metaphor of knowledge, see John Freccero, "Infernal Inversion and Christian Conversion (*Inferno* XXXIV)," *Italica*, 42 (1965), 35-41.

Pablo Neruda: The Poetics of Prophecy

Wiracocha, / Juan Coldeater, son of green star, / Juan Barefoot, grandson of the turquoise, / rise and be born with me, my brother.

The condor's assault, which has been threatened since the end of the eighth canto, fuses this negative symbol with the positive implications of the metaphor. The entire passage is made up of a single sentence whose initial adverb ("Cuando") dominates the temporal significance of the bird's beating against the speaker's temples—the site of poetic imagination. The attendant storm, moreover, casts the contest as a cosmic struggle that is resolved in the speaker's inability to see the assailant and later in his vision of a massive resurrection. One must note that the specific terms of the resolution—the poem's insistence on demonstrating a shift in the speaker's perception—do not allow for a simple reversal of terms: it is not so much that death becomes transubstantiated, in the precise sense of changing into a mystical body, as that the speaker can no longer recognize it as death. What suggests this change is the language employed in the description, which, in addition to emphasizing the specifically visual character of the scene, conveys a revision of *Residencia* in the discarded images of "polvo sombrío" and "ciego ciclo." The resurrection must be understood, then, as a trick of vision stemming from the meditation on death, a death that, though authentically acknowledged, is nonetheless transcended for the explicit purpose of yielding a poetic statement on history. In a move clearly designed to disclose the fictionality that permeates the canto, the speaker assigns allergorical surnames to the resurrected, who are thus born in the poet's naming.

The last canto in particular upholds this acknowledgment of death by forestalling any idealized return of the dead in the series of "No volverás" (You will not return). The renewed summons to rise and be born ("Sube a nacer conmigo, hermano") therefore refers to their future existence in language and, more specifically, in writing. As the dead extend their hands "desde la profunda zona" (from the depths) and look upon the speaker "desde el fondo de la tierra" (from the bottom of the earth), the symbolic nature of their kinship is further reinforced. This figurative meaning reaches a first climax in the image of "copa de esta nueva vida" (cup of this new life), which identifies the poem as a testament designed to redeem all the suffering endured in the convulsions of history. The Christian resonance of the image echoes the earlier "copa negra" (I, 173) and the "vaso" (I, 337), both of which prefigure this "copa," in addition to anticipating the more pointed "os crucificaron" (they crucified thee) later in the same stanza.[63] By the time the prophet announces, in a second climax, "Yo vengo a hablar por vuestra boca muerta" (I am going to speak through your dead mouth), we must view this "vocalization," as Rodríguez Monegal suggests, in its precise sense of *vox populi*, a commonplace figure that enhances the text's rhetorical presence.[64] This speech takes place, moreover, on behalf of the dead ("boca *muerta*,") an acknowledgment that is reinforced by later references to "silenciosos labios" (silent lips) and the recurrent "desde el fondo." As Felstiner notes, by this time the prophet has literally become a translator of silence and death.[65]

As the poem is brought to a close, once the prophet has suffered the victim's history, he sees himself as iron that is drawn to the magnetic dead: "Apegadme los cuerpos como imanes" (Let your bodies stick to me like magnets) (I, 334). The metaphor implicitly valorizes the poem's discourse as the fulcrum for otherwise scattered fragments. The elements of the last two lines, which invoke the speaker's blood and mouth, are inversely related, as if conjuring the figure of the cross, the ultimate sacrificial symbol, in the covenant with which the poem ends: "Acudid a mis venas y a mi boca. / Hablad por mis palabras y mi sangre" (Succour my veins and my mouth. / Speak through my words and my blood) (I, 344).

IV

It would be tempting to conclude this long chapter in a tone as uplifting as the one the poem seemingly adopts in its final lines. But such a morally admirable gesture would go against the

---

[63]The source of this image is Christ's words in Luke 22:20: "Esta copa es el nuevo pacto en mi sangre que por vosotros se derrama" (This cup is the new testament in my blood, which is shed for you). This passage is also part of the Eucharist liturgy in the Catholic mass.
[64]See *Neruda: El viajero inmóvil*, pp. 455-63. For the pertinence of the topic, see Walter J. Ong, *The Presence of the Word* (New Haven: Yale University Press, 1967), pp. 180-92.
[65]*Translating Neruda*, p. 178.

poem's greater insight, which warns us at every turn, even in its conclusion, of the dangers of empty praise. Neither an elegy nor a mystic poem, *Alturas de Macchu Picchu* is an allegory that asserts a negative knowledge as part of its statement on history and culture.

An allegory makes no pretense of direct observation. Figurative language excludes the possibility of direct perception or even of a dialectic of subject and object. Language and writing instead submit reality to their own purposes. In addition, the allegorical use of landscape relies overtly on allusive language inherited either from a typology or from literary history, as well as on a diction of rhetorical contrivance. The exclusion of presence in the poem, as we have seen, goes so far as to question the importance of the original site by introducing, through a supplementary letter in the title, a radical difference between text and experience. Even if we should regard Machu Picchu as a natural setting where the speaker seeks refuge, we must recognize that he bears no resemblance to it: Machu Picchu is dead, wholly other, a ruin. It is in such confrontation with death and otherness, however, that the possibility of an authentic historical destiny arises.

As the speaker, at a dramatic level, is aware of the difference between himself and the ruins, so the difference between the poem and the works to which it alludes constitutes an allegorical rhetoric. Instead of interacting with a safely external referent that would provide an unequivocal principle of explanation, the poem's allusive language maneuvers an enigmatic play among signs or texts. These texts, all of them milestones of Western tradition, constitute the signs of an anteriority that the poem implies but with which it can never coincide. The poem, like the speaker, *knows* this discontinuity, and it is on that knowledge that both elaborate an authentic time and history. There is, in fact, no way to deconstruct the poem, as we find the poem deconstructing itself in the acknowledgment of its own temporal/historical predicament. The discursive temporality of allegory is, in this sense, not unlike the discursive temporality of conversion insofar as both are determined by the unfolding of a demystified process that spreads the conditions of error (past) and wisdom (present) over a temporal axis.[66] To account for this predicament

[66]De Man, "Rhetoric of Temporality," pp. 206-7.

Prophecy of Writing

the poem advances a prophecy of writing, an irreducible space that at once presents Latin American consciousness and subverts the assumptions that afford such a possibility. Occupying that space, an avowedly *fictional* space, are the activities of reading and interpretation, now proposed as the instruments of the adoption of Western signs for the purpose of founding an "original" culture.

It is in this scandalous and profoundly historical sense, I believe, that we must understand the poem's political message. For to restrict the poem's politics to the pious theme of "social conscience" or to such platitudes as "empathy" and "solidarity," as critical tradition has in fact done, is to commit the same (political) error that the poem constantly avoids. In its precise, even meticulous revision of literary history, the poem flaunts a rhetorical manipulation of sources that amounts to a subversion of the Western library. Access to history is thereby shown to hinge on these critical activities that, far from being divorced from history and politics, are profoundly related as acts of disclosure of the historicity of the self. Not only is history exposed as the end product of (Western) power interests, but the poem goes one step further in establishing an interpretive act that unsettles the very notion of presence. The metaphor for this interpretive act is the ruin, the allegorical sign par excellence, whose very constitution demonstrates a fundamental gap between signifier and signified so that we are never able to grasp its ultimate meaning. We contemplate ruins, that is, much as we read allegories, constantly measuring the precarious distance that separates sign and meaning, knowing full well that their original sense has been suspended, and perhaps even lost, all the while we recreate a second meaning attesting to the loss of that original sense.[67]

Benjamin seems to have implied as much when he remarked that "allegories are, in the realm of thought, what ruins are in

---

[67]"The ruin is the actual form of past life, the present form of the past, not because of its content or residues, but as past as such" (my translation from Georg Simmel, "Las ruinas," in *Cultura femenina y otros ensayos*, trans. Eugenio Imaz et al. [Madrid: Revista de Occidente, 1934], p. 219). The ruins motif in Neruda recalls Carpentier's in the prologue to *El reino de este mundo* (1949), which grounds a meditation of "marvelous American reality." In a perhaps interesting coincidence, Carpentier visited the Haitian ruins of Sans-Souci in October 1943, the same month that Neruda visited Machu Picchu. In *Los pasos perdidos* (1953), his next novel, Carpentier evokes the ruins motif by having his anonymous

the realm of things."[68] Ruins, like allegories, are monuments to *lost* significance. Thus they are not monuments at all, since in them commemorative intention has been replaced by active interpretation. It is perhaps an irony of literary history that the criticism of *Alturas de Macchu Picchu* should have attempted to turn the poem into a monument to cultural identity when monumentality (in the sense of a petrification of meaning) is precisely what the poem rejects. No less responsible for these attempts have been Neruda's autobiographical recollections, which amount to anxious, self-serving, though perhaps unconscious strategies to rewrite a text that perhaps proved too bewildering or too embarrassing in its contradictions to be left on its own. It is as if Neruda attempted to rewrite the poem in order to erase the extra letter, the extra *c* that marks the difference between his visit and his poem. Yet far from neutralizing the poem's textuality, his recollections render it all the more obvious by repeating the very textuality that they intend to suppress. The poem sets forth at once an allegory of Latin American culture and the prophecy of writing that deconstructs that allegory, an inauguration of new signs and the knowledge that signs can never be new because they always form part of a system of differences.

To interpret against the past, to "invent" the myth of an origin even as that myth returns us to history, to repeat in the name of "originality"—such would be the "archeo-clastic" project of a (Latin) American poetics.[69] In pursuing this venture the poem refers us neither to the comfortable stability of cultural identity nor to the illusory safety of a self-referring text, but to the interpretive risks of exile. At the end of the poem, that is, we find

---

protagonist linger on lines from Rodrigo Caro's *Canción a las ruinas de Itálica* as an ironic allusion to Carpentier's own earlier "Americanism." The ironic distance between Carpentier's two novels could be the rhetorical equivalent of the allegorical tension built into Neruda's poem.

[68]Benjamin, *Origin of German Tragic Drama*, p. 178.

[69]I borrow the term from Joseph Riddel, "Decentering the Image: The 'Project' of 'American' Poetics?" in *Textual Strategies: Perspectives in Post-Structuralist Criticism*, ed. Josué Harari (Ithaca: Cornell University Press, 1979), p. 358. By "archeo-clastic" Riddel means "a myth of origins that puts the myth of origins in question." For Riddel's suggestive reading of a poet similar to Neruda, see his *Inverted Bell: Modernism and the Counterpoetics of William Carlos Williams* (Baton Rouge: Louisiana State University Press, 1974).

Prophecy of Writing

ourselves not in a mythical garden but, as the prologue anticipates, amid an *"exhausted* human spring." Not only is exile evoked in the setting, where ruins constitute a wilderness and the "heights" represent difference from an origin more than access to it; but the experience of exile, where meaning is always provisional and all readings are exposed to error, lies at the core of the poem's allegory.[70] And it is exile, finally, that provides the poem's rhetorical link to *Canto General,* the book in which Neruda included it in 1950. The link goes beyond mere thematics, as the prophet gradually becomes *el fugitivo,* and involves the precise structural role that the poem is called on to play within the sequence of the book, placed as it is between *La lámpara en la tierra* (The Lamp in the Earth), a first section on the myth of America's genesis, and *Los conquistadores.* Within this sequence, the section on the Conquest fulfills the prophet's covenant to become a historical spokesman, thus making his final "palabras" refer not so much to the poem we have just finished reading as to the book we are about to begin. How *Alturas* relates to the preceding first section may not be as clear, though, and we may conclude with a word on this crucial link.

A sequence of seven poems, of which the last six are a pointed analogue of the six days of creation in the biblical Genesis, make up *La lámpara en la tierra.* "Los hombres," the last poem, is a lyrical description of several Indian cultures, including the Inca ("Macchu Picchu" is mentioned explicitly) and the Araucanian. The Araucanians are of course the Indians of Chile, and the only ones personified in the poem in the form of "Arauco," presumably Neruda's *persona.* As the poem ends, the final scene anticipates several of the symbols we are about to find in *Alturas*:

> Mira el vacío de los guerreros.
>
> No hay nadie. Trina la diuca
> como el agua en la noche pura.
>
> Cruza el cóndor su vuelo negro.

---

[70]For this view of allegory as a "poetics of exile," see Mazzotta, *Dante,* especially pp. 227-74.

Pablo Neruda: The Poetics of Prophecy

No hay nadie. Escuchas? Es el paso
del puma en el aire y las hojas.

No hay nadie. Escucha. Escucha el árbol,
escucha el árbol araucano.

No hay nadie. Mira las piedras.

Mira las piedras de Arauco.

No hay nadie, sólo son los árboles.

Sólo son las piedras, Arauco.   [I, 329-30]

> Look at the warriors' vacuum. / There's no one. The flute trills / like water in the pure night. / The condor crosses the black flight. / There's no one. Do you hear? It's the step / of the puma in the air and the leaves. / There's no one. Listen. Listen to the trees, / listen to the Araucanian tree. / There's no one. Look at the stones. / Look at Arauco's stones. / There's no one, it's only the trees. / It's only the stones, Arauco.

The scene haltingly reveals an ironic culmination to the mythical sequence. In contrast to the exalted tone of the earlier sections, it is a desolate scene at a minus-zero point of history showing only the emptiness of war and the condor's deathly flight. Like a leitmotif, the recurrent "no hay nadie" underscores the speaker's failure to find a human agent; he must finally settle for the silent stones.

It is impossible to avoid this metaphorical context as we turn the page and begin to read *Alturas de Macchu Picchu*. Recalling the difference between Dante's two ascents, Neruda's two stony encounters form a sequence of failure and success which discards the fables of myth for those of history and turns the despondent "sólo son las piedras" (it's only the stones) into the joyful "permanencia de piedra y de palabra" (permanence of stone and of word). The sequence pivots, in other words, from mythical *origin* to historical *beginning*, dramatizing an intention while assuming the risks of rupture and discontinuity.[71] It could

---

[71]For this distinction see Edward W. Said, *Beginnings: Intention and Method* (New York: Basic Books, 1975), p. 143.

Prophecy of Writing

be said that it is this beginning that embodies the poem's politics, since it is here that the reader is asked to incur the interpretive risks that are involved in the poetic rewriting of history in *Canto General*. The allusion now is to Orpheus, the traditional figure of the poet, who after an unsuccessful visit to the underworld is able to move trees and rocks with the power of his singing. We realize now, finally, that the speaker's calling upon "amor americano" in the eighth canto refers back to "Amor América (1400)," the first of the seven poems in *La lámpara en la tierra* and the prologue to the book, which anticipates the covenant: "Yo estoy aquí para contar la historia" (I am here to relate history) (I, 315). The disclosure follows a series of statements on the scriptless marginality of America in respect to Western consciousness:

> Tierno y sangriento fue, pero en la empuñadura
> de su arma de cristal humedecido,
> las iniciales de la tierra estaban
> escritas.
>   Nadie pudo
> recordarlas después: el viento
> las olvidó, el idioma del agua
> fue enterrado, las claves se perdieron
> o se inundaron de silencio y sangre.   [I, 315]

> Tender and bloody was he, but on the hilt / of his wet crystal weapon / the earth's initials were / written. / No one could remember them later: the wind / forgot them, the language of water / was buried, the keys were lost / or were flooded with silence and blood.

By the end of *Alturas de Macchu Picchu* those initials have returned as a prophecy of writing. Beyond that lies the politics of the book.

4

Politics of the Book

I need the hypothesis of God to justify my style.
—Pierre Proudhon

Libro, déjame libre.
—Pablo Neruda, "Oda al libro"

I

Were we to reduce the end of *Alturas de Macchu Picchu* to the delivery of a historical covenant, we would risk slighting the dramatic context that validates its argument on history. As the ending of an account of a conversion, the poem's final lines show the emergence of an active prophet who, in contrast to the passive visionary of *Residencia en la tierra*, gains access to dramatic presence. This presence stems in part from the compelling pronouncement that creates a fictional audience out of the dead and turns the speaker into a spokesman. Equally compelling, though perhaps less obvious, are the biblical qualities of the new prophet, a strategy of characterization that appears in both the overt Christian imagery and the uplifting tone. Indeed, the Christian echo at the end of the poem is so strong that, in relation to the beginning, the prophet now seems to forsake his "empty net" in order to become a "fisher of men."

It would be equally wrong, of course, to reduce these formal characteristics to a defense of religion. But their effect on the reader cannot be simply dismissed if we are to explain the dramatic power of the historical covenant. Struck by the deliberateness of this Christian imagery, Pring-Mill, for example, linked it to "the general Catholic heritage of South America," viewing it as a rhetorical device similar to the Renaissance use of pagan mythology, by which "the textured associations of an extended frame of reference [come] into play without implying the literal truth of its conceptual framework."¹ Something similar could be said about the presence of biblical language in *Canto General*, and this chapter will deal largely with the way this language informs both the representation of the new prophet and the new textual theater, or scene of writing. As the rhetoric of conversion afforded a theological pattern for the articulation of a textual politics, so biblical language provides a rhetoric of history. And so by suggesting an analogy to scripture the text emphasizes the political urgency of its message. Most critics have missed the specifically textual nature of this politics as they continue to focus on the book's ideological wealth. And yet not only do the activities of reading and interpretation ground the politics of *Canto General*, but it could be shown that its use of biblical language signals a rhetorical kinship to the language of Marxism.

After a brief discussion of the circumstances in which Neruda wrote *Canto General*, I shall attempt to characterize both the book and its language. Given this broader focus, I am less concerned here with detailed explications of individual poems. My general aim, rather, is to show how Neruda's use of biblical language points up the textuality of his Marxist politics. My argument assumes, admittedly, the filiation of Marx with the prophetic tradition, a filiation which Neruda seems clearly to have identified. We shall find, however, that if Neruda freely adopts biblical rhetoric throughout *Canto General*, at the end of the book he recoils from it as a way of avoiding too formal a closure, and that the inscription of his own biography in the book of Latin American history will replace the long-awaited apocalypse.

II

By 1946, the year *Alturas de Macchu Picchu* was published, Neruda had already written more than a dozen of the poems that were destined for *Canto General*. Rodríguez Monegal has shown that the earliest one, written by Neruda on the occasion of his father's death, dates as far back as 1938.² Some of the

---

[1]Pablo Neruda, *The Heights of Macchu Picchu*, trans. Nathaniel Tarn, Introduction by Robert Pring-Mill (New York: Farrar, Straus & Giroux, 1969), pp. xiv–xv.
[2]See Emir Rodríguez Monegal, *Neruda: El viajero inmóvil* (Caracas: Monte Avila, 1977), pp. 311–12.

subsequent poems were part of *Canto General de Chile,* parts of which Neruda published privately in Mexico as a separate volume in 1943 and which later, revised and considerably expanded, became one of the fifteen sections of *Canto General.* By 1946, then, Neruda was well on his way to producing his magnum opus, although by his own admission writing such a poem as *Alturas de Macchu Picchu* helped him to widen the scope of his work. While he may not always have been aware of his enterprise, Neruda had spent more than a decade writing *Canto General* by the time he finally published it in 1950.

It seems important to dwell on such minor circumstantial details because we need first to demystify Neruda's writing of this book. Neither the spark of spontaneous genius nor the result of sudden political rage, *Canto General* was patiently thought out and planned for several years before Neruda completed and published it in the heat of a political controversy. During the period 1943–48, after the project for the book had crystallized, Neruda divided his time between writing *Canto General* and his duties in the Chilean senate. In the summer of 1947, moreover, a leave of absence granted by the Communist Party allowed him to take time off to complete the book, although by the end of that year he would return to denounce the Chilean government's break with the Communist bloc. The controversy soon involved Neruda in a heated controversy with then president Gabriel González Videla, which exploded early the following year when the Senate voted to impeach the poet. Refusing to surrender to the state police, who had orders to arrest him, Neruda went into hiding; and it was during one year of underground life that he completed *Canto General.* The entire affair proved an embarrassment to the González Videla regime, as writers and intellectuals the world over issued protests, and Neruda became an international hero, the recipient of several "homages" in European journals. Upon completing the book late in 1949, Neruda fled Chile as a voluntary exile, and he did not return until 1952, after González Videla had stepped down from office and there was no danger of reprisal.[3]

It is worth noting that the time Neruda devoted to completion of the book was brief in comparison with all the years he spent

---

[3]For a full account of this controversy, see ibid., pp. 142–52.

Politics of the Book

writing the bulk of the poetry. And yet it is surprising to find that the controversy with González Videla has dominated the way critics read *Canto General*. Journalistic readings were to some extent inevitable, of course, because the controvery forms one of the book's themes. But the *succès de scandale* that has since engulfed all discussion of *Canto General* can be attributed as much to the circumstances of its first publication as to its subversive content. The book has thus been extolled by critics whose noble piety has nevertheless failed to produce sober explications and has succeeded only in reducing the text to vulgar authorial directives. These misreadings have persisted even as the more orthodox Marxists in Latin America continue to reject what they perceive to be Neruda's often schematic version of historical dialectic. And while the dust of controversy has settled by now, few if any readings have gone beyond the book's more obvious thematic implications.[4]

The more we read *Canto General*, however, the clearer it becomes that it is a prophetic book (in a generic sense), and that an exclusively Marxist reading hardly suffices to explain its complexity. Its prophetic mode by itself would justify an alternate formalist reading, but more compelling still is the fact that a Marxist reading of *Canto General* must ultimately invoke the crucial role of prophetic tradition. The ideological link between Neruda and Marx as prophets never has, to my knowledge, been pointed out, and yet this is their common denominator.

Apart from all the problems involved in viewing Marx as a moral philosopher—specifically, the contradictions between the early, ethical Marx of the *Philosophical Manuscripts* (1844) and the later, scientific economist of *Capital* (1867)—there is ample evidence pointing to the prophetic design of his work.[5] Marx's vision of a world made new by the violent overthrow of privileged classes and the advent of a classless society has all the makings of a modern prophetic design. Marxism is in effect a modern, secular prophetic movement. And what could be

---

[4]See especially Roberto Salama, *Para una crítica a Pablo Neruda* (Buenos Aires: Cartago, 1957), and more recently Noël Salomon, "Un événement poétique: Le *Canto General* de Pablo Neruda," *Bulletin Hispanique*, 76 (1974), 92-124.

[5]For an excellent discussion of Marx as a moral philosopher, see Robert C. Tucker, *Philosophy and Myth in Karl Marx* (Cambridge: At the University Press, 1972).

viewed as the millenarian character of the Marxist vision is the result of its infusion with Hegelian providentialism, which, though radically demystified in Marx's text, characterizes the teleological thrust of all dialectical process. Marx replaces Hegel's "Absolute Spirit" with man and with the latter's struggle to achieve an ultimate self-consciousness that may allow his reconciliation with nature, with other men, and with himself. Marxists assert the hope of revolution with prophetic zeal, heralding a time when the exploitation of man by man will yield to a less alienated and more humanized society. Indeed, only if we regard Marxism as a prophetic movement can we explain its power despite the contradictions between Marx's claims for a scientific socialism and the inaccuracy of his predictions regarding capitalist society. "The extraordinary potency of Marxism becomes less paradoxical if Marx is seen as another kind of prophet—one in the tradition of the Hebrews of the Old Testament. In this sense, he was the greatest prophet of the secular religion of materialistic socialism."[6]

Inasmuch as ideology could be regarded as myth written in the language of science, we can read Marx as a prophetic mythology that stakes scientific and historical claims. It can be shown that Marx's visions of cataclysmic transformations, his appeals to violence and revolution as the means of effecting change and to proletarian ire against the bourgeoisie, all form part of an apocalyptic paradigm of biblical ancestry which Marx, as the imaginative writer he was, skillfully manipulated for rhetorical purposes.[7] There are, to be sure, startling parallels between Marxism and traditional apocalyptic thought. Marx's identification of the working-class struggle with the interests of all humanity allowed him to describe the world as made up of two factions—the capitalist and the proletarian—one evil, the other good, "whose final struggle would result in the overcoming of evil and the coming of a humanistic millennium."[8] Simi-

---

[6] Wilson H. Coates and Hayden V. White, *The Ordeal of Liberal Humanism* (New York: McGraw-Hill, 1970), p. 237.

[7] For a partial reading see Stanley Edgar Hyman, *The Tangled Bank: Darwin, Marx, Frazer, and Freud as Imaginative Writers* (New York: Antheneum, 1962), pp. 79–162.

[8] Eleanor Wilner, *Gathering the Winds: Visionary Imagination and Radical Transformation of Self and Society* (Baltimore: Johns Hopkins University Press, 1975), p. 154.

Politics of the Book

larly, a Marxist apocalypse follows the typical historical pattern in which crisis is resolved by apocalyptic vision. Finally, the content of such a humanistic millennium all but coincides with biblical versions: "a world of abundance, amity and equality, free of coercion and of divisions, both inner and outer, a world whose basic unity is that wholeness central to Marx's thought, the unity of the mental and material."[9]

It is the moral and ethical aspects of Marxism, then, that lend a prophetic character to *Canto General*. And even if we chose to read it exclusively as a Marxist pamphlet, we must ultimately contend with its prophetic form because the rhetorical fabric of Marxism itself stems from this tradition. True, Marxism is more than just a material doctrine of redemption; but such is Neruda's principal interpretation in his book, where it appears as a dramatic projection of the prophetic tradition. As Neruda carried Marx over from theory to poetry, he fashioned not simply a political tract but a peculiar kind of prophetic text.

That Neruda was intent on showing the affinities of his Marxist vision to prophecy can be gathered from the structure of *Canto General*. While Neruda's preference for the book or volume of poems to single or scattered texts is well known, nowhere else in his work is the idea of the book as unit so striking. It is Neruda's longest volume by far, sprawling over fifteen sections and more than three hundred poems. The first edition, which Neruda supervised, contained almost six hundred pages, and its huge pages and binding, eighteen inches long, made it bulky indeed. Neruda recognized its great size: "Some will like parts of a vast book like *Canto General*, some will like others. Many won't like it at all. I achieved my ambition in leaving it as a vast landscape."[10] And as if calling attention to its unity as a single volume, the last poem notes:

> Este libro termina aquí... Libro común de un hombre, pan abierto
> es esta geografía de mi canto... Así termina este libro... [I, 721-22]

---

[9]Ibid., p. 155. For further analogies between Marx and the prophetic tradition, see Martin Buber, "Prophecy, Apocalyptic, and the Historical Hour," in *Pointing the Way: Collected Essays,*, trans. and ed. Maurice Friedman (New York: Harper & Row, 1957), pp. 203-7.

[10]"Algo sobre mi poesía y mi vida," *Aurora*, 1 (1954), 16.

Pablo Neruda: The Poetics of Prophecy

This book ends here... A common book of a man, an open loaf / is this geography of my song... Thus ends this book....

All these salient features point to a central fact: *Canto General* is not simply a book but The Book, and its structure follows the principles of what Northrop Frye calls the encyclopedic form, an extensive literary pattern clustering a series of related episodes around a central theme.[11] The generic model of encyclopedic forms is the sacred or mythical book, such as the Western Bible or the Hindu Mahabharata, whose pre-Columbian counterparts are the Maya Popul Vuh and the Aztec Libro de Chilam Balam. Frye notes that every age of literature sees the formation of some such encyclopedic text, starting with sacred writings and working its way through "increasingly human analogies of scriptural revelation."[12] Neruda's is one of these modern human analogues, not unlike Whitman's *Leaves of Grass* (1855) or Hugo's *Légende des siècles* (1857), both of which are Romantic analogues of the Bible.

While the genre to which *Canto General* belongs may not be so readily obvious, evidence suggests that Neruda saw all of his poetry along similar lines. In a 1964 lecture on the occasion of his sixtieth birthday, he hinted that the encyclopedic form constituted a basic pattern in his work. This lecture has been seldom quoted, yet it provides some rare insights into Neruda's lifelong desire to become what he called "a cyclic poet," one whose expansive visions "would surpass a single moment and move onto a broader unity" (III, 709). Neruda refers to his repeated attempts to write cyclical poetry, from the callow *El hondero entusiasta* (The Passionate Shot Slinger) (1923, though not published until 1933) to the somewhat more successful *Tentativa del hombre infinito* (Attempt of the Infinite Man) (1925), all through *Alturas de Macchu Picchu* and *Canto General*, whose purpose was "to give a great unity to the world I wished to express" (I, 709). He further describes *Canto General* as "the crowning of my ambitious attempts," because it was "wide as a large fragment of time" and was able to span "the greater space in which all lives

---

[11] *Anatomy of Criticism* (Princeton: Princeton University Press, 1957), pp. 55-58, 315-26.
[12] Ibid., p. 56.

Politics of the Book

and people move, create and die" (I, 712). To Neruda, therefore, "cyclic poetry" was encyclopedic poetry, and his use of the term uncannily recalls Hugo's description of *La Légende des siècles* in its preface: "To express humanity in a kind of cyclic work, to paint it successively under all its aspects: history, fable, philosophy, religion, science..."[13]

Like all encyclopedic forms, *Canto General* takes an integrative, comprehensive view of history, from human beginnings to the near future. From the Bible to Blake's "Mental Traveller" to *Finnegans Wake*, all encyclopedic forms share this common structure.[14] It is this expansive scope, in fact, along with the historical perspective, that has often led to a reading of *Canto General* as an epic.[15] But while the book does contain certain epic elements of style and structure, such a reading seems too restrictive for a text that encompasses other modes and styles as well. The rhetorical thrust of *Canto General* seems more pointedly directed at what Gordon Brotherston calls "the Great Song of America," the project undertaken by numerous Latin American poets to write a single symbolic poem whose scope and size would simulate the continent's colossal dimensions.[16] Neruda's is the latest example of a tradition that includes, among others, Andrés Bello's unfinished *América* (1823), Rubén Darío's scattered New World lyrics, and Santos Chocano's turgid attempt at a sacred book in *Alma América* (1906). And while only *Canto General* attains any measure of success, it is perhaps significant that Neruda himself once included it in this tradition. "Many writers have felt primary duties toward the geography and citizenry of Latin America. To unite our continent, to discover and build it, was my purpose."[17] The same statement echoes eleven years

---

[13]My translation from *La Légende des siècles*, ed. Jean Gaudon (1859; Paris: Garnier-Flammarion, 1976), p. 3.

[14]See *Anatomy of Criticism*.

[15]See especially Elisabeth Siefer, *Epische Stilelemente im 'Canto General' von Pablo Neruda* (Munich: Fink, 1970); René de Costa, *The Poetry of Pablo Neruda* (Cambridge: Harvard University Press, 1979), pp. 105–44; and Manuel Durán and Margery Safir, *Earth Tones: The Poetry of Pablo Neruda* (Bloomington: Indiana University Press, 1981), pp. 81–83.

[16]*Latin American Poetry: Origins and Presence* (Cambridge: At the University Press, 1975), pp. 27–55. For an account of a similar (and sometimes parallel) tradition, see Roy Harvey Pearce, *The Continuity of American Poetry* (Princeton: Princeton University Press, 1954), pp. 59–136.

[17]Quoted in Rodríguez Monegal, *Neruda*, p. 185.

later in his lecture, in which *Canto General* becomes "a grand unity to the world I wished to express." The Book, then, imitates the continent by supplying a ready textual unity or integration otherwise unavailable in reality.

The fifteen sections of *Canto General* outline the parts that make up this textual unity, beginning with the cosmogony of *La lámpara en la tierra* and the allegory of *Alturas de Macchu Picchu*. These two opening sections, whose tone is as solemn as that of scripture, precede thirteen others that are arranged according to a historical sequence. Sections III and IV outline a Manichaean division of heroes and villains, *Los conquistadores* and *Los libertadores*, respectively, whose succession suggests an evolution toward increasing political freedom, though sections V and VI illustrate a regression into modern dictatorships and financial oligarchies. Section VIII, *Canto general de Chile,* proposes an idyllic view of Neruda's native country, though this is hardly the book's view of Chile's political corruption under González Videla. Section V, for example, ends with a long tirade against "González Videla, the traitor of Chile," which is further expanded in section XIII, *Coral de año nuevo para la patria en tinieblas* (New Year Chorale for the Fatherland in Darkness), as well as in other scattered texts. It is hardly surprising, then, that *Canto general de Chile* should be the book's middle section, the seventh of fifteen; its central position implies both that it forms the core of the book and that Chile's fall into corruption may be taken as paradigmatic of Latin American politics.

The seven sections in the first half of the book thus unfold a telescopic structure whose sequence of political degeneration finally focuses on the specific case of Chile. We see this pattern clearly enough even though the prophet who first emerges in *Alturas de Macchu Picchu* becomes relatively effaced in the remaining sections. Only in the subcycle that runs from sections VIII to XIII, which are among the book's more important, do we witness his gradual emergence. While in section VIII various members of Latin America's working classes relate individually their experiences of political oppression, in section IX, *Que despierte el leñador* (May the Rail-Splitter Awake), perhaps the single most prophetic speech in the volume, their voices converge in a single voice. Sections X and XI show in turn the bad and good moments of this prophet, who becomes successively *El fugitivo* (The Fugitive) and the strike leader of *Las flores de*

Politics of the Book

Punitaqui (The Flowers of Punitaqui). Finally, section XII, *Los ríos del canto* (The Rivers of Song), is a collection of epistolary poems addressed to Neruda's old friends, both dead and alive. In short, the subcycle begins with a series of separate though still highly dramatized poems, which are then followed by three sections that issue from a single prophetic speaker, a sequence that suggests the prophet's ability to organize into a single discourse what at first is a diffuse chorus. Section XIII, the last in the subcycle, recapitulates the sequence, and it is perhaps fitting that some of the most explicit references to his prophetic character should appear at this point. The last two sections, XIV and XV, closely parallel the first two: *El gran océano* (The Great Ocean) is another cosmogony, similar to the one in *La lámpara en la tierra*, while *Yo soy* (I Am) is an autobiography close to the allegory of *Alturas de Macchu Picchu*. Thus the book ends as it begins, with both a cosmogony and a first-person statement, a structural parallel that is designed to give the impression of a rounded unity.

These remarks should be sufficient to indicate the encyclopedic structure of *Canto General*. Far from being a loose aggregate of poems with a common title, as encyclopedic works so often are, the book is teleological, its beginning and end harmonized in an overall design. This structure becomes especially evident in sections III through XI, which expose a historical pattern of social injustice—a good beginning turned bad by corrupt politics and repeated foreign invasions. What renders this narrative sequence possible is the presence of an active prophetic voice that permeates all sections of the book and dramatizes the exposure of such a corrupt history. More important, it is this prophetic voice that organizes a reading of the book as scripture insofar as biblical language plays a crucial role in the rhetoric of *Canto General*. As the Bible is the West's sacred scripture, it becomes Neruda's readiest model for his encyclopedic form. Not only the structure, then, but the very language of *Canto General* promotes a secular analogy to scriptural revelation. This may explain why critics have often remarked on the poetry's biblical character though few have cited the Bible as a source.[18]

---

[18]In an early review of *Canto General* Ben Belitt called the book "a psalter of Isaianic salutations" ("Pablo Neruda and the Gigantesque Opinion," *Poetry*, 80 [1952], 116–18, later reprinted as part of his "Translator's Preface" to *Selected Poems of Pablo Neruda*, ed. and trans. Ben Belitt, with Introduction by Luis

Pablo Neruda: The Poetics of Prophecy

Only when we realize the implications of this biblical analogy does it becomes clear that a vast writing project underlies the argument of *Canto General*, beginning with the loss of "the earth's initials" (I, 315), of the codes buried under the "silence or blood" of history, followed by their recovery in the prophecy of writing of *Alturas de Macchu Picchu*, and culminating in its political implementation, as we shall see, in the remaining sections of the book. The recovered writing thus becomes incarnate, as it were, in the most textualized of forms by becoming an American bible: *biblos*, a book, The Book. In sweeping Hegelian fashion, *Canto General* views all of Latin American history as a vast movement toward the creation of an authentic Latin American writing.

One can hardly avoid noting that in following this model Neruda suspends all claims to an autonomous Latin American writing. What Dante and the poetry of ruins are to *Alturas de Macchu Picchu*, the Bible and biblical tradition are to the entire book. Yet we must, once again, view this tension as characteristic of Neruda's political message. Like the Bible, *Canto General* shows the history of a chosen people, from their pristine creation to their ultimate salvation. History appears in the form of a book that provides not only a ready concreteness but an imaginary dimension that demands the reader's interpretation in the here and now. Reading the Book of History, that is, will be much like reading the Bible, a text that invites and even commands interpretation as the reader accepts and interiorizes its redemptive message. As the Bible is God's Word speaking to Judeo-Christian peoples here and now, so will *Canto General* be History speaking to Latin Americans in their political present. And as reading and interpreting the Gospel yields the kind of faith that suggests Christ's resurrection, so reading the

---

Monguió [New York: Grove Press, 1962]). More recently Jean Franco has remarked that the character of *Canto General* recalls the Bible's ("Orfeo en Utopía," in *Simposio Neruda: Actas*, ed. Juan Loveluck and Isaac J. Levy [New York: Las Américas, 1975], p. 279). Similarly Robert Pring-Mill notes that *La lámpara en la tierra*, the first section of *Canto General*, is "almost a non-Christian Book of Genesis (needing no God)" (Introduction to Pablo Neruda, *A Basic Anthology*, ed. Robert Pring-Mill [Oxford: Dolphin, 1970], p. xlii). For similar comments regarding *La lámpara en la tierra*, see Siefer, *Epische Stilelemente*, pp. 148-51, and Gastón Soublette, *Pablo Neruda: Profeta de América* (Santiago de Chile: Nueva Universidad, 1980), pp. 27-56.

Politics of the Book

prophet's chronicle of political injustice will resurrect his redemptive message.[19] Neruda invests his biblical language, that is, with a sacramental quality that provides the symbolic bond between a prophet and his people. Thus at the end of the Book, after covering the entire span of Latin American history and denouncing countless injustices, the prophet can at last claim: "Soy libre adentro de los seres" (I am free within humans) [I, 721]. The interiorization of the Word has been made possible by the poem's becoming a "pan abierto" (open loaf), whose reading/eating is analogous to the Resurrection: "Y nacerá de nuevo esta palabra, / tal vez en otro tiempo sin dolores" (And this word shall be born again, / Perhaps in another time without pain) (I, 721).

III

Some of the most explicit uses of biblical commonplace appear in *La lámpara en la tierra,* the first section, where the catalogue of native American trees in "Vegetaciones" is modeled after the description of Eden in Genesis 2:9. Similarly, the subsections "Algunas bestias (Some beasts) and "Vienen los pájaros" (The birds come) recall Genesis 2:19, where Adam names the beasts in the garden. Perhaps the most striking biblical echo by far is the description of the Orinoco, Amazon, Tequendama, and Bío Bío, the four Latin American rivers that all but replace the four that flow out of Eden in Genesis 2:10.[20] Other allusions, such as the mock narrative of Creation in "La United Fruit Co." (I, 492), serve to unmask the myths promulgated by multinational corporations in Latin America. Even when such a commonplace is used satirically, it becomes significant in light of other instances. Excluding the more obvious epigraph from Luke in *Que despierte el leñador,* they appear, for example, in "A mi partido" (To My Party), one of the last poems, in which the speaker addresses the Community Party with the Petrine phrase "me hiciste contruir sobre la realidad como sobre una roca" (thou madest me build on reality as on a rock) (I, 721). The obverse of this motif

---

[19]For an illuminating discussion of the reader's role in the biblical text, see Walter J. Ong, "*Maranatha*: Death and Life in the Text of the Book," in his *Interfaces of the Word* (Ithaca: Cornell University Press, 1976), pp. 230-71.
[20]See Siefer, *Epische Stilelemente,* p. 150.

appears in the poem in *La arena traicionada* (The Betrayed Sand) in which González Videla is branded as "*Judas* enarbolando dientes de calavera" (*Judas* hoisting a skeleton's teeth) (I, 516; Neruda's italics).

All of these biblical allusions have the function of organizing a cultural model and a traditional language that locate Neruda's text within a literary framework. That is, they amount to a code that guides our reading through the voluminous mass of poetry and which repeatedly underscores the presence of scripture. And reinforcing these allusions are biblical characterizations that themselves function as extended references to the Manichaean scheme that runs throughout *Canto General*, references that identify both the good and the evil. The good, for example, appear as redeemers who defend the cause of human dignity, as in the case of Fray Bartolomé de Las Casas, the famed Dominican priest:

> Padre, fue afortunado para el hombre y su especie
> que tú llegaras a la plantación,
> que mordieras los negros cereales
> del crimen, que bebieras
> cada día la copa de la cólera.   [I, 379]

> Father, it was fortunate for man and his species / that you arrived at the plantation, that you bit the black cereals / of crime, that you drank / each day the cup of rage.

As the speaker identifies Las Casas' prophetic image, his initial reverence makes him request the legacy of "vino errante / y el implacable pan de tu dulzura" (errant wine / and the implacable bread of thy sweetness), two eucharistic symbols that may help in the struggle against a pervasive social injustice. And yet for all its pertinence, this poem cannot yield a clear sense of Neruda's mode of characterization. (To some extent, Las Casas could not have been portrayed as anything but a biblical prophet.) There are other instances, however, in which characterization is not so historically determined, as in the case of José Emilio Recabarren, the legendary union leader and founder of the Chilean Communist Party, to whom Neruda devotes an entire section of *Los libertadores*. Like Las Casas, Recabarren appears as a patriarch

Politics of the Book

whom the speaker even calls "Padre de Chile, Padre nuestro" (Father of Chile, our Father) (I, 450), in a line that all but quotes the Lord's Prayer. As a spokesman for mineworkers, Recabarren becomes "el capitán del pueblo" (the captain of the people) (I, 446), and the printed word of his newspapers constitutes the mineworkers' gospel:

> y el pueblo besó las columnas
> que por primera vez llevaban
> la voz de los atropellados
> . . .
> juntó una queja y otra queja,
> y el esclavo sin voz ni boca,
> el extendido sufrimiento,
> se hizo nombre, se llamó Pueblo,
> Proletariado, Sindicato,
> tuvo persona y apostura.   [I, 447]

> and the people kissed the columns / which for the first time carried / the voice of the trampled / . . . / he joined one protest to another, / and the voiceless, mouthless slave, / the extended suffering, / a name, it was called the People, / Proletarian, Syndicate, / acquired personhood and gentility.

Throughout this sequence, the speaker appears to be preparing the way for the arrival of Recabarren, who finally emerges in the tenth poem. In fact, their dramatic encounter uncannily recalls the meeting between Christ and John the Baptist:

> Y cuando tantos dolores
> reuní, cuando tanta sangre
> recogí en el cuenco del alma
> vi venir del espacio puro,
> de las pampas inabarcables,
> un hombre hecho de su misma arena,
> un rostro inmóvil y extendido,
> un traje con un ancho cuerpo,
>
> unos ojos entrecerrados
> como lámparas indomables.
>
> Recabarren era su nombre.   [I, 445]

Pablo Neruda: The Poetics of Prophecy

> And when so many pains / I joined, when so much blood / I gathered in the bowl of my soul, / I saw coming from the pure space, / from the infinite pampas, / a man made of his own sand, / a still and extended face, / a wide-bodied suit, / squinted eyes / like indomitable lamps. / Recabarren was his name.

Juan Villegas notes that Neruda here portrays the union leader as a redeemer who fulfills the birth of a new age, all attributes of a prophet.[21] Yet our interest in Recabarren's prophetic image ought not to overshadow the speaker's. It is he, after all, that joins pains, gathers blood, and has the vision of this "union Messiah," as it were. It is he, in fact, that becomes the most obvious and sustained prophetic character in the book, and around him cluster motifs related to the book's prophetic mode.

Perhaps the single most telling line in the volume is the one he delivers in the first poem: "Yo estoy aquí para contar la historia" (I am here to relate history) (I, 315). This image of the prophet as spokesman stems largely from his appearance in *Alturas de Macchu Picchu*, of course, but it is foreshadowed in this first poem, where the loss of writing determines his function as a retriever of history. As in the last section of *Alturas*, where interest shifts from writing to speech, "Amor América" de-emphasizes writing in favor of an oral presence that reverses the pattern that leads to the permanence of a written record:

> Tierra mía sin nombre, sin América,
> estambre equinoccial, lanza de púrpura,
> tu aroma me trepó por las raíces
> hasta la copa que bebía, hasta la más delgada
> palabra aún no nacida en mi boca. [I, 316]

> My land without a name, without America, / equinoxial stamen, purple lance, / your aroma rose through my roots / into

---

[21]"La mitificación del proletariado en el *Canto General*," *Mester*, 6 (1974), 90, now included in his *Estructuras míticas y arquetipos en el Canto General de Neruda* (Barcelona: Planeta, 1976), pp. 140-55. The meeting between Recabarren and the speaker suggests also an instance of "figural interpretation," which in the words of Erich Auerbach "establishes a connection between two events or persons, the first of which signifies not only itself but also the second, while the second encompasses or fulfills the first." See his essay "Figura" in *Scenes from the Drama of European Literature*, trans. Ralph Manheim (New York: Meridian, 1959), p. 53.

the cup I drained, into the most tenuous / word not yet born in my mouth.

The poem is the first in a series that seeks to create an oral fiction; and yet the same poem goes on to demonstrate that this oral rhetoric is circumscribed by the imperative of script and the preservation that forms the basis of historical record. Thus throughout the book such passages alternate with references to the importance and power of writing. All of these references structure a motif that defines the speaker as a scribe, a teacher of the sacred law in whose book he records for posterity the continent's silent history. Related to the book's analogy to sacred scripture, this aspect of the speaker's image has been consistently overlooked, yet it is a crucial thread in the overall argument. It becomes evident, for example, in the book's constant use of italics, as in the reference to González Videla as "*Judas.*" A more pointed instance occurs at the conclusion of *La arena traicionada*, where the tyrant's real name is spelled out, italicized and accompanied by invective:

> *Gabriel González Videla.* Aquí dejo su nombre,
> para que cuando el tiempo haya borrado
> la ignominia, cuando mi patria limpie
> su rostro iluminado por el trigo y la nieve,
> más tarde, los que aquí busquen la herencia
> que en estas líneas dejo como una brasa verde
> hallen también el nombre del *traidor* que trajera
> la copa de agonía que rechazó mi pueblo.   [I, 516]

> *Gabriel González Videla.* I leave his name here, / so that when time has erased / the infamy, when my country cleans / its face, lit by wheat and snow, / later those who here seek the heritage / that I leave in these lines like a green hot coal / may also find the *traitor's* name, who brought / the cup of agony that my people rejected.

Writing becomes a literal branding, an act of violence, which acquires a special status because of its ability to preserve what speech by itself cannot. Similarly, texts, written poems, become in the process legal or sacred documents that literally stain the memory of evil men. The scribe's revenge on the tyrant in the lines above has close parallels in other poems devoted to officers of the law no less corrupt, such as "Los jueces" (The Judges), in which the prophet records the legal injustices committed against the Indian population: "Así pasó y así lo dejo escrito. / Las vidas lo escribieron en mi frente" (Thus it happened and thus I leave it written. / Lives wrote it on my forehead) (I, 499). The passage becomes especially relevant because it conceals a subtle inversion of the well-known lines from Ezekiel 9:4, where God commissions the prophet to set a mark on the criers of abominations.[22] But whereas in Ezekiel, the prophet marks the forehead of the good, those who are to be spared, in Neruda the criers are the ones who brand the prophet's forehead, as if attempting to inscribe their complaints in his memory. The poem, as document, all but duplicates their inscription. It is perhaps significant that Neruda should allude again to the same passage from Ezekiel in a later poem ("Yo no sufrí," (I Did Not Suffer), in which the people give the prophet a similar task:

> Me dijeron: "Te debes a nosotros,
> eres el que pondrá la marca fría
> sobre los sucios nombres del malvado. [I, 644]

> They said to me: "Thou owest us, / thou art the one who put the cold mark / on the corrupt names of the wicked."

This time instead of branding the good, as in Ezekiel, the prophet marks the foreheads of the wicked—in effect, writing against such men. Erasure, the converse of this writing motif, becomes an existential threat, as in the speaker's cry against the tyrant's deletion of his name from the voting lists:

> Ya no soy ciudadano de mi país: me escriben
> que el clown indecoroso que gobierna ha borrado
> con otros miles de nombres el mío
> de las listas que eran la ley de la República.
> Mi nombre está borrado para que yo no exista. [I, 651]

---

[22]"And the Lord said unto him, go through the midst of the city, through the midst of Jerusalem, and set a mark upon the forehead of the men that sign and cry for all the abominations that be done in the midst thereof."

Politics of the Book

> I'm no longer a citizen of my country: they write me / that the indecent clown who governs has struck / my name along with other thousands / from the lists that were the law of the Republic. / My name has been erased so I won't exist.

The passage further emphasizes the writing motif by making the speaker learn of the tyrant's actions in a letter.

The speaker's identity as a scribe, then, to which are added other, less obvious characteristics, is a clear indication of the book's prophetic drama. There is a wealth of references, for example, to his life as a wandering exile or fugitive from political repression: "Soy errante hijo de lo que amo" (I am a wandering son of that which I love) (I, 644), and "Yo estoy errante, vivo la angustia de estar lejos / del preso y de la flor..." (I am a wanderer, I live the anguish of being far / from the prisoner and the flower) (I, 651). This is, of course, a description of Neruda during the year he fled the Chilean police and completed *Canto General*. But beyond this obvious biographical background, the speaker's peculiar wandering has a specific rhetorical effect that, when linked to other biblical images, acquires a dramatic function. Exile is the metaphor for the prophet's spiritual life, calling attention to a new age in which new values will prevail, beginning now, at this time and place. By thus espousing temporal or historical principles, the prophet implicitly devalues spatial or worldly attachments. Such physical uprooting is but the metaphor for the spiritual restlessness that the prophetic existence demands. By becoming a pilgrim the prophet opposes the moral complacency of sedentary life. "When the word becomes prophetic," writes Maurice Blanchot, "it isn't so much that we are given the future as that we are deprived of the present and of any other possibility of firm presence, stable or enduring."[23] Thus in *Canto General*, exile is the marginal position from which the poet delivers his statement on Latin American history. Not unlike Dante, the speaker "acts upon the world by being outside of it."[24]

The theme of exile, anticipated in *Alturas de Macchu Picchu*,

---

[23] "La Parole prophétique," in *Le Livre à venir* (Paris: Gallimard, 1959), p. 47.
[24] Giuseppe Mazzotta, *Dante, Poet of the Desert: History and Allegory in "The Divine Comedy"* (Princeton: Princeton University Press, 1979), p. 138.

permeates the entire book, but it acquires a special resonance in section X, *El fugitivo,* where the prophet repeatedly escapes from one hideout to the next: "de la puerta de un ser humano a otro, / de la mano de un ser a otro ser" (from the door of one human being to another, / from the hand of one being to another being) (I, 591), and "de noche en noche, / aquella larga hora, la tiniebla / hundida en todo el litoral chileno, fugitivo pasé de puerta en puerta" (from night to night, that long hour, the darkness / fallen on all the Chilean coast, a fugitive I passed from door to door) (I, 602). To be sure, none of these descriptions is explicit enough to constitute a biblical reference, save for the general image it helps to create. But other passages are far more telling. Let us return, for example, to section XXXVIII of *Los libertadores,* which precedes the appearance of Recabarren, the union leader. These poems are set in the mining desert of northern Chile. As the speaker comes on the scene of "El cobre" (Copper), the second poem in the sequence, he describes the desert in terms of an ongoing pilgrimage:

> Antes viví en muchos navíos,
> pero en la noche del desierto
> la inmensa mina resplandecía   [I, 439]

> I lived before in many ships / but in the desert night / the immense mine glitters.

It is this desert that is present throughout the entire section. The seventh poem even bears the title of "El desierto" and describes its physical roughness:

> el sol rompe sus vidrios en la extensión vacía
> y agoniza la tierra con un seco
> y ahogado ruido de la sal que gime,   [I, 443]

> The sun breaks its glass in the empty space, / and the earth agonizes with a dry / and drowning noise of crying salt,

in contrast with the cool, peaceful night in the following "Nocturno," in which the speaker enters "al circuito del desierto, a la alta aérea noche de la pampa" (the desert's compass, the high

Politics of the Book

night air of the pampa) (I, 444). Finally, in "El páramo" (The Desert), the last poem of the sequence, he summarizes life in the mines as the place where "el hombre vivía / mordiendo la tierra, aniquilado" (man lived / biting earth, destroyed) (I, 444). The final scene of poverty and wretchedness, the climax of the sequence, provides the appropriate setting for the emergence in the next section of the union leader Recabarren as a kind of secular Moses who led his people out of the (mining) desert and into the Promised Land (of unionization). The entire sequence is therefore designed to recall a traditional biblical setting—the desert as prophetic space. An endlessly provisional frontier, the desert holds out the promise "which is real in the emptiness of the sky and in the sterility of a naked land where man is never *here* but always outside."[25] It should hardly be surprising, then, that the section devoted to condemning Latin American dictators should be called *La arena traicionada,* The Betrayed Sand.

Such traditional biblical scenery, then, contributes to the speaker's identity as a prophet, even if in the above sequence he is far from being the redeemer figure one would expect. If we read the same poems purely as biography, on the other hand, we would counter that the above sequence in particular stems from Neruda's experiences during his tenure as senator from the northern provinces of Antofagasta and Tarapacá. These northern Chilean states, with which Neruda became acquainted during his election and on frequent trips during his years of service as senator, are almost entirely occupied by deserts rich in mineral deposits. In his *Memoirs* Neruda gave a moving description:

> Walking over the pampa was laborious and rough. It hasn't rained for half a century there, and the desert has done its work on the face of the miners. They are men with scorched features; their solitude and the neglect they are consigned to has been fixed in the dark intensity of their eyes. Going from the desert to the mountains, entering any needy home, getting to know the inhuman labor these people do, and feeling that the hopes of isolated and sunken men have been entrusted to you is not a light responsibility....

[25]Blanchot, "Parole prophétique."

Neruda adds that "as senator-elect of the inhabitants of this wilderness... I had to travel those deserts for many years.... Coming into those lowlands, facing those stretches of sand was like visiting the moon."[26]

If we compare this passage from the *Memoirs* with the sequence of poems, we readily notice that in both Neruda portrays himself as a dutiful public servant. But while the *Memoirs* are patterned after a strict historical sequence, the poems follow a more inventive course. They contain, for example, none of the references to Neruda's Senate seat which abound in the *Memoirs*. Nor do the chronologies coincide. The poems show Recabarren as a contemporary of the speaker's, while the *Memoirs* speak of him as a figure of the distant past: "I had a chance once to see Recabarren's printing presses, which had been through heroic service and were still doing the same job forty years later."[27] These striking differences point up Neruda's conscious adoption of the persona of a wandering prophet in the poems and his use of well-known biblical paradigms.

By far the clearest prophetic self-portrait occurs in "El regreso (1944)" (The Return) (I, 708), one of the last poems. The title refers to Neruda's return to Chile in 1944, when he was welcomed by "el rostro amarillo del desierto" (the yellow face of the desert), a reference to the miners who elected him to the Senate in 1945. Farther on in the poem he reveals the meaning of his mission: "peregriné sufriendo / de árida luna en cráter arenoso..." (suffering I traveled / from arid moon to sandy crater...), while claiming to have had visions despite the region's barrenness: "Pero sin vegetales, sin garras, sin estiércol, / me reveló la tierra su dimensión desnuda" (But without plants, without claws, without dung, / the land revealed to me its naked dimension). His pilgrimage, like Moses's, becomes a way of knowing his brethren:

> Me entregué a los desiertos y el hombre de la escoria
> salió de su agujero, de su aspereza muda
> y supe los dolores de mi pueblo perdido.

---

[26]*Memoirs*, trans. Hardie St. Martin (New York: Farrar, Straus & Giroux, 1976), pp. 166-67. For Neruda's contemporary chronicle of one of his visits, see "Viaje al norte de Chile," II, 580-600.

[27]*Memoirs*, p. 168.

Politics of the Book

> I delivered myself up to the deserts and the man of the slag /
> came out of his hole, his mute harshness, / and I knew the
> sorrows of my lost people.

And the already heightened biblical resonance reaches a climax in the following stanza:

> Entonces fui por calles y curules y dije
> cuanto vi, mostré las manos que tocaron
> los terrones ahitos de dolor, las viviendas
> de la desamparada pobreza, el miserable
> pan y la soledad de la luna olvidada.
>
> Y codo a codo con mi hermano sin zapatos
> quise cambiar el reino de las monedas sucias.   [I, 708]
>
> And then I went through streets and curules and told / everything I saw, I showed the hands that touched / the lumps full of pain, the lodgings / of forsaken poverty, the miserable / bread and the loneliness of the forgotten moon. / And elbow to elbow with my barefoot brother / I tried to change the kingdom of dirty coins.

A typical prophetic formula, incorporating the prophet's wandering and his visionary reportage, opens the first stanza. The unusual "curules"—which means principally the ceremonial chairs used by Roman magistrates—highlights the biblical resonance, and the allusive effect echoes further in the later invective against "el reino de las monedas sucias," which is an obviously Christian turn of phrase. A similar messianic ring brings the poem to a close: "Y en la sombra mi voz es repartida / por la más dura estirpe de la tierra" (And in the shadow my voice is scattered / by the hardier stock of the earth).[28] Unlike the earlier desert sequence, then, the poem focuses entirely on the speaker's messianic character instead of prefiguring the arrival of another, more qualified redeemer. No other poem in

---

[28] For a similar re-creation of the same experience, see the poem "Saludo al norte (1945)," which contains the following striking lines: "Recabarren el Padre, comenzó su jornada, / de orilla a orilla del desierto..." (Recabarren the Father began his journey / from end to end of the desert) and "Autoriza mi voz en tus desiertos / entre tu brava gente, entre tus muertos..." (Magnify my voice in thy deserts / among thy brave people, among thy dead) (III, 657-58).

Pablo Neruda: The Poetics of Prophecy

Canto General, with the exception of *Alturas de Macchu Picchu*, focuses so explicitly on the speaker as prophet.

IV

We have seen so far that the thematics of political condemnation determines the speaker's dual role as scribe and exile. These roles depend on one another for their effectiveness: while the prophet discovers compelling social injustice everywhere he goes, his wandering is itself part of the same injustice imposed by his enemies as punishment for writing in the first place. It is this dialectic that structures *Canto General* and moves the speaker to foretell a final day of judgment, a millennial vision pointing toward an imminent apocalypse of social and political redemption. Such visions bear out my earlier remarks about the affinities between Marxism and traditional apocalyptic thought, affinities that are borne out in "Llegará el día (The Day Will Come), the final poem of *Los libertadores:*

> No renunciéis al día que os entregan
> los muertos que lucharon. Cada espiga
> nace de un grano entregado a la tierra,
> y, como el trigo, el pueblo innumerable
> junta raíces, acumula espigas,
> y en la tormenta desencadenada
> sube a la claridad del universo. [I, 459]

> Give not up the day that was given thee / by the fighting dead. Each ear of wheat / is born from a seed given to the earth, / and like wheat the numberless people / gather roots, lay up ears, / and on the unchained storm / mount to the light of the universe.

The day of final judgment will be a literal storm that will unchain an enslaved people, and the poem conveys this sense in the political metaphor of underground revolution, subtly concealed in its vegetable imagery. In another poem from *La arena traicionada* the same uprising appears in similar terms:

> pero ellos saldrán de la tierra
> a cobrar la sangre caída
> en la resurrección del pueblo. [I, 459]

Politics of the Book

but they shall come out of the earth / to collect the spilled blood / in the resurrection of the people.

It is in *Que despierte el leñador,* the ninth section, that we find the most sustained sequence of apocalyptic announcements. This section, as I pointed out earlier, falls within the subcycle that runs from sections VIII to XIII, in which the prophet gradually reemerges and assumes a central dramatic role. It is perhaps the first text that Neruda wrote after going underground, a circumstance that may explain its caustic tone. (It was first circulated clandestinely in mimeographed copies that bore the unorthodox imprint "May 1948, somewhere in Latin America"). Like *Alturas de Macchu Picchu, Que despierte el leñador* was first published separately and acquired a fame of its own before becoming one of the better known sections of *Canto General.* It is certainly as powerful a text as *Alturas,* and its strategic position in the second half of the book in a way balances the first, which is dominated by *Alturas.* Its six sections present an anti-imperialistic warning to the United States, whose *leñador* is the spirit of justice embodied in Abraham Lincoln, widely known as "the rail-splitter."

The epigraph from Luke 10:15, where Christ curses the evil ways of Capernaum, one of three sinning cities mentioned in this chapter of the New Testament, is the first indication of the poem's prophetic intent. The epigraph signals that the poem is a cry of judgment addressed to another nation in the manner of a traditional Old Testament speech, a fact confirmed by the poem's structure. As Klaus Westermann shows, this type of text usually consists of five parts: the commissioning of a messenger, the prophet's summoning of an audience, an accusation of wrongdoing, a messenger formula (such as "Thus saith the Lord"), and a prophetic announcement or foretelling.[29] The poem's six sections follow roughly the same outline. While section I enacts a commission, II and III reverse the traditional sequence of summons and accusation. Section IV has a negative announcement or warning that contains the messenger formula, and section V presents a hortatory speech or positive announce-

---

[29]See Klaus Westermann, *Basic Forms of Prophetic Speech,* trans. Hugh Clayton White (Philadelphia: Westminster Press, 1967), p. 206.

ment that contains the core of the warning. Section VI, finally, delivers a blessing and farewell.

The prophet's commission comes, in this instance, not from above but from within. Love is his credential: "Al oeste de Colorado River / hay un sitio que amo" (West of the Colorado River / there is a place I love) (I, 572). As he repeats his professed love ("Amo el pequeño hogar del *farmer*" [I love the little home of the farmer]) (I, 573), a discreet shift of pronouns implies that his single voice becomes a collective chorus and turns him into a spokesman for the masses: "Es tu paz lo que amamos, no tu máscara" (It is thy peace we love, not thy mask) (I, 573). Section II charges the United States government with the political crimes of racial oppression, yellow journalism, McCarthyism, and support of Latin American dictatorships, all as part of the depiction of a chaotic American society that contrasts, in the following section, with an idealized view of a Stalinized Soviet Union. The ensuing appeals to the American people adopt a formulaic language similar to that of biblical speeches: "a todos / hablo y digo: afirma el paso, abre tu oído al vasto mundo humano..." (to all / I speak and say: Make firm thy step, open thine ear to the vast human world) (I, 583).

Sections IV and V warn and invite, respectively. A conditional clause, typical of the announcement sections in judgment speeches, precedes the warning: "Pero si armas tus huestes, Norte América... / saldremos de las piedras y del aire para morderte" (But if thou armest thy hosts, North America, ... / we shall come forth from the rocks and the air to harry you) (I, 584). Twelve injunctions, levied against the United States on behalf of several countries in Latin America and elsewhere, culminate in the following warning:

> Si tocáis ese muro, caeréis
> quemados como el carbón de las usinas,
> las sonrisas de Rochester se harán tinieblas
> que luego esparcirá el aire estepario
> y luego enterrará para siempre la nieve.
> Vendrán los que lucharon desde Pedro
> hasta los nuevos héroes que asombraron la tierra
> y harán de sus medallas pequeñas balas frías
> que silbarán sin tregua desde toda
> la vasta tierra que hoy es alegría.

Politics of the Book

> Y desde el laboratorio cubierto de enredaderas
> saldrá tambien el átomo desencadenado
> hacia vuestras ciudades orgullosas. [I, 587]

> If thou touchest that wall, thou shalt fall / burned like factory coal, / Rochester's smiles shall become a darkness / to be spread by the shrublike air / and buried forever under snow. / Those who fought shall come, from Peter / to the new heroes who astonished the earth, / and from their little medals they shall make cold bullets / that shall whistle without ceasing from all / the vast land that today is a rejoicing. / And from the ivy-covered laboratory / shall come forth also the unchained atom / toward thy proud cities.

Never did the American empire sound so close to Babylon or the words of a Marxist more prophetic than in the above passage. The "wall" referred to in the first line is one made of "stone and blood" (I, 587), a boundary of the twenty million Soviet bodies lost in battle during World War II. Trespassing against that wall would mean an atomic conflagration to be followed by natural upheavals, such as the wind- and snowstorms that the passage describes with traditional apocalyptic imagery. Aside from these biblical echoes, there even seems to be some deliberate ambiguity in Neruda's unqualified reference to "Pedro," which in context appears to refer to Peter I of Russia, known as Peter the Great (1672-1725), but which also evokes Peter, Christ's apostle and founder of his church. Indeed, the same effect seems to be at work in the next section, the "invitation" part of the prophetic speech. At one level "Abraham" obviously refers to Lincoln, but at another it evokes Abraham the Hebrew patriarch:

> Que despierte el Leñador.
> Que venga Abraham con su hacha
> y con su plato de madera
> a comer con los campesinos. [I, 587]

> Let the Rail-splitter awake. / Let Abraham come with his ax / and his wooden dish/ to eat with the farmers.

Ambiguity stems from the fact that here the American president is called by his first name, whereas an earlier section speaks of "el viento sobre Lincoln" (the wind over Lincoln) (I, 426-28);

there the rail-splitter sleeps in his grave while the waves of racial oppression sweep over him. Thus Lincoln's awakening as "Abraham" in this later section signifies the emergence of an American redeemer who will correct the very charges levied in the second section:

> Que venga Abraham, que hinche
> su vieja levadura la tierra
> dorada y verde de Illinois,
> y levante el hacha en su pueblo
> contra los nuevos esclavistas,
> contra el veneno de la imprenta,
> contra la mercadería
> sangrienta que quieren vender.   [I, 588]

> Let Abraham come, let raise / its ancient yeast the land / of Illinois, gold and green, / and let him raise his ax on his people / against the new slave traders, / against the poison of the press, / against the bloody / merchandise they wish to sell.

Both of the concluding speeches in section VI depart radically from the structure of the traditional judgment speech. While the litany seems to be modeled after New Testament forms (perhaps Christ's Sermon on the Mount, Matt. 5-7), the farewell is a peculiar Nerudian addition that rounds off the poem. Its effect, however, is hardly an easy one because in the end the speaker's prophetic identity ceases to be clear. While he still displays a distinctive nomadic character ("ando errante por el mundo que amo / en mi patria encarcelan mineros" [I go wandering through the world I love / in my country they are jailing miners]) (I, 589), his last lines are riddled by a strange uncertainty of purpose:

> Yo no vengo a resolver nada.
> Yo vine aquí para cantar
> y para que cantes conmigo.   [I, 590]

> I come to solve nothing. / I came here to sing / and to have you sing with me.

Such a statement would not have been possible at the conclusion of *Alturas de Macchu Picchu*, as nothing could be further removed from its vision than this playful acknowledgment of the prophet's limits before an international conflict. Indeed, this final irony exposes a more crucial aspect of *Canto General:* the lack of an explicit apocalypse. Despite many passages that announce a coming day of judgment, such as the end of *Alturas* or even section IV of *Que despierte el leñador,* none of these intimations amounts to the cosmic drama that is required for apocalypse. We become increasingly aware of this disparity as we approach the end of the book, because apocalypse is the one expectation that remains unfulfilled by the otherwise consistently scriptural tone. That is, Neruda's Book begins with a clear enough Genesis but it ends with the author's autobiography instead of a Book of Revelation.

By thus acknowledging a gap between history and writing, Neruda pointedly avoids an ending that would make his text coincide with its biblical model. The suggestion of a sacred history, which serves to emphasize political urgency, ultimately yields to the contingencies of human time. Not only does this suspension of apocalypse return the scene of writing, the biblical theater, to an unillusioned human history, but it also makes of apocalypse a condition of the reading act itself. No passage in *Canto General* bears out these issues better than *Las flores de Punitaqui,* the eleventh section, whose similarities to *Alturas de Macchu Picchu,* beginning with the poet's ascent over "El valle de las piedras" (The valley of stones) (I, 607) and ending with his participation in a worker's strike, makes it a virtual though less exalted replay. Although the poem repeatedly suggests a violent confrontation between workers and management, it avoids depicting such a resolution. Instead, "La letra" (The Letter), the last poem in the section, dramatically subordinates the expectation of apocalypse to the activity of reading:

> Así fue. Y así será. En las sierras
> calcáreas, y a la orilla
> del humo, en los talleres,
> hay un mensaje escrito en las paredes
> y el pueblo, sólo el pueblo, puede verlo.
> Sus letras transparentes se formaron
> con sudor y silencio. Están escritas.

Pablo Neruda: The Poetics of Prophecy

> Las amasaste, pueblo, en tu camino
> y están sobre la noche como el fuego.
> . . .
> Sobre esta claridad irá naciendo
> la granja, la ciudad, la minería,
> y sobre esta unidad como la tierra
> firme y germinadora se ha dispuesto
> la creadora permanencia, el germen
> de la nueva ciudad para las vidas. [I, 620)

> Thus it was. And thus it shall be. On the ridges / of limestone and at the rim / of the smoke, in the workshops, / a message is written on the walls / and the people, only the people, can see it. / Its transparent letters were made / of sweat and silence. They are written. / You molded them, people, on your road / and they hover over the night like fire. / . . . / Over this brightness will be born / the farm, the city, the mine, / and over this unity like the earth / firm and germinating has been created / the creative permanence, the germ / of the new city for the lives.

The entire passage is built on biblical models that suggest a millennial pattern. It makes use, notably, of two biblical commonplaces: Daniel 5:5, King Belshazzar's discovery of the writing on the wall, and Exodus 12:39, Israel's baking of unleavened bread on the road out of Egypt. The two combine in a metaphor whose "brightness" lights the way for the "new city," Neruda's version of the New Jerusalem, which in Revelation 21:2 descends in bridal array to join Christ after the destruction of the old earth. The day of reckoning is clearly at hand, and the passage further reinforces its imminence by invoking the same "permanencia" that in the seventh canto of *Alturas* had redeemed the ruined city. Apocalypse, then, is written on the wall for the exclusive consumption of "the people," but it forms no part of Neruda's own text.

By replacing an apocalyptic vision at the end of the book, the poet's autobiography dissolves the closure that would have provided a retrospective unity. Unlike the conversion text, which describes the progress of the self from the coherent prospect of the end, the Book of History ends by denying the possibility of a privileged vantage point from which one could discern pattern

Politics of the Book

and order in random events. Instead, the irreducibly poetic enterprise of narrating one's own life closes the scene of writing while at the same time opening it to all its attendant contradictions. The most flagrant of these contradictions, perhaps, is the statement toward the end of *Yo soy* (I Am) where the speaker attempts the dissolution of his own medium:

> No escribo para que otros libros me aprisionen
> ni para encarnizados aprendices de lirio...
> Escribo para el pueblo aunque no pueda leer mi poesía con sus ojos rurales.   [I, 715]
>
> I do not write so that other books may confine me / or for inflamed apprentices of lily... / I write for the people even though they cannot read my poetry with their country eyes.

Condemned to the mediated death of writing, the scribe posits the resurrection of an "oral reading," so to speak, whose effect on the real world of history will one day make recitation no longer necessary.

Canto General was Neruda's most ambitious attempt by far at a prophetic book, even though its lack of a fully realized apocalypse may suggest a failure of vision. Its encyclopedic structure reveals a scriptural parallel that is reinforced by the sheer number of biblical allusions and the speaker's characterization as a prophet. But what appears to be Neruda's failure can be called that only if we read the book retrospectively and take into account his later prophetic poetry, in which the earlier lack of apocalypse becomes the obsessive compulsion to produce one. As in the first sections of *Alturas de Macchu Picchu*, which rewrite the poetry of *Residencia en la tierra*, Neruda's late apocalyptic mode performs a creative self-correction of *Canto General*. The scope of this rewriting extends through several texts and culminates finally in *La espada encendida* (The Flaming Sword), a little-known text published in 1970, the same year that Neruda was awarded the Nobel Prize. As its title suggests, it, too, parallels scripture, though it is closer to Blake than to Hugo or Whitman. It took Neruda more than twenty years to rewrite *Canto General*, but in the end he did so to create an explicit apocalypse as well as his last prophetic book.

5

Apocalypse

> The trees bring forth sweet Extacy
> To all who in the desart roam;
> Till many a city there is built
> And many a pleasant shepherd's home.
> —William Blake, "The Mental Traveler"

I

The avoidance of apocalypse that we witness at the end of *Canto General* represents more than just an aesthetic choice. The turning away from a political solution signals a return to history. Nor does the substitution of Neruda's autobiography for an apocalyptic ending amount to a regression to the self's idolatrous fictions. *Yo soy* is a deliberate textual construct made up of verifiable dates and events which remains, like any other autobiography, rhetorically open so as to justify its own writing. "Yo no voy a morirme" (I am not going to die away) (I, 720), warns one of its last dated entries. It is perhaps no accident that as the book ends, it opens itself to history, as if inviting the reader to share the opening implicit in the pointed avoidance of an apocalypse by revolution.

Whether such an avoidance attests to a political softening on Neruda's part is, of course, difficult to say. Neruda remained a Communist, though not always with the same degree of militancy, until his death. His first book after *Canto General* was *Las uvas y el viento* (The Grapes and the Wind) (1954) a pious travelogue through the postwar world which followed the strictest canons of socialist realism. Later in the decade he became an avid supporter of the Cuban Revolution—he devoted an entire volume of praise to it: *Canción de gesta* (Epic Song) (1961)—and remained so despite the public disparagement to which the

Apocalypse

Cuban intelligentsia subjected him in the mid-1960s. In 1964, moreover, Neruda participated actively in Salvador Allende's second try for the Chilean presidency (he had first run and lost in 1958), and five years later he even yielded his own Communist Party candidacy on behalf of Allende's coalition. After the election, Neruda served as Chile's ambassador to France. It was during the coup that killed Allende that Neruda died, of an unrelated illness made worse by his despair at the collapse of the government he had helped to form.[1]

But if militancy was evident in Neruda's actions, it was not always reflected in the poetry he wrote after *Canto General*. Besides *Las uvas y el viento* and *Canción de gesta*, only one of his late books could be considered strictly political: *Incitación al nixonicidio y alabanza de la revolución chilena* (Incitement to Nixoncide and Praise for the Chilean Revolution) (1973), written on the occasion of Chile's parliamentary elections. I mention this not to suggest any particular flaw in Neruda's politics but to note a fact of his work which is seldom recognized if not deliberately concealed. A subtle rift between poetry and politics underlies much of what Neruda wrote after *Canto General*, and any political content was put at the service of a poetry of introspection. The publication of *Estravagario* (Book of Vagaries) in 1958, Neruda's most sustained attempt at whimsical verse, is usually cited as a turning point, but it could be shown that *Estravagario* is the end result of an introspective trend that began a few years earlier and which is particularly noticeable in several key poems, from *Odas elementales* (Elemental Odes) (1954) to *Plenos poderes* (Full Powers) (1962). This final chapter focuses on these poems, less because they reflect Neruda's changing politics than because they form a conceptual bridge between *Canto General* and the three apocalyptic books that Neruda wrote toward the end of his life. The earlier turn away from apocalypse marks the beginning of an introspective pattern, a shift from external revolution to internal regeneration; this pattern culminates in the apocalypse of mind of *La espada encendida* (1970).

In *Fin de mundo* (World's End) (1969), *La espada encendida*, and *2000* (1974) we find that "godless apocalypse" which Amado

---

[1]For additional details of Neruda's life during these years, see Emir Rodríguez Monegal, *Neruda: El viajero inmóvil* (Caracas: Monte Avila, 1977), pp. 183–239.

Pablo Neruda: The Poetics of Prophecy

Alonso, in an innocent reference to *Residencia en la tierra*, once unwittingly predicted.[2] The three books constitute, in effect, a prophetic cycle of their own, a kind of Nietzschean "twilight of the gods" derived from biblical tradition. Neruda wrote all three—including *2000*, whose posthumous publication probably belies an earlier writing—within a four-year period. According to Robert Pring-Mill, Neruda wrote *Fin de mundo* and *La espada encendida* at the same time, almost as if exploring the same mode from different perspectives, one historical and satirical, the other mythical and solemn.[3] In fact, the gradual adoption of an apocalyptic mode recalls Neruda's earlier attempts at a conversion poem. As earlier, he tested the same rhetorical pattern in several texts only to find that the constraints of historical immediacy hindered formal success. In each case, success would mean the rhetorical coherence resulting from the shedding of abstraction and the infusion of language with the dramatic power of allegory or myth.

Neruda's insistent use of these patterns itself confirms their conceptual affinity. Conversion and apocalypse are both metaphors of regeneration which describe patterns of change at spiritual and historical levels. As in conversion the old man is put off for the new, so in apocalypse the old heaven and earth are shed for the new and redeemed. If we can view conversion as an internalized apocalypse, in which the change in the self enacts metaphorically the eschatological drama of the destruction of an old creation, then we can similarly understand apocalypse in terms of a cosmic conversion. I may seem to be oversimplifying, but if a conceptual affinity between conversion and apocalypse does exist, it should help us to identify more than just the recurrence of a rhetorical pattern in Neruda's poetics of prophecy. M. H. Abrams has described how the Romantic secularization of a millenarian pattern of thinking gradually evolved from "faith in an apocalypse by revelation" to "faith in an apocalypse by revolution" and eventually to "faith in an apocalypse by imagination or cognition."[4] The underlying as-

---

[2]*Poesía y estilo de Pablo Neruda* (Buenos Aires: Sudamericana, 1968), p. 34.
[3]Introduction to *Pablo Neruda: A Basic Anthology* (Oxford: Dolphin, 1975), p. lxv.
[4]*Natural Supernaturalism: Tradition and Revolution in Romantic Literature* (New York: Norton, 1971), p. 334.

Apocalypse

sumption of such a pattern is the pertinence of apocalypse as an internal metaphor—"the external means... replaced by an internal means of transforming the world"[5]—and the wealth of examples that Abrams cites is enough to confirm it. What Abrams' statement suggests, in fact, is that the course of Romanticism proves apocalypse to be *nothing but* an internal metaphor, and further that the link between the two patterns consists not so much of the relation of human to historical change as of the interdependence of two modes whose difference resides in the degree of their dramatic scope.

While the dramatically successful conversion rests on a dialectic between two selves who converge gradually in an ethical and structural coherence, the successful apocalypse rests on the unfolding of a pattern of crisis, judgment, and salvation. Working on a dramatic model of history, apocalypse "has a crisis, a dénouement and an end, creating if not a drama, at least a set of visualizable scenes that are designed to impress upon the reader the imminence of definitive change."[6] What does seem to be crucial to both apocalypse and conversion, at any rate, is the dramatic specificity that prevents the reduction of process to an abstract statement. As earlier, Neruda set himself to create that visionary drama as though taking up a challenge.

II

In "El hombre invisible" (The Invisible Man), the prologue to *Odas elementales*, the poet claims that "sólo yo no existo... yo soy el único / invisible" (I alone do not exist... I am the only / invisible one) (II, 11), the positive corollary of which appears as

> yo quiero
> que todos vivan
> en mi vida

---

[5]Ibid.
[6]Ernest L. Tuveson, *Millennium and Utopia: A Study in the Background of the Idea of Progress* (Berkeley: University of California Press, 1949), pp. 4-5. For discussions on the dramatic nature of apocalyptic literature, see Amos N. Wilder, "The Rhetoric of Ancient and Modern Apocalyptic," *Interpretation*, 25 (1971), 436-53, and Bernard McGuinn's Introduction to his *Visions of the End: Apocalyptic Traditions in the Middle Ages* (New York: Columbia University Press, 1979).

Pablo Neruda: The Poetics of Prophecy

y canten en mi canto,
yo no tengo importancia.   [II, 13]

I want / everyone to live / in my life / and sing in my song, / I have no importance.

By claiming invisibility, the poet suppresses the self as a subject for poetry in favor of an objectivist aesthetic, the rendering of objects purely and directly. Such was Neruda's latest statement on his poetics of prophecy, only this time the poet's mediating role is stressed to the point of eliminating all subjective content. Somewhat like a secular mystic, Neruda's prophet wishes to empty himself on behalf of the object's boundless presence.

The poetics of the "elementary ode" implies a poetic self whose suppression allows for the transvaluation of common objects—air, onions, artichokes, thread, and bread—which normally would not form part of poetic "experience," or at least that experience as defined by classical tradition. By gaining insight into the grandeur of the lowly and into the sublimity of the trivial, the odes set out to liberate the reader from the bondage of classical poetry and thus to open the world to imaginative re-creation. Nor should we overlook the fact that this undertaking transposes political categories into the sphere of poetic perception. The elevation of common objects constitutes a leveling of poetic subject and the breaking down of class distinctions, as if reducing all things to the same standard by investing the lowliest with a humble dignity of their own. Whether in fact such transvaluations can occur only at the expense of the self is of course questionable, and Neruda himself suggests as much in "El hombre invisible." While the "invisible" prophet disparages his precursors ("los viejos poetas," the old poets) for being too self-centered and for their self-indulgent use of the first-person pronoun, he himself uses that pronoun lavishly from the outset. In fact, halfway through the poem and after repeatedly claiming his own unimportance, we see him pausing to indulge in the very distractions he disparaged earlier: "estrellas" (stars), "la dulce que amo" (the sweet one I love), and "la ola de los misterios" (the wave of mysteries) (II, 13). In what amounts to an acknowledgment of self-indulgence, these words

Apocalypse

go beyond restating the creative cycle glimpsed earlier in "Arte poética" and expose rhetorical "invisibility" as a convention of self-effacement that all but reinforces the role of the visionary self. Not unlike Wordsworth's *Lyrical Ballads* and the Romantic conception they reflect, Neruda's ode discloses the presence of "an original Writer," whose genius shows through in applying "powers to objects on which they had not been exercised before," so as to produce "effects hitherto unknown."[7] It is not so much the author, then, as the speaker who must efface himself before the object. The distinction is implicit in "El hombre invisible," which makes self-effacement part of an economy of representation and thereby proposes its own ironic reading. The object shines no brighter when the speaker is made to disappear—the politics of perception inherent to this transvaluative poetics only makes it seem so.

After *Odas elementales* Neruda continued to pursue this internalized politics, though only by misreading this potential ironic content for the sake of reconstituting the self's imaginative role. We can detect a rewriting of "El hombre invisible," for example, in such a later poem as "Pido silencio" (I ask for silence) (in *Estravagario*), in which the speaker shuts off the object and withdraws from poetic duties:

> Ahora me dejen tranquilo.
> Ahora se acostumbren sin mí.
> Yo voy a cerrar los ojos. [I, 602]

---

[7]"Preface to *Poems of 1815*," in *Literary Criticism of William Wordsworth*, ed. Paul M. Zall (Lincoln: University of Nebraska Press, 1966), pp. 182, 184. For a discussion of the theory of Romantic transvaluation, see Abrams, *Natural Supernaturalism*, pp. 390-99. The extant studies on Neruda's odes do not fully account for the Romantic origins of this transvaluative poetics. See, among others, Walter Holzinger, "Poetic Subject and Poetic Form in the *Odas elementales*," *Revista Hispánica Moderna*, 36 (1970-71), 41-49; Luis de Arrigoitia, "Las *Odas elementales* de Pablo Neruda," *Sin Nombre*, 3 (1972), 31-43; Jaime Alazraki, "Observaciones sobre la estructura de la *oda elemental*," *Mester*, 4 (1974), 94-102; Eliana Suárez-Rivero, "La estética esencial en una oda nerudiana," in *Simposio Neruda: Actas*, ed. Isaac Jack Levy and Juan Loveluck (Columbia: University of South Carolina-Las Américas, 1975), pp. 79-96; René de Costa, *The Poetry of Pablo Neruda* (Cambridge: Harvard University Press, 1979), pp. 144-74; Robert Pring-Mill, "El Neruda de las 'Odas elementales,'" in *Coloquio internacional sobre Pablo Neruda (la obra posterior al "Canto General")*, ed. Alain Sicard (Poitiers: Publications du Centre de Recherches Latino-Américaines, 1979), pp. 261-300.

Pablo Neruda: The Poetics of Prophecy

Now leave me in peace. / Now get used to being without me. / I am going to close my eyes.

Self-fulfillment has replaced self-effacement, and the revision reaches as far back as the visionary raids of *Residencia en la tierra*, an echo of which is heard a few lines later: "sucede que voy a vivirme. / Sucede que soy y que sigo" (it happens that I am going to live. / It happens that I am and that I go on) (II, 603). That is, instead of "walking around" and losing himself in the object, the poet demands a leave of absence in order to devote himself to introspection:

> adentro
> de mí crecerán cereales...
> y dentro de mí soy oscuro...
> Déjenme solo con el día.
> Pido permiso para nacer.   [II, 603]

> within / me grains will grow... / and within me I am dark... / Leave me alone with the day. / I beg permission to be born.

Neruda's discreet reconversion, his latest break with the past, requires a silent rest after the exhausting stocktaking of four volumes of "elementary odes." The new quietist mode, echoed in "A callarse" (To Keep Silent), another text from *Estravagario*, determines a quest for a still unsatisfied self-knowledge:

> tal vez un gran silencio pueda
> interrumpir esta tristeza,
> este no entendernos jamás
> y amenazarnos con la muerte.   [II, 607]

> perhaps a great silence will be able to / interrupt this sadness, / this never understanding ourselves / and threatening ourselves with death.

To enter into such a meditation is of course to risk exchanging a stable self for a plural self, to allow introspection to feed on retrospection and to find, as in "Regreso a una ciudad" (Return to a City), a parade of masks and disguises:

Apocalypse

> Ahora me doy cuenta que he sido
> no sólo un hombre sino varios
> y que cuantas veces he muerto,
> sin saber cómo he revivido,
> como si cambiara de traje
> me puse a vivir otra vida... [II, 608]

> Now I realize that I have been / not just one man but several, / and that as many times as I've died, / without knowing how I've been reborn, / as if changing suits, / I started to live another life...

Such a discovery amounts to more than just an admission of change. It signals the wholesale subversion of the speaker. As earlier a politics of perception leveled class distinctions by conferring value on the trivial, so now the internalization of that politics exposes the futility of proposing an immutable individual consciousness. The effects of this introspective politics show through in "Partenogénesis" (which may be construed as "self-birth"), in which the speaker differentiates himself from "sujetos estimables, / políticamente profundos" (estimable subjects, / politically deep), and is confirmed in "Testamento de otoño" (Autumn Testament), *Estravagario*'s last poem, which all but rewrites the last will and testament of *Canto General*:

> Dejé mis bienes terrenales
> a mi Partido y a mi pueblo,
> ahora se trata de otras cosas,
> cosas tan oscuras y claras
> que son sin embargo una sola. [II, 700–701]

> I left my earthly possessions / to my Party and my people, / now it's a matter of other things, / things so dark and bright / that they are nonetheless a single thing.

"Cosas tan oscuras y claras" refers to the contradiction between the bright orthodoxy of socialist realism and the dark irony of an unillusioned politics. Unlike the odes, in which "a final pirouette always manages to turn pain into hope, death into rebirth and envy into love," the later poetry exposes "life's light and shadow without making concessions to any one belief."[8]

---

[8] Rodríguez Monegal, *Neruda*, p. 384.

Pablo Neruda: The Poetics of Prophecy

One must stress the specifically political origins of this metaphorical conflict, although it would be wrong to reduce it entirely to Neruda's ostensible response to the de-Stalinization that was taking place in the Soviet Union during those years. In reconverting to an ironic view of self and world following a period of Marxist orthodoxy, Neruda rescues the earlier dialectic of irony and melancholy and applies it to a description of political revisionism and its effects on existential issues. Among these issues is the role of poetry in everyday life. Not only does poetry reveal to the reader both the value of the trivial and the self's internal contradictions, but, as we see in "Deber del poeta" (The Poet's Duty), the preface to *Plenos poderes*, it assumes a liberating role in breaking down the barriers of faulty perception:

> llego y abro la puerta del encierro
> y un sin fin se oye vago en la insistencia
> . . .
> para que donde esté el encarcelado,
> donde sufra el castigo del otoño,
> yo esté presente con una ola errante.   [II, 973]
>
> I arrive and open the door of confinement / and infinity is heard vaguely upon persistence... / so that wherever the prisoner may be, / wherever he may suffer the punishment of autumn, / I may be there with a rambling wave.

The "punishment of autumn" is the menace of time, whose meaning poetry will nevertheless rescue from the threat of death. And in "Plenos poderes," the last poem, which together with the first frames the volume, as it were, the theme of internal liberation recurs in the same metaphorical terms:

> El trigo negro de la noche crece
> mientras mis ojos miden la pradera
> y así de sol a sol hago las llaves:
> busco en la oscuridad las cerraduras
> y voy abriendo al mar las puertas rotas
> hasta llenar armarios con espuma.   [II, 1017]
>
> The black wheat of night grows / while my eyes measure the meadow, / and so I make the keys from dusk to dawn. / I search in darkness for the keyholes / and start opening to the sea the broken doors / until the cabinets are filled with foam.

Apocalypse

Here the earlier metaphors of political outlook form part of a temporal dialectic in which poetic vision plays a central role. After forging the keys according to the measurements of the melancholy ground, the poet opens the doors to the prison and floods it with the "rambling waves" of the first poem. External dichotomy gives way to an internal dialectic governed by a coincidence of opposites. And so, while in *Estravagario* the poet ventures to say in the abstract that "toda claridad es oscura" (all lightness is dark) (II, 701), he now claims proudly, "A plena luz camino por la sombra" (In full daylight I walk in shadow) (II, 1017).

It is not my purpose to reduce Neruda to a few symbolic texts or to embark on an "ideological" reading. The avoidance of apocalypse in *Canto General* marks the origin of an introspective tendency that runs through the subsequent poetry; it stands out clearly in the poems quoted above. And if apocalypse marks the poetry's point of departure, it also signals its final destination, insofar as it provides a climactic pattern for the representation of the self's internal renewal. That is, a rhetoric of conversion whose adequacy is rendered doubtful by the recent discovery of a plural self is replaced by an inward thrust that culminates in the definitive transvaluations of apocalypse. The apocalyptic mode will encompass all possible conversions within a single drama.

At least two antecedents of this mode can be identified in texts dating from the same period as that of the new introspective lyrics: "Escrito en el año 2000" (Written in the Year 2000) in *Canción de gesta* (1960) and "Cataclismo" (Cataclysm) in *Cantos ceremoniales* (Ceremonial Songs) (1962). Each of these poems may be regarded as an attempt to rewrite the end of *Canto General* and to disengage from the creative specter of that earlier book, even though both owe their dramatic patterns to *Alturas de Macchu Picchu*. The first of these poems, included in Neruda's brief tribute to the Cuban Revolution, comprises the last section of "Meditación sobre la Sierra Maestra" (Meditation on the Sierra Maestra), whose title refers to the mountains where Castro waged his guerrilla war. Atop the new heights, the speaker surveys a broad spatial and temporal expanse:

> tengo derecho al sueño soberano
> a descansar con los ojos abiertos,

Pablo Neruda: The Poetics of Prophecy

entre los ojos fatigados,
y mientras duerme el hombre con su tribu,
cuando todos los ojos se cerraron,
los pueblos sumergidos en la noche,
el cielo de rosales estrellados
dejo que el tiempo corra por mi cara
como aire oscuro o corazón mojado
y veo lo que viene y lo que nace,
los dolores que fueron derrotados,
las pobres esperanzas de mi pueblo
los niños en la escuela con zapatos,
el pan y la justicia repartiéndose
como el sol se reparte en el verano.[9]

I have a right to the sovereign dream, / to rest with open eyes / among exhausted eyes, / and while man sleeps with his tribe, / when all the eyes are closed, / the peoples submerged in the night, / the sky starred with roses, / I let time stroke my face / like dark air or wet heart, / and see what comes and is born, / pains that were routed, / the poor hopes of my people, / children in school with shoes on, / bread and justice being spread / as the sun is spread in summer.

The scene recalls the last canto of *Alturas*, in which the soaring condor thrusts against the speaker's forehead, in the less well-wrought image of time stroking the poet's face as a prophetic investiture. In a subtle inversion of the earlier sequence the brooding specter of the poet's anguished past follows the initial redemption, but it soon gives way to a millennial hope that is cast as a cyclical renewal. Similarly, the metaphor of the city, which the poem uses as a sign of historical beginning, appears at the end:

[9]*Canción de gesta*, 4th ed. (1960; Montevideo: El Siglo Ilustrado, 1970), p. 100. Neruda never included this book in the Losada editions of his *Obras completas*, probably in order to avoid problems with the Argentine authorities. In a note appended to this fourth edition, the Uruguayan publisher states that Neruda had promised to include a second and final poem titled "Juicio Final" (Last Judgment) in this section. But perhaps that title was meant less as an index of apocalypse than as Neruda's last word in his ongoing quarrel with Cuba's intellectuals. The title echoes, at least, in his preface to the third edition (1968): "Those who read these poems in the coming years will be able to judge [juzgarán] and will meditate on the works and lives of all of us," (p. 10). Neruda expanded on his disaffection from the Cuban intelligentsia in his *Memoirs*, trans. Hardie St. Martin (New York: Farrar, Straus & Giroux, 1976), pp. 324-28.

Apocalypse

> levantemos la ciudad dichosa
> con los brazos de los que ya no viven
> y con manos que no han nacido ahora.   [II, 104]

> we shall build the happy city / with the arms of those no longer living / and with hands that have not yet been born.

What is new in the poem, then, is not its visionary aspect, whose echo of *Alturas* is almost crippling, but the millenarianism of the title. The reference to the millennium, a vantage point in time when an old age ends and a new and healthier era is about to begin, foreshadows the apocalyptic mode and prefigures, in fact, both the title of *2000* and the references to a millennium in *Fin de mundo*. What is wholly missing, of course, is a cosmic apocalypse, the punitive destruction of the old earth by natural holocaust, as if the external politics of *Canto General* still weighted too heavily to allow such a dramatization.

We only begin to discern the apocalyptic pattern in "Cataclismo," in *Cantos Ceremoniales* (1961), whose title suggests it. The poem appeared only two years after "Escrito en el año 2000," but those two years seem to have been enough to make the difference that is reflected in the title of the volume. "In opting for the 'ceremonial,'" Ben Belitt has noted, "Neruda is removing himself from the 'general,'" as if signaling a change for "the decidedly meditative and exploratory cast" and thus building more "time into the unfolding of the mind's apprehension of itself."[10] It is more significant, however, that a Chilean earthquake should provide an occasion for introspection. The earth tremors described in the first section, for example, elicit a literal fear and trembling, as if the shaking of the earth exposed the speaker to the nakedness of his own being:

> Hombre soy, por qué nací en la tierra?
> Dónde está mi mortaja?
> Esta es la noche?   [II, 948]

> I am a man, why was I born on earth? / Where is my shroud? / Is this the night?

---

[10]Introduction to *Pablo Neruda: A New Decade (Poems 1958-1967)*, ed. and trans. Ben Belitt and Alastair Reid (New York: Grove Press, 1969), pp. xxiv and xxv.

Pablo Neruda: The Poetics of Prophecy

The three probing questions lend an immediacy to the dynamics of existence in response to the erosion of all structures, psychic as well as physical. The questions address plainly the confounding fear that plagues the population during the holocaust. Following a description of the wintry forty-day prelude to the earthquake, fear ("el miedo") joins the falling debris along with smoke, lava, and the sea. The earth itself appears frightened ("de nuevo borraba su nombre con espanto" [again it obliterated its name with terror]) (II, 949) in exposing the clash of life and death, light and darkness, order and chaos. And as the poet addresses several of the inhabitants by name (in a distant echo of canto XI of *Alturas*), he ventures an economic image, casting the trembling earth as a demanding landlord and the people as its frightened tenants:

> Ahora la gran deuda de la vida fue pagada con miedo,
> fue volcada en la tierra como una cosecha
> de la que todos huían rezando, llorando y muriendo,
> sin comprender por qué nacimos, ni por qué la tierra
> que esperó tanto tiempo a que madurara el trigo
> ahora, sin paciencia, como una brusca viuda
> borracha y crepitante se hiciera pagar de golpe
> amor y amor, vida y vida, muerte y muerte.   [II, 949]

> Now the great debt of life was paid with fear, / was overturned on earth like a harvest / from which all fled praying, crying and dying, / without understanding why we are born or why the earth, / which waited so long for the wheat to ripen, / now, with no patience at all, like a rude widow, / drunk and noisy, demands immediate payment, / love and love, life and life, death and death.

The image is striking for its association of the inhabitants' fear with the personification of the earth. By section VII, the middle of the poem, Chile's volcanoes have been elevated to the rank of angered deities ("Dioses perdidos, renegados / dioses sustituídos" [Lost gods, apostate / surrogate gods]) to whom the speaker appeals and to whom he attributes, in the next section, the "terror" felt by the inhabitants. This association continues in section IX, where it is dramatized by a lover's despondent

Apocalypse

monologue, and it reaches a climax in the short section X, which expands on its meaning:

> El miedo envuelve los huesos como una nueva piel,
> envuelve la sangre con la piel de la noche,
> bajo la planta de los pies mueve la tierra:
> no es tu pelo, es el miedo en tu cabeza
> como una cabellera de clavos verticales
> y lo que ves no son las calles rotas
> sino, dentro de ti, tus paredes caídas,
> tu infinito frustrado, se desploma
> otra vez la ciudad, en tu silencio sólo se oye
> la amenaza del agua, y en el agua
> los caballos ahogados galopan en tu muerte. [II, 952-53]

> Fear wraps the bones like a new skin, / wraps the blood with the skin of night, / moves the earth under your feet; / it isn't your hair, it's the fear in your head / like a wig of vertical nails, / and what you see is not broken streets / but, within you, your own fallen walls, / your frustrated infinity, the city / collapses once again, in your silence one can hear only / the threat of water, and in that water / the drowned horses gallop into your death.

The ultimate cataclysm is, of course, fear itself, which, besides "causing" the earthquake and making hair seem as sharp as construction nails, casts shattered illusions as broken streets. Its most insidious effect by far is the deceptive shrinking of the horizon of possibility. The speaker remarks, for example, in a statement that dominates the end of the poem, that the city has collapsed *once again* ("otra vez"), as if reminding us of earlier catastrophes in order to belie a discouraging end. This internal sense culminates in the "amenaza del agua," which refers both to the title (a cataclysm is a great flood) and to the puddle of tears shed in the silent expectation of death.

The upbeat turn of the last three sections comes partly in response to this knowledge. The message of unillusioned hope implies the rebuilding of the city out of its ruins, much as Nature nurtures herself by the irrigation of human tears. And at the end of the poem, the prophet appears as an apocalyptic angel sheltering the frightened population "bajo mis alas mojadas" (beneath my wet wings). Yet this safety stems not from the angel's figurative presence but from an inner historicity implicit in a view of existence as a succession of renewed beginnings:

> vistámonos de nuevo de hombre y de mujer desnudos:
> construyamos el muro, la puerta, la ciudad:
> comencemos de nuevo el amor y el acero:
> fundemos otra vez la patria temblorosa.   [II, 954]

> let us dress ourselves anew as naked men and women: / let us build the wall, the door, the city: / let us begin anew the love and the steel: / let us found again the trembling fatherland.

"Cataclismo," then, does not provide a full-blown apocalypse either. But unlike "Escrito en el año 2000," it contains a few hints that suggest Neruda's growing awareness of the formal possibilities of apocalypse, including its pertinence as an internal metaphor. Perhaps the most telling of these hints, beyond the scattered descriptions of seismic turmoil, is the allusion to Genesis at the end, an allusion that, while not integrally related to apocalypse, ends the poem with a patently biblical stamp. The allusion, moreover, forms part of the final redemptive act as the speaker pleads for the wisdom of innocence, a kind of Nietzschean "willful forgetfulness" that would permit a return to Paradise despite awareness of apocalypse. It also prefigures, as we shall soon learn, the central metaphor of *La espada encendida*. Tentatively, at least, this allusion identifies Neruda's creative disengagement from *Canto General* as a gradual immersion in myth, even if that myth also stems from a biblical source. For the moment, though, we must first turn to *Fin de mundo* and *2000*, whose lapse into the external politics of *Canto General* renders what are perhaps two less accomplished versions of apocalypse.

III

Fin de mundo (World's End) is in many ways a rewriting of *Canto General*. It, too, has an encyclopedic form, consisting of 122 poems in eleven sections linked by a recurring critique of the twentieth century. Like *Canto General*, it is a chronicle, though its historical outlook, unlike that of the earlier work, is pervaded by a tragic awareness of the planet's imminent self-destruction.

Apocalypse

Faced with an approaching millennium, Neruda shifts from the role of denouncer of social injustice in Latin America to that of critic of the nuclear age. This thematic shift signals an ideological change as the narrower aspects of Marxism appear to be discarded for a balanced view in which the right and the left are equally to blame for the world's chaos.

According to Hernán Loyola, the original title of *Fin de mundo* was *Juicio Final* (Last Judgment).[11] In discarding that title for the second time, Neruda seems to have chosen a more oblique approach, though a telling sign appears from the outset in the first poem, "La puerta" (The Door), whose title alludes to the passages in Revelation that describe the arrival of the Son of Man. Initially, the door identifies the speaker's privileged vantage point: "Yo estoy en la puerta partiendo y / recibiendo a los que llegan" (I am at the door parting from / and welcoming those who arrive), a neutral enough statement that becomes more pointed in the next few lines: "Por eso, en la puerta espero / a los que llegan a este fin de fiesta: / a este fin de mundo" (That is why at the door I wait / for those who come to this party's end: / to this world's end) (II, 359). The context generally recalls the words of Christ in Revelation 3:20 ("Behold, I stand at the door and knock: if any man hear my voice, and open the door, I will come in to him"), which still echo at the end of the poem: "Entro con ellos pase lo que pase. / Me voy con los que parten / y regreso" (I go in with them, come what may. / I leave and return with those who leave) (III, 360). Obviously, Neruda does stray from the biblical source somewhat, but the echoes resound strongly after the suggestive title and the preceding eleven stanzas, which describe the century's wars and manmade disasters.

The speaker describes this as a "siglo permanente" (permanent century) that is about to disappear with the advent of a new millennium. Whether its conclusion will bring about a "revolución idolatrada" (idolized revolution) or the "mentira patriarcal" (Patriarchal lie) (III, 357), a new kingdom of God, remains all the more uncertain as the century has been one of frustrated expectations of peace. Its string of manmade disasters has ended with the advent of the nuclear age, which forebodes the planet's even-

---

[11]*Pablo Neruda: Antología esencial,* ed. Hernán Loyola (Buenos Aires: Losada, 1971), p. 34.

tual annihilation. And yet not even the massive stockpiling of atomic weapons seems enough to cause despair, for after many a lament the speaker still clings to a saving hope: "Sí se ha resuelto, gracias: / nos queda la esperanza" (It has indeed been resolved, thanks: / hope remains to us) (III, 359). It is no accident that these words, which dramatize the redemptive hope appropriate to the apocalyptic mode, appear strategically between the two echoes of Revelation. The counterpoint between hope and the threat of destruction is perhaps the central motif of *Fin de mundo*, and its first poem all but anticipates the book's final resolution.

Neruda's apocalyptic imagination associates the advent of a new millennium, reflecting a patent eschatological consciousness, with the imminence of a nuclear holocaust. In "El siglo muere" (The Century Dies), for example, the millennium is ushered in with apocalyptic trumpets and fires, and a three-poem sequence in section VI dramatizes the last events. The clutter of modern technology in "Se llenó el mundo" (The World Filled Up) heralds "limones de aluminio" (aluminum lemons), "intestinos eléctricos" (electric intestines), and a "Niágara sintético" (synthetic Niagara) (III, 413). Even the teardrops elicited by this dirge are turned into an artificial substance: "Y recordándolo derramo lágrimas de penicilina" (And remembering it I shed penicillin tears) (III, 414). The irony in this satire on the future somewhat reduces prophetic urgency. Yet we find no such relief in "Bomba [Bomb] (I)," one of two poems devoted to the threat of nuclear war, in which the "usina total de la muerte" (whole factory of death) is made to resemble a latter-day Damocles' sword "colgando sobre la cabeza del mundo" (hanging over the world's head) (III, 414). "Muerte de un periodista" (Death of a Journalist), the third poem, returns to a satirical note in the tale of a journalist's death under a Russian tank during the uprising in Prague in the spring of 1968. As the journalist was "eaten up," so must we all be prepared to be devoured by the steel monsters:

> Debo cumplir con mi deber:
> hacerme aceitoso y sabroso
> para que me coma una máquina." [III, 416]

Apocalypse

> I must do my duty: / make myself oily and tasty / so that a machine may eat me.

This realization prompts the readiest acknowledgment of apocalypse:

> Es nuestra época pesada
> la edad de las patas de fierro,
> el siglo sangriento y redondo,
> y debemos reconocer
> las ruedas del Apocalipsis. [III, 416]

> Our heavy era is / the age of iron claws, / the bloody and round century, / and we must acknowledge / the wheels of the Apocalypse.

As the chronicle of an age, *Fin de mundo* deals with many subjects, ranging from international politics to the new Latin American novel to Neruda's most personal obsessions. It is this historical quality, in fact, that makes of it another version of the sacred book—a Century Book, to be precise—though in a less sustained sense than *Canto General*. The dramatic weakness of *Fin de mundo* stems in part from the absence of a clear historical pattern that would define an analogy with scripture and thus clarify the political role that writing assumes—this despite a number of references to the speaker's identity as a scribe, as in "Tristísimo siglo" (Most Sorrowful Century), one of the last poems, which invokes the commonplace analogy of book to world:[12]

> El siglo de los desterrados,
> el libro de los desterrados,
> el siglo pardo, el libro negro,
> esto es lo que debo dejar
> escrito y abierto en el libro,
> desenterrándolo del siglo
> y desangrándolo en el libro. [III, 458]

[12]For a survey of this topic in Western literature, see Ernst Robert Curtius, *European Literature and the Latin Middle Ages,* trans. Willard R. Trask (New York: Harper & Row, 1953), pp. 302-47.

Pablo Neruda: The Poetics of Prophecy

> The century of exiles, / the book of exiles, / the dark century, the black book, / this is what I must leave / written and open in the book, / unearthing it from the century / and bleeding it in the book.

It is as if Neruda wished to fill a time capsule with the century's anxieties for the benefit of future generations of readers. At one point, the speaker reveals his identity as a prophetic scribe:

> Yo soy el cronista abrumado
> por lo que puede suceder y lo que debo predecir   [III, 388-89]
>
> I am the chronicler overwhelmed / by what can happen and what I must foretell,

And some of the final poems clarify that image further as he calls himself "un centinela secreto" (a secret sentinel) and

> el hombre sonoro
> testigo de las esperanzas
> en este siglo asesinado.   [III, 464]
>
> the sonorous man, / witness to the hopes / betrayed in this century.

Toward the end, with the waning of the century, he includes a further note of optimism, though the foreseen future is only partly redemptive. Man's survival, that is, appears to be unrelated to the world's, condemned as it is to end in self-destruction. Spoken as if moments after the nuclear holocaust, his last words are thus hardly reassuring:

> Cansados de ir y volver
> encontraremos la alegría: en el planeta mas amargo.
> Tierra, te beso y me despido.   [III, 465]
>
> tired of going and returning, / we shall find joy: in the bitterest planet. / Earth, I kiss you and I take my leave.

While the motif of impending doom does provide a loose unity to *Fin de mundo,* the book ultimately fails to dramatize the

Apocalypse

events of a traditional apocalypse. Like *Canto General*, from which it cannot be completely separated, and such poems as "Escrito en el año 2000" and "Cataclismo," it only tells of apocalypse instead of showing it. It is particularly noteworthy, for example, that the final poems show the speaker standing at the literal end of the world despite the absence of a dramatic holocaust. This truncated ending seems to be related to the absence of redemption, as the renewal of the earth seems impossible after a nuclear disaster, and man appears to be condemned to an endless wandering in search of another elusive millennium. These two flaws attest to Neruda's bitter vision of the future, and they may well have driven him to pursue the very different view of apocalypse that we find in *La espada encendida*.

The conceptual bridge between the two books may be *2000*, a minor volume of nine poems whose satirical tone is so reminiscent of *Fin de Mundo* that one might surmise that Neruda had excised them from the earlier book and rearranged them as a separate volume.[13] Like *Fin de mundo*, *2000* bewails the destruction leading up to the millennium, but its festive tone forbids a somber conclusion. Its "characters," who parade though the book as in a *danse macabre* in celebration of the new age, condemn the century. Among them are a future door-to-door salesman who peddles an absurd "botón para cambiar el mundo" (button to change the world) (p. 14) and a dismal bureaucrat who refuses to join in the celebration:

> Qué tengo yo que ver
> con los tres ceros que se ostentan gloriosos
> sobre mi propio cero, sobre mi inexistencia?   [p. 34]

> What have I to do / with the three zeros that boast of their glory / above my own zero, above my nonexistence?

And yet "La Tierra" (The Earth), the key middle poem, sounds a redemptive note very different from the bitterness of both the rest of the poems and the earlier *Fin de mundo*:

> Este mismo planeta, la alfombra de mil años
> puede florecer pero no acepta la muerte ni el reposo.   [p. 233]

[13]All quotations refer to *2000* (Buenos Aires: Losada, 1974).

This same planet, the carpet of a thousand years, / can bloom but does not accept death or repose.

It is impossible, of course, to know the extent to which this shift attests to an "evolution" in Neruda's treatment of the millenarian theme. Not only was *2000* published posthumously, so that its precise relation to *Fin de mundo* is impossible to determine, but it is a minor and uneven volume whose interest lies mainly in the light it can shed on Neruda's other works. *La espada encendida*, Neruda's third and most accomplished apocalyptic book, seems to develop the redemption theme that is only suggested in *2000*. And in finally dramatizing a cosmic apocalypse, it corrects both the thinness of *2000* and the diffuse bitterness of *Fin de mundo*, which was written about the same time.

IV

The best summary of *La espada encendida* is its prefacing "Argument":

> This fable tells the story of a fugitive from the great devastations that did away with mankind. Founder of a kingdom located in the spacious Magellanic solitudes, he decides to be the last of the world's inhabitants until a damsel, escaping from the Golden City of the Caesars, appears in his territory.
> The fate that led them to come together raises against them the ancient flaming sword of the new savage and solitary Eden.
> Upon God's anger and death, in a setting illuminated by the great volcano, these Adamic beings become conscious of their own divinity. [III, 471]

The word "fable" indicates the poem's mythopoeic conception. Rhodo and Rosía, Neruda's "last" couple, are also his "first," as the title tells us; its biblical source (Gen. 3:24) serves as the epigraph to the book: "So he drove out the man; and he placed at the east of the Garden of Eden Cherubims and a flaming sword which turned every way, to keep the way of the tree of life." Neruda replaces the Bible's prelapsarian garden with a "savage and solitary Eden," a renewed beginning that is already

Apocalypse

postapocalyptic. Rhodo is a fugitive from history's last nightmare; his disgust for his race has driven him to attempt self-extinction. Rosía, too, is a fugitive, though from the world of myth rather than history, a survivor of the "Golden City of the Caesars," the Chilean source myth, which appears in a note at the end of the book.[14] Their sexual encounter and subsequent love therefore reenact the Edenic myth, but only after history and myth have run their full course. And their achievement of a love beyond sexual desire amounts to their joint attempt to reenter Paradise and partake of the tree of life, an attempt avenged by the rising of the flaming sword against them in the form of a more deadly apocalypse.

La espada encendida creates an apocalypse by rewriting Genesis, thus suggesting a profound cyclical identity between Revelation and Creation, between the earth's destruction and its renewal. The text duplicates this identity by opposing the epigraph from Genesis to the final note on the Chilean source myth, as if pointing to a similar synthesis between biblical imagination and American mythology. Neruda's overt use of all these texts highlights the poem's bookishness and thus underscores the fable's nonmimetic character. In addition to these biblical passages (and several more that will become evident in due course), its texts include both the end of "Cataclismo" and Neruda's 1923 translation of "L'incendie terrestre," a short story by Marcel Schwob, which is virtually grafted onto the poem.[15] Schwob's story was also about a "last couple," who, like Rhodo and Rosía, escape a final conflagration by floating down to the sea. Its most

---

[14]Neruda's source for the myth, as he states in the *Nota*, is Julio Vicuña Cifuentes, *Mitos y supersticiones de Chile* (Santiago de Chile, 1919), For further bibliography on the legend of the City of the Caesars, see Carlos Keller, *Mitos y leyendas de Chile* (Santiago de Chile: Jerónimo de Vivar, 1972), pp. 58–64.

[15]Eliana Suárez Rivero has pointed out these biblical allusions in "Fantasía y mito en la obra de Pablo Neruda: *La espada encendida*," in *Otros mundos, otros fuegos: Fantasía y realismo mágico en Iberoamérica, Memoria del XVI Congreso de Literatura Iberoamericana,* ed. Donald A. Yates (Pittsburgh: K & S Enterprises [for] Michigan State Council on Latin American Studies, 1975), pp. 199-204. Neruda's translation of Schwob, under the pen name Sachka, was first published in *Zig-Zag*, 974 (October 20, 1923), and is reprinted in III, 759-62. The story was originally part of Schwob's collection *Le Roi au masque d'or*, which Neruda had reviewed a few months earlier, under the same pen name, in *Claridad*, 95 (July 21, 1923). Luis Sáinz de Medrano refers to Schwob's text in his paper "El último Neruda," in *Otros mundos, otros fuegos*, p. 192.

telling passage, perhaps, was rendered by Neruda as follows: "Y, en ese vieja barca, primer instrumento de la vida inferior, ellos eran un Adán jovencito y una pequeñita Eva, únicos sobrevivientes del Infierno terrestre" (And in that old boat, the first instrument of the lower life, they were a young Adam and a little Eve, the sole survivors of the earthly Inferno) (III, 762). Whether or not the couple survives is a question that Schwob leaves open at the end of the story, and we could regard Neruda's later graft as an attempt to supply a resolution for its uncertain ending: "Ella se levantó y se desvistió. Desnudos, la luz universal iluminaba sus miembros frágiles y pálidos. Se tomaron las manos y se besaron. —Amémonos, dijo ella" (She arose and undressed. Nude, the universal light shone on her frail and pale limbs. They held hands and kissed. "Let us love each other," she said) (III, 762). This climactic Edenic gesture, which recalls the end of "Cataclismo," reaffirms the value of desire in the face of Apocalypse, as if invoking a creative force in the midst of physical destruction. In *La espada encendida* the defense of desire recurs so forcefully that it requires nothing less than the agency of William Blake, whose poetry mediates Neruda's late immersion in myth.

Ever since 1935, when Neruda translated "Visions of the Daughters of Albion" and "The Mental Traveller," critics have speculated about Blake's possible influence on Neruda.[16] But nothing in Neruda's earlier works shows Blake's influence so clearly as this late book. In addition to recalling Blake's mythical "Giant Forms," Rhodo and Rosía enact a Blakean erotic drama whose argument is perhaps best summarized in Plate 14 of *The Marriage of Heaven and Hell*:

> The ancient tradition that the world will be consumed in fire at the end of six thousand years is true, as I have heard from Hell.
> For the cherub with his flaming sword is hereby commanded
> to leave his guard at the tree of life, and when he does, the whole creation will be consumed, and appear infinite and holy

---

[16]Neruda's translations of Blake first appeared in *Cruz y Raya* (Madrid), 20 (November 1943), and are reprinted in III, 767-80.

Apocalypse

whereas it now appears finite and corrupt.
This will come to pass by an improvement of sensual
enjoyment. . . .
If the doors of perception were cleansed everything would
appear to man, as it is, infinite.
For man has closed himself up, till he sees all things
thro' narrow chinks of his cavern.[17]

Blake proposes an apocalypse of mind that would liberate the body through "sensual enjoyment" and thereby cleanse "the doors of perception." Neruda adopts Blake's metaphorical pattern, which links the removal of the "flaming sword" from the tree of life by means of an apocalyptic conflagration, and gives it an overtly sexual meaning that in Blake is only implicit. In Plate 14 of *The Marriage*, Blake relates apocalypse to his work as poet and engraver, to his printing "in the infernal method, by corrosives," whose heat melts "apparent surfaces away."[18] Neruda reads a sexual meaning in Blake's apocalypse of poetic engraving and thereby links his own argument with Blake's more sexually explicit texts, notably "Visions of the Daughters of Albion."

Blake's motto in "Visions," published in the same year as *The Marriage*, is that "the Eye sees more than the Heart knows." Applied to *La espada encendida*, the motto means that Rhodo and Rosía, like Blake's Theotormon and Oothoon, are tortured souls who attempt to teach the heart to catch up with the pleasures enjoyed by the eye. Both couples attempt, that is, to carry innocence into experience through sexual release and thereby reconcile conscience with desire. Rhodo's obsession with the past, his simultaneous disgust and nostalgia, makes of him a new Theotormon, though Neruda seems also to have endowed him with the titanic prowess and bad faith of Bromion, the third and villainous character in the mythical triangle of Blake's "Visions." Rosía seems clearly patterned on Oothoon, "the soft soul of America" and Blake's true protagonist, though she fails to dis-

---

[17]*The Poetry and Prose of William Blake*, ed. David V. Erdman, with commentary by Harold Bloom (New York: Doubleday, 1965), pp. 38-39.
[18]Ibid., p. 38. Blake's (as well as Schwob's and Neruda's) source for the image of apocalypse by fire is II Peter 2:8-13. For a discussion of Blake's fire symbolism, see Northrop Frye, *Fearful Symmetry: A Study of William Blake* (Princeton: Princeton University Press, 1947), pp. 194-201.

play the subtle ironic growth of her predecessor. With Rosía, and following Blake, Neruda seeks to fashion a geographical allegory in which American myth may incorporate its tortured history and achieve a total liberation. The design harks back to *Canto General,* of course, but the new internal argument suggests a subtle critique. As in Blake, "the ethics of sexual release... would renovate mankind and end all mind-forged tyrannies, not just the political ones."[19] Yet Blake, too, seems to be criticized, as Rhodo and Rosía achieve the union that eludes Theotormon and Oothoon. Neruda's apocalypse is a response to Blake's irony.

Rhodo's first reaction to Rosía, in the second of the book's eighty-seven poems, contains the germ of the crisis: "la vió sin verla" (he saw her without seeing her), a Blakean displacement of the heart by the eye which the speaker restates a few lines later: "Rhodo la destinó, sin saberlo, al silencio" (Rhodo destined her, without knowing it, to silence) (III, 473). As a prisoner of the past (perhaps the violent past of *Fin de mundo*), Rhodo can only experience a desire that submits its object to his own self-imposed fate—"La muerte lo enlutó de manera espaciosa ... hasta que decidió dedicarse al silencio" (Death slowly enveloped him... until he decided to dedicate himself to silence) (III, 475).[20] Rhodo's state of mind is conveyed by the collection of seventy salt statues of his former wives, on which he lingers nostalgically in an ironic recasting of the story of Lot (Gen. 19:26). Rosía's intrusion on this silent exile rekindles Rhodo's desire, though his act of possession is corrupted by his obsession with the past. This is Rhodo's "hallazgo" (discovery) in the ninth poem, where Rosía's own silence torments him enough to drive him to a jealous fit. But Rhodo's violence arouses Rosía and turns both into the "savages" of the following poem:

> Se deseaban, se lograban, se destruían,
> se ardían, se rompían, se caían de bruces
> el uno dentro del otro, en una lucha a muerte,
> se enmarañaban, se perseguían, se odiaban,

[19]Harold Bloom, *Blake's Apocalypse: A Study in Poetic Argument* (New York: Doubleday, 1965), p. 110.
[20]Alain Sicard, *El pensamiento poético de Pablo Neruda,* trans. Pilar Ruiz Va (Madrid: Gredos, 1981, p. 545.

Apocalypse

> se buscaban, se destrozaban de amor,
> volvían a temerse y a maldecirse y a amarse,
> se negaban cerrando los ojos. [III, 479]

> They desired, achieved, destroyed, / burned, broke each other, they fell headlong / one inside the other, in a fight to the death, / they scratched, pursued, hated, / searched for, destroyed each other for love, / they feared and cursed and loved each other over again, / they withdrew from each other closing their eyes.

The couple's sexual violence, which puts each "entre el amor y el odio" (between love and hate) (III, 480), stems from the fury of a mediated desire that turns sex into a challenge and lovers into contenders. That Neruda intended the theme of mediated desire as a gloss on Genesis seems to be confirmed by Poem XI, where Rhodo's age is given as 130, Adam's age when he begat Seth (Gen. 5:3), and in the titles of the next two poems, "El conocimiento" (Knowledge) and "La culpa" (Guilt).[21] The departure from Genesis comes in poem XIV, where the speaker half-mockingly remarks the crucial difference:

> Ahora, el que cuenta esta historia te pregunta, viajero,
> si Dios no visitó sus patagonias,
> si allí en el último Edén, el de los dolores,
> nadie apareció sentado en el cielo,
> quién o qué cosa, trueno o árbol o falso dios
> dictó de nuevo el castigo para los amorosos? [III, 482]

> Now, the one who tells this story asks you, voyager, / if God didn't visit his Patagonias, / if there in the last Eden, the one of sorrows, / no one appeared seated in heaven, / who or what, thunder or tree or false god, / dictated anew the lovers' punishment?

The question becomes rhetorical when the obvious answer is withheld: that Rhodo and Rosía are their own judges and the "flaming sword" is a projection of their guilt. Neruda's "guilt," however, goes beyond a narrowly moral sense and is identified not with the breaking of a divine command but with the kind of

---

[21]See Suárez Rivero, "Fantasía y mito," p. 202.

physical desire that stems from an inauthentic relation to time such as Rhodo's. The Bible's linkage of pleasure to suffering, Neruda's gloss seems to say, cannot be read in isolation from the temporal inauthenticity imposed by God in providing the garden or from the human propensity to escape the rigors of the present, an inauthenticity that Genesis conceals, Neruda's gloss further implies, by portraying Eden as a beneficent gift. Pleasure and suffering are related, then, not as a result of man's first disobedience but as a function of the garden's deceptions:

> El sufrimiento fue como una sangre negra
> que por las venas subió sin descanso
> cuando el goce bajaba del árbol de la vida.   [III, 481]
>
> Suffering was like a black blood / that rose through the veins without pause / when pleasure fell from the tree of life.

Hence the lust that begins and ends with the body and which borders on hatred as much as on love.

Neruda's metaphor for this inauthentic desire is the holocaust, which the couple transfers imaginatively onto the landscape and whose principal agent is the fire that smolders within the volcanoes of passion. As pleasure posits its own suffering and guilt, so does lust eventually erupt and cause widespread destruction. The metaphorical association of lust with fire is not new, of course, but here again a passage from Blake's "Visions" proves instructive. Bromion's rape of Oothoon is witnessed by Theotormon "with secret tears," while imprisoned "in religious caves beneath the burning fires / Of lust, that belch incessant from the summits of the earth."[22] Theotormon's "religious caves" are his hideaway from lust, but his jealous witnessing still takes the form of a volcano about to burst with the passion of mediated or mimetic desire. Rhodo and Rosía's "heat," like Theotormon's, is a "consumption/consummation" gone wrong that dictates an economy of diminishing returns ("mientras más la tuvo ... él parecía consumirla menos" (when most he possessed her ... he seemed to consume her least) (III,

---

[22]*Poetry and Prose*, p. 45. Neruda renders these lines literally: "cavernas religiosas bajo los fuegos ardientes / de la lujuria, vomitando incesante desde las alturas del mundo" (III, 769).

Apocalypse

479), and which stands to be corrected with the all-consuming fire of apocalypse, the ultimate wedding or union in love.[23]

This internal meaning becomes gradually obvious in the book's counterpoint equation of character and landscape, spiritual and geological turmoil. The first sign of this equation is the earth tremor ("un estertor o un trueno / manifestó la tierra (the earth gave a death rattle or a thunderclap) (III, 477) which follows closely after the couple's first copulation in poem VIII. The speaker remarks then on the creation of "un nuevo mundo interno como un panal salvaje" (a new inner world like a savage honeycomb) (III, 478). Similarly, in poem XXVII, "La cadena" (The Chain), Rhodo and Rosía make love "mientras... el reino despiadado temblaba" (while... the cruel kingdom trembled), simultaneous actions that are paralleled in "Estaban presos en su paroxismo, / y estaban presos en su propio Edén" (They were prisoners in their paroxysm, / and they were prisoners in their own Eden) (III, 493). It is only in poem XXXII, where Rhodo's admission of temporal inauthenticity yields a statement of affection, that we begin to witness some spiritual improvement: "Si bien tu amor me volvió al sufrimiento / abrió la dicha pura" (Although your love returned me to suffering, / it unlocked pure happiness) (III, 499). But this statement seems to be contradicted in "La espada se prepara" (The Sword Is Readied), the next poem, which describes the birth and growth of a volcano. Poems XXXVIII to LXXX alternate no fewer than fifteen times between descriptions of the couple's anxieties and those of seismic turmoil. The latter all bear the same title, "Volcán" (Volcano), and they follow in a crescendo that erupts in LXXI, the title poem. In "Advenimiento" (Advent), the poem that immediately precedes it, the equation receives its fullest treatment when Rosía's passion parallels volcanic activity:

> Ella sintió crecer adentro de ella:
> no la razón, sino una rosa dura,
> una pasión como una cruz de piedra,
> un grito vegetal de sus raíces.
> De la tierra erizada brota el humo,

---

[23]For the general problematic of mediated desire, violence, and religion, see René Girard, *La Violence et le sacré* (Paris: Bernard Grasset, 1972).

Pablo Neruda: The Poetics of Prophecy

incierta torre, lista
para caer, bocina de los truenos,
río de los dolores.   [III, 529]

> She felt growing inside her / not reason, but a hard rose, / a passion like a stone cross, / a vegetable scream of her roots. / Smoke burst forth from the bristling earth, / uncertain tower, ready / to fall, trumpet of thunders, / river of pain.

In the next poem the flaming sword erupts "ardiendo encima de la boca nevada" (burning atop the snow-covered mouth) (III, 529), but by now we know that "mouth" refers as much to Rosía as to the volcano. The eruption, at this point in the poem, signals that Rhodo and Rosía have attained mutual love and thus threaten to reenter Paradise. Rhodo's earlier admission of love in poem LXIV, for example, is preceded by the forging of "la espada del castigo" (the sword of punishment) (III, 523). But this surface explanation does not fully account for the inner argument. Metaphorically, the flaming sword rises against the couple as their own flames of lust become gradually extinguished. The violence of mediated desire is thus transferred to the idea of God, the ultimate mediator. Yet apocalypse, in this latter-day Genesis, will not mean simply another expulsion from the garden, but the wholesale destruction of that garden along with the very idea of God or mediation itself. What appears to be the lovers' punishment, then, is actually their liberation, as Neruda follows closely Blake's injunction, in *The Marriage of Heaven and Hell*, for the removal of the Flaming Sword and the world's rebirth as "infinite and holy."

The turmoil and clamor of volcanic activity represent the death throes of a God who, in resorting to violence, proves to be jealous of human love:

> Gemía Dios
> como un encarcelado
> que fue quemado vivo.
> Se derretía Dios
> en sus derrotas
> y desde su pasión, tortura y muerte,
> Dios, muerto para siempre,
> amenazó a los hombres con su espada encendida.   [III, 530]

Apocalypse

> God groaned / like a prisoner / being burned alive. / God was melting / in his defeats / and out of his passion, torture, and death, / God, dead forever, / threatened men with his flaming sword.

Here the analogy between divine defeat and volcanic eruption rests on the serious pun of "derrotas" (defeats) and "derretía" (melted), earlier implied in the last stanza of poem IX, as if to suggest a linguistic fatalism in which the melting of God's sword embodies his defeat. By thus attributing to God the same pun used earlier to dramatize the couple's predicament ("Rhodo reconoció su *derrota* /... y ella se estremeció como si / la *quemara* un rayo de oro" (Rhodo recognized his *defeat* /... and she shuddered as if / *burned* by a ray of gold) (III, 479), the poem demonstrates the extent to which God's violence has replaced man's. The lovers realize this in poem LXXIX as they are about to crash down a waterfall in their makeshift Noah's ark, which once again becomes filled with the world's fauna. Their fall dramatically reenacts the original Fall, but the new immersion in water also suggests a redemptive baptism:

> sólo allí comprendieron
> que eran dioses,
> que cuando el viejo Dios levantó la columna
> de fuego y maldición, la espada ígnea,
> allí murió el antiguo,
> el maldiciente,
> el que había cumplido y maldecía su obra,
> el Dios sin nuevos frutos
> había muerto y ahora
> pasó el hombre a ser Dios.
> Puede morir, pero debe nacer
> interminablemente:
> no puede huir: debe poblar la tierra,
> debe poblar el mar: sólo los nuevos dioses
> mordieron la manzana del amor.   [III, 536-37]

> only then did they understand / that they were gods, / that when the old God raised the column / of fire and cursing, the fiery sword, / there died the ancient one, / the cursing one, / the one who fulfilled and cursed his own work, / the God without new fruits / had died and now / man went on to become God. /

Pablo Neruda: The Poetics of Prophecy

> He can die but he must be born / endlessly. / He cannot escape. He must populate the earth, / he must populate the sea: only the new gods / bit the apple of love.

Unlike Adam and Eve, Rhodo and Rosía interpret God's violence as a sign of his exhaustion and their exile from Eden as confirmation of their own divinity. Yet Neruda's idea of divinity, like his conception of guilt, is mostly figurative: divinity is freedom from restraints and mediations, including the authority of an avenging God. Thus as the lovers float toward the open sea they discover that "la venganza del fuego quedó atrás. / El volcán abdicó su profecía" (the fire's vengeance remained behind. / The volcano revoked its prophecy) (III, 538). The couple's survival, that is, belies the prophecy of the world's end. And if fire has consumed the world (as Blake duly noted), the fire of imagination lives on. Once the lovers reach their new land, Rosía attests to their regeneration: "Rompimos la cadena" (We broke the chain) (III, 541). Her words allude to the earlier poem "La cadena," poem XXVII, in which the couple had made love as a snowstorm threatened. Her last statement is also the book's: "Sobre esta piedra / esperaré para encender el fuego" (On this rock / I shall stay to light the fire) (III, 542). By subverting the obvious Petrine phrase, Rosía points toward the founding of a new church: the temple of human love.

In *La espada encendida* Neruda gave final form to the apocalypse he had essayed in numerous earlier texts by fusing it with a late introspective poetics. The rewriting of Genesis thus becomes a creative self-correction that extends as far back as the truncated apocalypse of *Canto General* and reappears, in various degrees of explicitness, in several poems and books. Beyond the bitter chronicle of *Fin de mundo*, Neruda's argument is that apocalypse lies not at the end of history or at the behest of a deceptive God, but within the halting tremors of the human soul.

Postscript

After a life spent training for the sight!
What in the midst lay but the Tower itself?
—Robert Browning, "Childe Roland to the
Dark Tower Came"

When I write I'm absent,
and when I return I've already left.
—Pablo Neruda, "Return to a City"

El campanario de Authenay
(from *Geografía infructuosa*, 1972)

Contra la claridad de la pradera
un campanario negro.

Salta desde la iglesia triangular:
pizarra y simetría.

Mínima iglesia en la suave extensión
como para que rece una paloma.

La pura voluntad de un campanario
contra el cielo de invierno.

La rectitud divina de la flecha
dura como una espada

con el metal de un gallo tempestuoso
volando en la veleta.

(No la nostalgia, es el orgullo
nuestro vestido pasajero

Pablo Neruda: The Poetics of Prophecy

y el follaje que nos cubría
cae a los pies del campanario.

Este orden puro que se eleva
sostiene su sistema gris

en el desnudo poderío
de la estación color de lluvia.

Aquí el hombre estuvo y se fue:
dejó su deber en la altura,

y regresó a los elementos,
al agua de la geografía.

Así pude ser y no pude,
así no aprendí mis deberes:

me quedé donde todo el mundo
mirara mis manos vacías:

las construcciones que no hice:
mi corazón deshabitado:

mientras oscuras herramientas
brazos grises, manos oscuras

levantaban la rectitud
de un campanario y de una flecha.

Ay lo que traje yo a la tierra
lo dispersé sin fundamento,

no levanté sino las nubes
y sólo anduve con el humo

sin saber que de piedra oscura
se levantaba la pureza

en anteriores territorios
en el invierno indiferente.)

Oh asombro vertical en la pradera
húmeda y extendida:

Postscript

una delgada dirección de aguja
exacta, sobre el cielo.

Cuántas veces de todo aquel paisaje,
árboles y terrones

en la infinita estrella horizontal
de la terrestre Normandía,

por nieve o lluvia o corazón cansado,
de tanto ir y venir por el mundo,

se quedaron mis ojos amarrados
al campanario de Authenay,

a la estructura de la voluntad
sobre los dominios dispersos

de la tierra que no tiene palabras
y de mi propia vida.

En la interrogación de la pradera
y mis atónitos dolores

una presencia inmóvil rodeada
por la pradera y el silencio:

la flecha de una pobre torre oscura
sosteniendo un gallo en el cielo.   [III, 588-91]

Against the meadow's brightness / a black belfry. / It stands out from the triangular church: / blackboard and symmetry. / A minimal church on the smooth space / as if made for a dove to pray. / The pure will of a belfry / against the winter sky. / The arrow's divine rectitude, / hard as a sword, / with the metal of a stormy rooster / flying on the weathervane. / (Not nostalgia but pride / is our fleeting dress, / and the foliage that once covered us / falls at the belfry's feet. / This pure rising order / holds up its gray scheme / in the naked dominion / of the rain-colored season. / Here man once was and left: / he left his duty at the height / and returned to the elements, / to the water of geography. / Thus I could be and could not, / thus I learned not my duties: / I remained where everyone / could look at my empty hands: / the constructions I built not, / my uninhabited heart: /

Pablo Neruda: The Poetics of Prophecy

while dark tools, / gray arms, dark hands / raised the rectitude / of a belfry and of an arrow. / Alas, what I brought to earth / I scattered without foundation, / I raised but clouds / and only walked around with smoke / without knowing that out of dark stone / purity was raised / in previous territories / in the indifferent winter.) Oh, vertical amazement on the meadow / moist and spacious, / direction of spire, / exact, upon the sky. / How many times out of all that landscape, / trees and lumps of earth, / on the infinite horizontal star / of earthy Normandy, / through snow or rain or heart tired / from so much coming and going through the world, / my eyes fixed / on the belfry at Authenay, / on the structure of will / over the scattered dominions / of the wordless earth / and of my own life. / Upon the meadow's interrogation / and my amazed pains, / a still presence surrounded / by the meadow and silence: / the arrow of a poor dark tower / holding up a rooster in the sky.

Each of the poem's three sections corresponds to a different reaction of the speaker's. In the first section, made up of the first six couplets, he describes the vision. In the second section, the fifteen parenthetical couplets, he meditates on the vision's meaning. In the third, the rest of the poem, he externalizes his amazed reaction and proposes a conclusion.

The initial impression is cast in symmetrical couplets written in impassive telegraphese. The belfry appears dark from mold or age. It stands out starkly against the winter sky of Normandy, a fortress bearing its steeple as though it were an arrow or a sword. The confrontation appears at the outset in the use of the preposition "contra" (against), the first word of the poem, which recurs in the fourth couplet. This opposition between belfry and landscape sets up a primary contrast of black and white which suggests the image of a blackboard, the poem's metaphor for Neruda's writing, on which a series of moral qualities are inscribed. The steeple's "divine rectitude" is superimposed on the structure's "pure will" and both are crowned by the weathervane's stormy "rooster," the symbol of virility.

The following parenthetical meditation reveals the meaning of the vision, at whose feet the speaker now humbles himself like a pilgrim before an altar. The belfry presents "un orden puro que se eleva," a pure rising order or symbolic structure that seeks transcendence over immanent obstacles. The belfry's "altura" of course recalls that of Machu Picchu, whose own anonymity had embodied a similar sign of plenitude, and thus identifies the structure as the speaker's negative image. The belfry is what he is not: a reminder of faults, the X ray of desire.

Like all belfries, this one signifies watchtower and music, vision and song. In Neruda, as we know by now, bells are the symbol of poetic experience—"mi profesión de campana" (my bell vocation [III, 601]), he says elsewhere in the same book. Yet never before has a belfry appeared in his poetry. The belfry at Authenay is Neruda's vision of poetry incarnate, the origin of all songs and the source of all visions, though in this case the poet admits that he had nothing to do with achieving this particular incarnation. Hence his despondency when he finds it, feeling "empty hands" and an "uninhabited heart," since the structure embodies in the simplest terms the absolute presence that his own work has always attempted but failed to express. After a life spent training for the sight, the prophet keeps his appointment with the original vision, but all he learns are the limits of his creative enterprise and the poverty of his own text. Rubén Darío, good symbolist that he was, wrote once that his style was but "the bud of thought seeking to be the rose." At the end of the same poem, however, Darío found not the limits of vision but a poetic Unknown that offered a cryptic "cygnet's neck, questioning." Neruda places himself beyond Darío's question, at the moment when the bud of creation has already bloomed into a rose, only to find the misery of his own creation and the errors of visionary reading.

Why the error? The belfry is dark, built by dark tools and hands, and its scheme is gray. Far from signifying the negativity that its somberness suggests, the belfry proves to be purity itself, "divine rectitude" rising out of darkness. What the vision tells the poet, then, is that his language has been wrong all along: darkness, not brightness, is the true purity, and the "winter sky" is but the void against which the dark tower rises. That is, the error lies in the poet's reading, his interpretation, which, in siding with the forces of brightness, chose the immaterial "clouds" and "smoke" over the fundamental "dark stone."

The poem's last section begins with an apostrophe that acknowledges the structure's superiority. Whereas in the initial reaction the belfry appears "*against* the meadow's brightness" and "*against* the winter sky," now the steeple looms "*upon* the sky" and "*over* the scattered dominions." While both the meadow and the sky spread out horizontally, dispersing all meaning, the belfry rises vertically upon the "wordless earth"—the poet's impoverished text. To the pain caused by his discovery of such a "still presence," the speaker responds with a final irony in which he admits the poverty of his work in contrast to the wealth of a humble belfry. In this sense, the last couplet is but a replay of the initial reaction, though this time the speaker, as if showing that he has learned his lesson, strips the scene of all interpretation and reduces it to a pure object: the steeple is but an "arrow," the belfry "a poor dark tower," the weathervane "a rooster in the sky," and yet all three are enough to embody the presence, as well as the error, of all past and future poetry.

Every poet dwells in a belfry of his own, the poetic "scheme" that comprehends his work. Within that scheme he inscribes his probes into reality and establishes a dialogue with himself. We call such schemes an author's "poetics," but often the term conveys the impression of an ordering consciousness and a body of beliefs that cause and control each and every aspect of the poem. A poetics, however, can never be complete, can never be the whole of a poet's "theories." Neither language nor literary tradition allows the author to control all of the rules and principles that define his text because the text functions as a sign within systems of meaning that exceed the limits of an ordering consciousness. Language, then, not the poet or the reader, is the true author of the poem, and the acknowledgment of that fact alone constitutes the truest sign of authenticity.

Authenay, authenticity, author. Could it be that this poem is but a fable of the modern author, and in particular of the Romantic poet who codifies his work according to a tradition that exposes him to the possibility of error? Almost fatefully, Neruda had to arrive at Authenay, a Normandy village so small that it does not even appear on most maps, to acknowledge his tradition and confess his authenticity. For how else could the prophet lay the groundwork for our residence on earth?

Bibliography

I. Works by Pablo Neruda

BOOKS

Canción de gesta. 4th ed. Montevideo: El Siglo Ilustrado, 1960.
A New Decade: Poems 1956-1967. Ed and trans. Ben Belitt and Alastair Reid. New York: Grove Press, 1969.
Toward the Splendid City: Nobel Lecture. New York: Farrar, Straus & Giroux, 1972.
Obras Completas. 4th ed. 3 vols. Ed. Margarita Aguirre, Alfonso Escudero, and Hernán Loyola. Buenos Aires: Losada, 1973.
2000. Buenos Aires: Losada, 1974.
Confieso que he vivido: Memorias. Barcelona: Seix Barral, 1974.
Memoirs. Trans. Hardie St. Martin. New York: Farrar, Straus & Giroux, 1977.
Isla Negra. Trans. Alastair Reid. Afterword by Enrico Mario Santí. New York: Farrar, Straus & Giroux, 1981.
―――― with Héctor Eandi: *Correspondencia durante "Residencia en la tierra."* Ed. Margarita Aguirre. Buenos Aires: Losada, 1980.

ESSAYS

"Palabras de Pablo Neruda (al dar las gracias por el homenaje que el pueblo panameño le hizo la noche del 3 de septiembre de 1943 por invitación de la Sociedad Española de Beneficencia)." *Repertorio Americano,* 24 (October 13, 1943), 274.
"Pablo Neruda habla." *El Siglo,* December 5, 1943, p. 12.
"Algo sobre mi poesía y mi vida." *Aurora,* 1 (1954), 10-21.

II. Works Cited

BOOKS

Abrams, Meyer H. *Natural Supernaturalism: Tradition and Revolution in Romantic Literature.* New York: Norton, 1971.

Pablo Neruda: The Poetics of Prophecy

Agamben, Giorgio. *Stanze, la parola e il fantasma nella cultura occidentale.* Turin: Einaudi, 1977.

Alonso, Amado. *Poesía y estilo de Pablo Neruda: Interpretación de una poesía hermética.* 2d ed. 1940; Buenos Aires: Sudamericana, 1968.

Auerbach, Erich. *Scenes from the Drama of European Literature.* Trans. Ralph Mannheim. New York: Meridian Books, 1959.

Bays, Gwendolyn. *The Orphic Vision: Seer Poets from Novalis to Rimbaud.* Lincoln: University of Nebraska Press, 1964.

Benjamin, Walter. *The Origin of German Tragic Drama.* Trans. John Osborne. 1928; London: NLB, 1977.

Bergmann, Emilie L. *Art Inscribed: Essays on Ecphrasis in Golden Age Poetry.* Cambridge: Harvard University Press, 1979.

Bingham, Hiram. *The Lost City of the Incas.* New York: Duell, Sloan, 1948.

Bizzarro, Salvatore. *Pablo Neruda: All Poets the Poet.* Metuchen, N.J.: Scarecrow Press, 1979.

Blanchot, Maurice. *Le Livre à venir.* Paris: Gallimard, 1959.

Bloom, Harold. *Blake's Apocalypse: A Study in Poetic Argument.* New York: Doubleday, 1965.

Borges, Jorge Luis. *Historia de la eternidad.* 1936; Buenos Aires: Emecé, 1953.

Brotherston, Gordon. *Latin American Poetry: Origins and Presence.* Cambridge: At the University Press, 1975.

Buber, Martin. *Pointing the Way: Collected Essays.* Ed. Maurice Friedman. New York: Harper & Row, 1957.

Camacho Guizado, Eduardo. *Pablo Neruda—Naturaleza, historia y poética.* Madrid: Sociedad General Española de Librería, 1978.

Cano Ballesta, Juan. *La poesía española entre pureza y revolución (1930-1936).* Madrid: Gredos, 1971.

Cardona Peña, Alfredo. *Pablo Neruda y otros ensayos.* Mexico City: Andrea, 1955.

Clifford, Gay, *The Transformations of Allegory.* London: Routledge & Kegan Paul, 1974.

Coates, Wilson H., & Hayden V. White. *The Ordeal of Liberal Humanism: An Intellectual History of Modern Europe.* New York: McGraw-Hill, 1970.

Costa, René de. *The Poetry of Pablo Neruda.* Cambridge: Harvard University Press, 1979.

Culler, Jonathan. *Structuralist Poetics: Structuralism, Linguistics, and the Study of Literature.* Ithaca: Cornell University Press, 1975.

Curtius, Ernst Robert. *European Literature and the Latin Middle Ages.* Trans. Willard R. Trask. New York: Harper, 1953.

Darío, Rubén. See García Sarmiento, Félix Rubén.

Bibliography

Demaray, John G. *The Invention of Dante's Commedia*. New Haven: Yale University Press, 1974.

Derrida, Jacques. *Of Grammatology*. Trans. Gayatri Chakravorty Spivak. Paris, 1967; Baltimore: Johns Hopkins University Press, 1976.

―――. *Writing and Difference*. Trans. Alan Bass. Paris, 1967; Chicago: University of Chicago Press, 1978.

―――. *Positions*. Trans. Alan Bass. Paris, 1972; Chicago: University of Chicago Press, 1981.

Durán, Manuel, and Margery Safir. *Earth Tones: The Poetry of Pablo Neruda*. Bloomington: Indiana University Press, 1981.

Erdman, David, ed. *The Poetry and Prose of William Blake*. With commentary by Harold Bloom. New York: Doubleday, 1965.

Felstiner, John. *Translating Neruda: The Way to Macchu Picchu*. Stanford: Stanford University Press, 1980.

Fletcher, Angus. *Allegory: The Theory of a Symbolic Mode*. Ithaca: Cornell University Press, 1964.

Foucault, Michel. *The Order of Things: An Archaeology of the Human Sciences*. Paris, 1966; New York: Random House, 1970.

Freccero, John, ed. *Dante: A Collection of Critical Essays*. Englewood Cliffs, N.J.: Prentice-Hall, 1970.

Frye, Northrop. *Fearful Symmetry: A Study of William Blake*. Princeton: Princeton University Press, 1947.

―――. *Anatomy of Criticism: Four Essays*. Princeton: Princeton University Press, 1957.

García Sarmiento, Félix Rubén (Rubén Darío). *Poesías completas*. Ed. Alfonso Méndez Plancarte and Antonio Oliver Belmás. Madrid: Aguilar, 1968.

Gilman, Stephen. *The Tower as Emblem*. Frankfurt am Main: Vittorio Klostermann, 1967.

Girard, René. *La Violence et le sacré*. Paris: Bernard Grasset, 1972.

Goldstein, Laurence. *Ruins and Empire: The Evolution of a Theme in Augustan and Romantic Literature*. Pittsburgh: University of Pittsburgh Press, 1977.

González Echevarría, Roberto. *Alejo Carpentier: The Pilgrim at Home*. Ithaca: Cornell University Press, 1977.

Grandgent, C. H., and Charles S. Singleton, eds. *La Divina Commedia*. Cambridge: Harvard University Press, 1972.

Hagstrum, Jean H. *The Sister Arts: The Tradition of Literary Pictorialism in English Poetry from Dryden to Gray*. Chicago: University of Chicago Press, 1958.

Hartman, Geoffrey. *Beyond Formalism: Literary Essays, 1958–1970*. New Haven: Yale University Press, 1970.

Heredia, José María. *Poesías completas.* Ed. Angel Aparicio Laurencio. Miami: Universal, 1970.
Heschel, Abraham J. *The Prophets.* New York: Harper & Row, 1962.
Hugo, Victor. *La Légende des siècles.* Ed. Jean Gaudon. 1859; Paris: Garnier-Flammarion, 1976.
Huidobro, Vicente. *Manifestes.* Paris: Revue Mondiale, 1925.
Hyman, Stanley Edgar. *The Tangled Bank: Darwin, Marx, Frazer, and Freud as Imaginative Writers.* New York: Atheneum, 1962.
Isidore of Seville. *Etymologiarum sive originum libri XX.* Ed. W. M. Lindsay. Oxford: Claredon Press, 1966.
Jameson, Fredric. *The Prison-House of Language: A Critical Account of Structuralism and Russian Formalism.* Princeton: Princeton University Press, 1972.
Jíménez, Juan Ramón. *Españoles de tres mundos.* Buenos Aires: Losada, 1942.
Keller, Carlos. *Mitos y leyendas de Chile.* Santiago de Chile: Jerónimo de Vivar, 1972.
Kermode, John Frank. *Romantic Image.* 1953; New York: Random House, 1957.
Larrea, Juan. *Del surrealismo a Machupicchu.* Mexico City: Joaquín Mortiz, 1967.
Lehmann, A. G. *The Symbolist Aesthetic in France, 1885–1895.* 1950; 2d ed. Oxford: Basil Blackwell, 1968.
Levy, Isaac J., and Juan Loveluck, eds. *Simposio Neruda: Actas.* New York: Las Américas, 1976.
Lindblom, Johannes. *Prophecy in Ancient Israel.* Philadelphia: Muhlenberg Press, 1962.
Loyola, Hernán. *Ser y morir en Pablo Neruda (1918–1945).* Santiago de Chile: Santiago, 1967.
Lozada, Alfredo. *El monismo agónico de Pablo Neruda: Estructura, filiación y sentido de "Residencia en la tierra."* Mexico City: B. Costa Amic, 1971.
Lyons, Bridget Gellert. *Voices of Melancholy: Studies in Literary Treatments of Melancholy in Renaissance England.* New York: Norton, 1971.
McFarland, Thomas. *Romanticism and the Forms of Ruin: Wordsworth, Coleridge, and Modalities of Fragmentation.* Princeton: Princeton University Press, 1980.
McGuinn, Bernard. *Visions of the End: Apocalyptic Traditions in the Middle Ages.* New York: Columbia University Press, 1979.
Man, Paul de. *Blindness and Insight: Essays in the Rhetoric of Contemporary Criticism.* New York: Oxford University Press, 1971.
Martínez Bonati, Félix. *La estructura de la obra literaria.* 1961; 2d ed. Barcelona: Seix Barral, 1972.

Bibliography

Mazzotta, Giuseppe. *Dante, Poet of the Desert: History and Allegory* in *"The Divine Comedy."* Princeton: Princeton University Press, 1979.

Montes, Hugo. *Para leer a Pablo Neruda.* Buenos Aires: Francisco de Aguirre, 1974.

_____, ed. *Machu Picchu en la poesía.* Santiago de Chile: Nueva Universidad, 1972.

Moore, Edward R. *Miscellaneous Essays.* Studies of Dante, 3d ser. 1903; New York: Greenwood Press, 1968.

Nicolson, Marjorie Hope. *Mountain Gloom and Mountain Glory: The Development of the Aesthetics of the Infinite.* Ithaca: Cornell University Press, 1959.

O'Gorman, Edmundo. *The Invention of America: An Inquiry into the Historical Nature of the New World.* Bloomington: Indiana University Press, 1961.

Ong, Walter J. *The Presence of the Word: Some Prolegomena for Cultural and Religious History.* New Haven: Yale University Press, 1967.

_____. *Interfaces of the Word: Studies in the Evolution of Consciousness and Culture.* Ithaca: Cornell University Press, 1977.

Paz, Octavio. *Xavier Villaurrutia en persona y en obra.* Mexico City: Fondo de Cultura Económica, 1978.

Pearce, Roy Harvey. *The Continuity of American Poetry.* Princeton: Princeton University Press, 1954.

Piehler, Paul. *The Visionary Landscape.* London: Edward Arnold, 1971.

Poggioli, Renato. *The Theory of the Avantgarde.* Trans. Gerald Fitzgerald. 1962; New York: Harper & Row, 1971.

Pring-Mill, Robert, ed. *Pablo Neruda: A Basic Anthology.* Oxford: Dolphin, 1975.

Quiñones, Ricardo J. *The Renaissance Discovery of Time.* Cambridge: Harvard University Press, 1972.

Riddel, Joseph. *The Inverted Bell: Modernism and the Counterpoetics of William Carlos Williams.* Baton Rouge: Louisiana State University Press, 1974.

Rimbaud, Arthur. *Complete Works: Selected Letters.* Trans. and ed. Wallace Fowlie. Chicago: University of Chicago Press, 1966.

Rivas González, Mario. *Exégesis del poema "Alturas de Macchu Picchu."* Santiago de Chile, 1955.

Rivers, Elias, ed. *Renaissance and Baroque Poetry of Spain.* New York: Dell, 1965.

Rodríguez Monegal, Emir. *Neruda: El viajero inmóvil.* 1966; 2d rev. ed. Caracas: Monte Avila, 1977.

Said, Edward W. *Beginnings: Intention and Method.* New York: Basic Books, 1975.

Pablo Neruda: The Poetics of Prophecy

Salama, Roberto. *Para una crítica a Pablo Neruda*. Buenos Aires: Cartago, 1957.

Saxl, Fritz, Erwin Panofsky, and Raymond Klibansky. *Saturn and Melancholy*. London: Thomas Nelson, 1964.

Schwartzmann, Félix. *Del sentimiento de lo humano en América*. Santiago de Chile: Universidad de Chile, 1953.

Seward, Barbara. *The Symbolic Rose*. New York: Columbia University Press, 1960.

Sicard, Alain. *El pensamiento poético de Pablo Neruda*. Trans. Pilar Ruiz Va. Lille, 1977; Madrid: Gredos, 1981.

———, ed. *Coloquio internacional sobre Pablo Neruda (la obra posterior al Canto General)*. Poitiers: Publications du Centre de Recherches Latinoaméricaines, 1979.

Siefer, Elisabeth. *Epische Stilelemente im "Canto General" von Pablo Neruda*. Munich: Fink, 1970.

Simmel, Georg. *Cultura femenina y otros ensayos*. Trans. Eugenio Imaz et al. Madrid: Revista de Occidente, 1934.

Soublette, Gastón. *Pablo Neruda: Profeta de América*. Santiago de Chile: Nueva Universidad, 1980.

Starobinski, Jean. *The Invention of Liberty, 1700-1789*. Trans. Bernard C. Swift. Geneva: Albert Skira, 1964.

Tucker, Robert C. *Philosophy and Myth in Karl Marx*. 1961; 2d ed. Cambridge: At the University Press, 1972.

Tuveson, Ernest L. *Millennium and Utopia: A Study in the Background of the Idea of Progress*. Berkeley: University of California Press, 1949.

Valcárcel, Luis E. *Machu Picchu*. Buenos Aires: EUDEBA, 1964.

Villegas, Juan. *Estructuras míticas y arquetipos en el "Canto General" de Pablo Neruda*. Barcelona: Planeta, 1976.

Volney, C. M. *Les Ruines, ou méditations sur les révolutions des empires*. Paris, 1791.

Waisbard, Simone. *Machu Picchu: Cité perdue des Incas*. Paris: Robert Laffont, 1974.

Westermann, Klaus. *Basic Forms of Prophetic Speech*. Trans. Hugh Clayton White. Philadelphia: Westminster Press, 1967.

Willard, Nancy. *Testimony of the Invisible Man: William Carlos Williams, Francis Ponge, Rainer Maria Rilke, Pablo Neruda*. Columbia: University of Missouri Press, 1969.

Wilner, Eleanor. *Gathering the Winds: Visionary Imagination and Radical Transformations of Self and Society*. Baltimore: Johns Hopkins University Press, 1975.

Wordsworth, William. *The Literary Criticism of William Wordsworth*. Ed. Paul M. Zall. Lincoln: University of Nebraska Press, 1966.

Bibliography

ESSAYS AND ARTICLES

Alazraki, Jaime. "El surrealismo de *Tentativa del hombre infinito*." *Hispanic Review*, 40 (1972), 31–39.

———. "Observaciones sobre la estructura de la *Oda elemental*." *Mester*, 4 (1974), 94–102.

———. "Punto de vista y recodificación en los poemas de auto-exégesis de Pablo Neruda." *Symposium*, 32 (1978), 184–97.

Alonso, Amado. "The Stylistic Interpretation of Literary Texts." 1942; rpt. in *Velocities of Change: Critical Essays from MLN*, ed. Richard Macksey. Baltimore: Johns Hopkins University Press, 1974.

Arrigoitia, Luis de. "Las *Odas elementales* de Pablo Neruda," *Sin Nombre*, 3 (1972), 31–43.

Bernini, Rodolfo. "Origine, sito, forma e dimensioni del Monte del Purgatorio e dell'Inferno dantesco." *Rendiconti della Reale Accademmia di Lincei*, 5th ser., 25 (1916), 1015–1129.

Cabrera, Sarandy. "Primera teoría del *Canto General*." *Número*, 13–14 (1951), 189–95.

Caillois, Roger. "La Cité et le poème." *Europe*, 537–53 (1974), 57–61.

Cano Ballesta, Juan. "Pablo Neruda and the Renewal of Spanish Poetry during the Thirties." In *Spanish Writers of 1936*, ed. Jaime Ferrán and Daniel P. Testa, pp. 94–106. London: Tamesis Books, 1973.

Cantón, Wilberto. "Neruda en México (1940–1943)." *Anales de la Universidad de Chile*, 157–60 (1973), 263–70.

Carrillo, Gastón. "La lengua poética de Pablo Neruda: Análisis de *Alturas de Macchu Picchu*." *Boletín del Instituto de Filología de la Universidad de Chile*, 21 (1970), 293–332.

Concha, Jaime. "Interpretación de *Residencia en la tierra*." *Mapocho*, 2 (1963), 5–39.

Engler, Kay. "Image and Structure in Neruda's *Las Alturas de Macchu Picchu*." *Symposium*, 27 (1974), 130–45.

Felstiner, John. "La danza inmóvil, el vendaval sostenido: *Four Quartets* de T. S. Eliot y Alturas de Macchu Picchu." *Anales de la Universidad de Chile*, 157–60 (1971), 176–96.

Freccero, John. "Infernal Inversion and Christian Conversion (*Inferno*, XXXIV)." *Italica*, 42 (1965), 35–41.

———. "Dante's Prologue Scene." *Dante Studies*, 84 (1966), 1–25.

———. "Medusa: The Letter and the Spirit." *Yearbook of Italian Studies*, 1 (Florence, 1972), 1–18.

García, Pablo. "Interpretación de Alturas de Macchu Picchu." *Pro Arte*, 57–58 (1949), 17–22.

Goić, Cedomil. "*Alturas de Macchu Picchu*: La torre y el abismo." *Anales de la Universidad de Chile*, 157–60 (1971), 153–66.

Gómez Paz, Julieta. "Aproximación al poema de Neruda 'Alturas de Machu Picchu.'" *Sin Nombre*, 7 (1976), 57-70.
González-Cruz, Luis F. "El viaje trascendente de Pablo Neruda: Una lectura de *Tentativa del hombre infinito*." *Symposium*, 32 (1978), 197-207.
Gullón, Agnes. "Pablo Neruda at Macchu Picchu." *Chicago Review*, 27 (1974), 138-45.
Gullón, Ricardo. "Relaciones Pablo Neruda-Juan Ramón Jiménez." *Hispanic Review*, 39 (1971), 141-66.
Hart, Francis R. "Notes for an Anatomy of Modern Autobiography." *New Literary History*, 1 (1970), 485-511.
Higman, Perry Christian. "*Alturas de Macchu Picchu* en la obra de Pablo Neruda." Ph.D. dissertation, University of Iowa, 1976.
Holguín, Andrés. "Tres conferencias de Pablo Neruda." *Revista de las Indias*, 56 (1943), 267-70.
Holzinger, Walter. "Poetic Subject and Poetic Form in the *Odas Elementales*." *Revista Hispánica Moderna*, 36 (1970-71), 41-49.
Jiménez, Juan Ramón. "Carta a Pablo Neruda." *Repertorio Americano*, 23 (January 17, 1942), 12.
———. "¿América sombría?" *Repertorio Americano*, 24 (August 14, 1943), 209-11.
Jitrik, Noé. "*Alturas de Macchu Picchu*: Una marcha piramidal a través de un discurso poético incesante." *Nueva Revista de Filología Hispánica*, 26 (1976), 510-55.
Kaske, Carol V. "Mount Sinai and Dante's Mount Purgatory." *Dante Studies*, 89 (1971), 1-18.
Lipschutz, Alexander. "*Alturas de Macchu Picchu* de Pablo Neruda, visión indiana americana." *Repertorio Americano*, 45 (November 10, 1949), 345-46.
Loveluck, Juan. "*Alturas de Macchu Picchu*: Cantos I-V." *Revista Iberoamericana*, 39 (1973), 175-88.
———. "Tributo y despedida, Pablo Neruda (1904-1973): 'Más notas sobre Neruda en Oriente.'" *Hispania*, 57 (1974), 976-78.
Loyola, Hernán. "Los modos de autoreferencia en la obra de Pablo Neruda." *Aurora*, 3-4 (1964), 64-125.
———. "Itinerario de Pablo Neruda." *Anales de la Universidad de Chile*, 157-60 (1971), 9-23.
Man, Paul de. "The Rhetoric of Temporality." In *Interpretation: Theory and Practice*, ed. Charles S. Singleton, pp. 173-209. Baltimore: Johns Hopkins University Press, 1969.
Mazzotta, Giuseppe. "The *Canzoniere* and the Language of the Self." *Studies in Philology*, 75 (1978), 271-96.

Bibliography

Montes, Hugo. "Acerca de *Alturas de Macchu Picchu.*" *Mapocho,* 2 (1964), 120-34.

Morales, Leonidas. "Estructura mítica de *Alturas de Macchu Picchu.*" *Estudios Filológicos,* 1 (1965), 167-84.

Pérus, Françoise. "Arquitectura poética de *Alturas de Macchu Picchu.*" *Atenea,* 425 (1972), 104-30.

———. "Hauteurs de Macchu Picchu." *Europe,* 537-53 (1974), 86-110.

Pring-Mill, Robert. "Preface." In Pablo Neruda, *The Heights of Macchu Picchu,* trans. Nathaniel Tarn, pp. vii-xix. New York: Farrar, Straus & Giroux, 1967.

Revueltas, José. "América sombría." *Repertorio Americano,* 23 (May 9, 1942), 140-41.

Riddel, Joseph. "Decentering the Image: The 'Project' of 'American' Poetics?" In *Textual Strategies: Perspectives in Post-Structuralist Criticism,* ed. Josué Harari, pp. 322-58. Ithaca: Cornell University Press, 1979.

Rodríguez Fernández, Mario. "Exégesis del poema *Alturas de Macchu Picchu* de Pablo Neruda." *Anales de la Universidad de Chile,* 102 (1956), 128-31.

———. "El tema de la muerte en *Alturas de Macchu Picchu.*" *Anales de la Universidad de Chile,* 131 (1964), 23-50.

Rose, William. "Rilke and the Conception of Death." in *Rainer Maria Rilke: Aspects of His Mind and Poetry,* ed. William Rose and G. Craig Houston, pp. 41-84. New York: Gordian Press, 1970.

Saalmann, Dieter. "Der Tod als Sinnbild Aesthetischer Affinität zwischen Rainer Maria Rilke und Pablo Neruda." *Deutsche Vierteljahrsschrift für Literaturwissenschaft und Geistesgeschichte,* 48 (1974), 197-227.

———. "The Role of Time in Neruda's *Alturas de Macchu Picchu.*" *Romance Notes,* 18 (1977), 169-77.

Salomon, Noël. "Un événement poétique: Le *Canto General* de Pablo Neruda." *Bulletin Hispanique,* 76 (1974), 92-124.

Stackelberg, Jürgen von. "Ein Kommentar zur Dichtung." In *Die Höhen von Macchu Picchu,* trans. Rudolf Hagelstange, pp. 21-26. Hamburg: Hoffmann & Campe, 1965.

Starobinski, Jean. "Ironie et mélancholie (I): Le Théatre de Carlo Gozzi." *Critique,* 227 (1966), 291-308.

———. "Ironie et mélancholie (II): *La Princesse de Brambilla* de E. T. A. Hoffmann." *Critique,* 228 (1966), 438-57.

Suárez Rivero, Eliana. "Fantasía y mito en la obra de Pablo Neruda: *La espada encendida.*" In *Otros mundos, otros fuegos: Fantasía y realismo mágico en Iberoamérica,* ed. Donald A. Yates. Transactions of the 16th

Congress of the International Institute of Ibero-American Literature. Pittsburgh: K & S Enterprises for Michigan State Council on Latin American Studies, 1975.

Uriel García, José. "Sumas para la historia del Cuzco (I)-(III)." *Cuadernos Americanos,* Vol. 104, No. 3 (1959), 133-151; No. 4 (1959), 140-61; No. 5 (1959), 152-86.

———. "Machu-Picchu." *Cuadernos Americanos,* 106 (1961), 161-251.

Wardropper, Bruce W. "The Poetry of Ruins in the Golden Age." *Revista Hispánica Moderna,* 35 (1969), 295-304.

Wilder, Amos N. "The Rhetoric of Ancient and Modern Apocalyptic." *Interpretation,* 25 (1971), 436-53.

Wilson, Edward M. "Sobre la 'Canción a las ruinas de Itálica.'" *Revista de Filología Española,* 23 (1936), 20-31.

Index

Abrams, Meyer H., 14, 22–23, 25n, 150, 208–9
Alazraki, Jaime, 36n, 98n
Alberti, Rafael, 27, 43
Allegory, 107–8, 136–38, 162n, 170–72
Allende, Salvador, 13
Alonso, Amado, 19–21, 26n, 28n, 30n, 36, 39, 71–72, 97–98, 139, 207–8
Alturas de Macchu Picchu, 19, 21–22, 104–75, 176–78, 184–85, 198–99, 203, 216–17
Americanism, 108–25
Apocalypse, 180–81, 198–236
Arguijo, Juan de, 153
Aristotle, 40–41
Auto-exégesis (self-exegesis), 36

Baudelaire, Charles, 34–35, 42
Bays, Gwendolyn, 26n
Belitt, Ben, 185n, 217
Bello, Andrés, 183
Benjamin, Walter, 140, 171–72
Bible, 185–87, 203, 226–36
Bingham, Hiram, 105
Blake, William, 183, 205, 228–30
Blanchot, Maurice, 16, 193, 195
Bloom, Harold, 45, 230
Borges, Jorge Luis, 13, 16–17, 112
Brotherston, Gordon, 183

Canción de gesta, 206–7, 216n
 "Escrito en el año 2000," 215–17
Cano Ballesta, Juan, 67n
Canto General, 22, 122, 173–207
 Arena traicionada, La, 184, 187, 191, 195
 "González Videla, el traidor de Chile," 184, 191
 "Jueces, Los," 192
 Canto General de Chile, 117, 178
 Conquistadores, Los, 184
 Coral de año nuevo para la patria en tinieblas, 184
 Flores de Punitaqui, Las, 184–85
 "Letra, La," 203–4
 Fugitivo, El, 184, 194–95, 205

Gran Océano, El, 185
Lámpara en la tierra, La, 173–75, 184–85, 187
 "Algunas bestias," 187
 "Amor América (1400)," 175, 190
 "Hombres, Los," 173–74
 "United Fruit Co., La," 187
 "Vegetaciones," 187
 "Vienen los pájaros," 187
Los libertadores, 184, 194
 "Bartolomé de Las Casas," 188
 "Cobre, El," 194
 "Desierto, El," 194
 "Llegará el día," 198
 "Nocturno," 194
 "Páramo, El," 195
Que despierte el leñador, 184, 187, 199–203
Ríos del canto, Los, 185
Yo soy, 185
 "A mi partido," 187
 "Regreso, El," 196–97
 "Yo no sufrí," 192
Cantos ceremoniales:
 "Cataclismo," 215, 217–20, 227–28
 "Sobrino de Occidente, El," 15
Cardona Peña, Alfredo, 28n
Caro, Rodrigo, 138–40, 144, 153, 171–72n
Concha, Jaime, 56n
Conversion:
 in *Alturas de Macchu Picchu*, 103, 127–28, 170–72
 and apocalypse, 208–9
 in "Entrada a la madera," 83, 89
 in *Tercera residencia*, 97–103
Cycle, 47n, 56–58. *See also* Encyclopedia.

Dante Alighieri, 147–52, 161–62, 167n, 174–75, 193
Darío, Rubén. *See* García Sarmiento, Félix Rubén.
De Man, Paul, 18, 41, 70n, 156n, 170
Derrida, Jacques, 30n, 162n, 163n
Diary or journal form, 57–58, 82
2000 (*Dos mil*), 207, 217, 225–26

253

Index

Eandi, Héctor, 17n, 29, 43–44, 47, 57n
Ecphrasis, 144–45, 160–61
Encyclopedia, 182–85
Epic, 183
Espada encendida, La, 22, 205, 207–8, 220, 226–36
Estravagario, 207
  "A callarse," 212–13
  "Partenogénesis," 213
  "Pido silencio," 211–12
  "Regreso a una ciudad," 212–13
  "Testamento de otoño," 213
Ezekiel, 191–93

Felstiner, John, 30n, 34n, 67n, 169
Fin de mundo, 207–8, 217, 220–25, 230
  "Bomba," 222
  "Muerte de un periodista," 222
  "Puerta, La," 221
  "Se llenó el mundo," 222
  "Siglo muere, El," 222
  "Tristísimo siglo," 223
Foucault, Michel, 35
Franco, Jean, 186n
Freccero, John, 89n, 148n, 149n, 155n, 167n

García Lorca, Federico, 17, 43
García Sarmiento, Félix Rubén (Rubén Darío), 112, 122, 152, 183, 241
Geografía infructuosa, 237–42
  "Campanario de Authenay, El," 237–42
Gilman, Stephen, 133n
González-Cruz, Luis, 36n
González Echevarría, Roberto, 113–14
González Vera, José Santos, 29, 47
González Videla, Gabriel, 22, 178–79, 191
Guillén, Jorge, 43

Hartman, Geoffrey, 156–57
Hegel, G. W. F., 114, 180–81, 186
Heredia, José María, 152
Hondero entusiasta, El, 182
Hugo, Victor, 22, 182–83
Huidobro, Vicente, 43–46

Incitación al nixonicidio y alabanza de la revolución chilena, 207
Irony, 29, 41–42, 70
  as *auto-exégesis,* 36

Jiménez, Juan Ramón, 110–14, 122–25

Kermode, Frank, 25

Larrea, Juan, 122–25, 139n, 152, 160–61
Lincoln, Abraham, 199, 201–2
Loveluck, Juan, 29n
Loyola, Hernán, 106n, 121n, 221
Lozada, Alfredo, 26n, 30n, 32n, 36n

Machu Picchu, Neruda's visit to, 116–21
Marx, Karl, 179–81
Mazzotta, Giuseppe, 83n, 148n, 151n, 193n
Melancholy:
  in *Alturas de Macchu Picchu,* 161–62
  in *Residencia en la tierra,* 39–42
Memory, 56–58
Milton, John, 40n

Nerval, Gérard de, 37, 40n
Nietzsche, Friedrich, 16

Odas elementales, 207, 209–11
  "Hombre invisible, El," 209–10
O'Gorman, Edmundo, 151
Ong, Walter J., 187n
Ortega y Gasset, José, 43, 114

Panofsky, Erwin, 40n, 161n
Paz, Octavio, 27, 108
Plato, 148
Plenos poderes, 207
  "Deber del poeta," 214
Poetics, 13, 18–19, 237–42
Poggioli, Renato, 45
Pring-Mill, Robert, 125n, 146n, 162–63n, 176–77, 186n, 208–9, 211n
Prophecy, 14–17
  in *Alturas de Macchu Picchu,* 160–75
  in *Residencia en la tierra,* 42

Recabarren, José Emilio, 188–90, 194–96
Residencia en la tierra:
  allusions to, in *Alturas de Macchu Picchu,* 125–33, 150–51, 168
  Amado Alonso's reading of, 19–21
  in Jiménez–Revueltas dispute, 110–13, 122
  1 (1925–1931), 26–65
    "Alianza (Sonata)," 50–51
    "Arte poética," 36–42, 71
    "Caballo de los sueños," 52–53
    "Colección nocturna," 46
    "Comunicaciones desmentidas," 46
    "Débil del alba," 53–56, 79–80
    "Galope muerto," 29–36, 48–49, 76–77, 134, 160
    "Significa sombras," 62–65
    "Sistema sombrío," 60–62, 102, 130
    "Sonata y destrucciones," 58–59
    "Tango del viudo," 91–92
    "Unidad," 48–50, 79, 129
  2 (1931–1935), 66–96
    "Agua sexual," 74–75
    "Entrada a la madera," 83–90
    "Josie Bliss," 90–96
    "No hay olvido (Sonata)," 80–82
    "Un día sobresale," 67–69
    "Vuelve el otoño," 75–79
    "Walking around," 70–74

Index

Reverdy, Pierre, 44
Revueltas, José, 110–14
Rilke, Rainer, Maria, 57n, 131–34, 146
Rimbaud, Jean Arthur, 25–26, 49–50
Rodríguez Monegal, Emir, 14n, 26n, 27n, 39, 57n, 67n, 108n, 109n, 169, 177
Ruins, 137, 140–41, 143–46, 148, 154, 171–73
   poetry of, 138–39

Santos Chocano, José, 183
Scene of writing, 29–30, 82–83
Schwob, Marcel, 227–28
Sicard, Alain, 36n, 56n
Singleton, Charles, 149
Spanish Civil War, 67, 97–101, 108–9
Spengler, Oswald, 114–15
Starobinski, Jean, 41n, 139n
Suárez-Rivero, Eliana, 211n

Tentativa del hombre infinito, 36, 182
Tercera residencia (1935-45):
   "Canto sobre unas ruinas," 139–40
   "Furias y las penas, Las." 99
   "Nuevo canto de amor a Stalingrado," 102–3
   "Reunión bajo las nuevas banderas," 100–102
Translation, poetics of, 155–61

Uvas y el viento, Las, 206–7

Vega, Garcilaso de la, 138
Villegas, Juan, 190
Vision, 24–26
   as aural mode, 30

Wardropper, Bruce W., 139n
Westermann, Klaus, 199
Whitman, Walt, 13, 22, 182–83
Wordsworth, William, 211

Library of Congress Cataloging in Publication Data

Santí, Enrico Mario.
  Pablo Neruda, the poetics of prophecy.

  Includes bibliographical references and index.
  1. Neruda, Pablo, 1904–1973—Criticism and interpretation.   I. Title.
PQ8097.N4Z775   861   82-4878
ISBN 0-8014-1472-5   AACR2